VIRGINIA HISTORICAL SOCIETY DOCUMENTS

*Volume 2*

*FOUR YEARS IN THE CONFEDERATE ARTILLERY*
THE DIARY OF PRIVATE HENRY ROBINSON BERKELEY

HENRY ROBINSON BERKELEY
*A Photograph taken in Richmond in March, 1862*

# *FOUR YEARS IN THE CONFEDERATE ARTILLERY*

---

The Diary of
Private Henry Robinson Berkeley

Edited by

William H. Runge

Virginia Historical Society

Richmond 1991

*For Landon Robinson Berkeley*

# ACKNOWLEDGMENTS

Many hands go into the preparation of a publication of this kind, and I would like to acknowledge them here. First of all, I would like to express my grateful appreciation to Mr. Landon Robinson Berkeley of Yorktown, Virginia, the diarist's son, for having so generously presented his father's diary to the Virginia Historical Society, under whose auspices it is being published. Mr. Berkeley also gave freely of his time in answering questions raised during the preparation of the manuscript for publication, and placed at my disposal pictures of his parents, letters, and an account book kept by his father, which shed much light on the diarist's postwar years. My several interviews with him were one of the great pleasures encountered in this work. My sincere thanks are due also to Mrs. Helen J. Campbell of Yorktown, Virginia, who was largely responsible for bringing the diary to the attention of the Society. Mrs. Ewing Mc-Michael of Nokesville, Virginia, Henry Robinson Berkeley's niece, presented to the Society pictures and a letter written by her uncle while in prison. She was also generous with her time in answering questions relating to the family, which places me in her debt. Mr. Harrison C. Berkeley of Charlottesville, Virginia, a nephew of the diarist's wife Nannie, has been most helpful in providing me with information concerning the family and Hanover County, for which he has my sincere thanks. The valuable and helpful criticism of portions of the manuscript made by Professors Edward Younger and Robert L. Kellogg, of the University of Virginia faculty, is gratefully acknowledged. It is impossible for me to thank adequately Mr. L. A. Beaurline, also of the University of Virginia faculty, for assistance far above and beyond the call of duty. To Miss Mary Topping and Mrs. Robert L. Plaster, I would like to express my thanks for their typing of the manuscript. I would like also to thank the following people for the help they cheerfully gave at various stages of the preparation of this manuscript: Mrs. Rosewell Page, Mr. Rosewell Page, Jr., Mr. Thomas S. Kirkpatrick, (now deceased), Mr. Meade Winston, Mr. Richard B. Harwell, Mr. James I. Robertson, Jr., Mr. Francis L. Berkeley, Jr., Mr. John Cook Wyllie, and Mr. N. Harvey Deal. Needless to say, I am greatly indebted to the Virginia Historical Society for the privilege and pleasure of preparing this diary for publication. My particular thanks go to the Society's editor, Mr. William M. E. Rachal, for his continuous help and many valuable criticisms. Additional thanks go to the editorial staff of the University of North Carolina Press. I would like also to acknowledge the help of my wife, Beverly Hackett Runge, whose time was cheerfully given at every point in the preparation of the diary for publication.

WILLIAM H. RUNGE

*University of Virginia*
*September 5, 1960*

# CONTENTS

# ILLUSTRATIONS

# MAPS

# INTRODUCTION

Henry Robinson Berkeley, the author of the diary here published for the first time, was born on March 27, 1840, at "White House," his parents' home near the Old Fork Church in Hanover County, Virginia. His mother and father were first cousins, both descended from the Berkeleys of "Barn Elms," a distinguished family that had served Virginia since the seventeenth century. Berkeley's mother, Susan Elizabeth, was the daughter of Lewis and Elizabeth Darracott Berkeley of "Montout," the farm adjacent to "White House." She was born in 1808 or 1809. His father, Edmund, was the son of the fifth Nelson Berkeley of "Airwell" and his second wife, Lucy Robinson. Edmund Berkeley of "White House" was a farmer all of his life. Active in political life, he was a member of the Virginia House of Delegates for the 1824-25 session.[1]

Nothing is known of Berkeley's boyhood days. His early education must have been informal and irregular if one can judge from his penmanship, spelling, and literary style at the age of twenty. Robin, as Henry Robinson was called by his family and friends, registered at the Hanover Academy for the 1859-60 session through the kindness of his aunt, Mary Berkeley Latané, who paid his tuition.

Hanover Academy, located a few miles down the road from Robin's home, was founded in 1850 by Lewis Minor Coleman. In 1859, when Coleman accepted the Chair of Latin at the University of Virginia, he was succeeded as principal by Hilary P. Jones, one of his assistants. Jones and almost all of the assistants were graduates of the University of Virginia, a school which had an exceptional reputation as a training place for young men. The Academy consisted of four schools: English Language and Liter-

---

[1] The sources used throughout this discussion of Berkeley are as follows unless otherwise noted: Interviews with Landon R. Berkeley; Frances Berkeley Young, *The Berkeleys of Barn Elms* (New Haven, 1954); and manuscript genealogical notes concerning the author's immediate family now in the Virginia Historical Society. All quotations are from the diary itself.

ature, Ancient Languages, Modern Languages, and Mathematics. Each of the school's two literary societies, the Concord and the Hanover, had its own hall, and jointly they owned a library of about a thousand volumes, in those days a sizable library for an academy.[2]

Young Berkeley spent two sessions at the Academy, the second of which was interrupted in its final days by the threat of war. He must have matured greatly during those two years; certainly they gave him a good grounding in the rudiments. His education must have been continued under his own direction in his later years, for he gained a reputation as an able teacher of students preparing for college, and there is no record of his attending school after the war.

On Saturday, May 17, 1861, Robin records in his diary that he attended at Hanover Junction (now Doswell) a rally of the Hanover Artillery and that while there he enlisted as a private in the unit. Many of his classmates and most of the Academy's faculty did likewise. The Hanover Artillery had been formed a month before under the leadership of William Nelson of "Oakland." Nelson, a kinsman of Robin's, was fifty-three years old at the time he became the first commanding officer of the company. He uniformed the men at his own expense.

Nelson, born in 1807 at "Oakland," lived as a bachelor all of his life at this charming old Hanover farm. A pious churchman, he was noted for his sincerity, kindness, and strictness in matters of discipline. He was a superb horseman and continued to ride strenuously up to the time of his death in 1892 at the age of eighty-five. Several times during the war he had his horse shot from under him. Though he had not the soldier's dashing, reckless nature, as did so many of his contemporaries, he could always be spotted by the silk top hat which he wore even on the battlefield. During the first, inactive year of the war his men resented his strictness in discipline, and when the time came for the re-election of the company officers in April of 1862, Nelson was not confirmed in his command. Robin Berkeley recorded in his diary that, later in the war, most of the men "learned to know him better and to love and admire his stern courage and noble qualities of mind and heart, and were ready to follow him wherever he might lead."

After his failure to be re-elected, Nelson's qualities as a field officer were recognized in his appointment to the command of an artillery bat-

2 For the Hanover Academy, see John Wesley Boitnott, "Secondary Education in Virginia, 1845-1870" (Doctoral dissertation, University of Virginia, 1935), pp. 73-77; Rosewell Page, *Hanover County: Its History and Legends* (Richmond, 1926), p. 56; and the catalogues of the Academy published at various times.

talion with the rank of major. In the winter of 1863-64 he was promoted to lieutenant colonel, and a year later to colonel, the rank he held at the end of the war. Nelson was in action without interruption for the length of the war though men much younger were not able to stand the strain. In his "Burial of the Guns," Thomas Nelson Page modeled the "Old Colonel" after his uncle, Colonel Nelson, and in this story is much of the flavor of the old gentleman's character. The "Old Colonel" died on a Sunday morning in 1892, while kneeling at his bed in prayer.[3]

A little more than a month after the organization of the company, Nelson received orders to proceed with his battery to Richmond, where on May 21 the men were enrolled in the service of Virginia for one year. They were first assigned to a river battery on Jamestown Island. The restlessness of Robin Berkeley and his comrades produced by the inactivity of this assignment, when there was "nothing to change the dullness of camp life, except to drill, to do guard duty, work on our fortifications, and have dress parade every evening," undoubtedly had much to do with their dissatisfaction with the commanding officer.

In early October, the dullness of Robin's camp life was interrupted, but unhappily by typhoid fever. He was sent home seriously ill, and remained there to recuperate until March, when he re-enlisted in the Hanover Artillery for the remainder of the war. During his absence, his company had been sent to Yorktown where it became a part of the field artillery.

On the Yorktown-Warwick River Line, Robin, on April 5, had his baptism under fire. "This was the first time I was under fire and I thought we would all be killed." He added, "However, no one was hurt, not even a horse."

It was in April, behind the Yorktown-Warwick River Line, that the men of Berkeley's battery replaced William Nelson as the company's commanding officer with George Washington Nelson, then but twenty-two years of age and a kinsman of the older man. The men of the battery were soon to regret their action. Wash, as his friends called him, was a brave and able soldier, but he had little ability as a commander. Not many months went by before Robin's mess occupied "itself during its leisure

[3] For Colonel Nelson, see the biographical sketch in Jed Hotchkiss, *Virginia* (Atlanta, 1899), pp. 1073-74; Vol. III of the *Confederate Military History*, Clement G. Evans, editor; Jennings C. Wise, *The Long Arm of Lee or The History of the Artillery of the Army of Northern Virginia* (Lynchburg, Va., 1915), *passim*, especially pp. 878-79. Interviews with Mrs. Rosewell Page and Mr. Rosewell Page, Jr., were also most helpful.

time in abusing Wash and his lieutenants" for their negligence and laziness.

After the Confederate withdrawal from its line across the Peninsula, Berkeley took part in little action until the engagement at White Oak Swamp, where he was in the thick of the battle. After this engagement, he saw no action at all until Fredericksburg in December. In the interval, the battery rapidly disintegrated as a fighting unit. During the several weeks following the Seven Days Campaign, the battery's "horses died like anything for want of proper care." Robin added, "The company is going to the dogs, and unless something is done, and done very soon, it will go to pieces. Wash is a brave man . . . but bravery alone will not keep up a battery. It requires a hard-working, industrious man of good executive ability; one who never tires, and is always on the lookout for his men and horses."

The end of the Hanover Artillery came soon. On October 5, 1862, rumors spread through the battery's camp near Winchester that their company, as well as others in the same condition, were to be mustered out and the men assigned to other units. The rumors proved to be accurate. The men of the Hanover Artillery were to be given the choice of transferring to Pichegru Woolfolk's Ashland Battery or Thomas J. Kirkpatrick's Amherst-Nelson Battery, which was in Major William Nelson's Battalion. Robin and his mess chose to join Kirkpatrick's Battery.

Thomas Jellis Kirkpatrick, although much younger than Major Nelson, in whose battalion he served, was made of much the same stuff as his commander. A sincerely religious man, he was not the dashing type. Brave and courageous, Kirkpatrick was one of the many workhorses without whom the war could never have been fought. He was on continuous duty throughout the war.

Born in Cumberland County, Virginia, in 1829, he was the son of John Kirkpatrick, a Presbyterian minister of Scotch-Irish descent, and Jane Jellis of Lynchburg. He was educated at Washington College (now Washington and Lee University) and in 1852 married Fortunata Sydnor of Lynchburg. A lawyer, he was an ardent States' righter in the years before the war. With the rising threat of war, he recruited a company of artillery in the spring of 1861 and served as its commanding officer until the end of hostilities. He was promoted to the rank of major during the final two months of the war.

Following the war, Major Kirkpatrick returned to his law practice in Lynchburg and once again became active in many local and statewide projects. In 1869, he was elected to the Virginia State Senate as a Funder. He died in 1897.[4]

The first battle that Robin fought in under his new commander, Major Kirkpatrick, was at Fredericksburg in December, 1862. Berkeley's gun saw little action in this engagement although he was under severe shelling.

Following Chancellorsville and Jackson's death, General Lee reorganized his army into three corps, commanded by Generals James B. Longstreet, Richard S. Ewell, and A. P. Hill. At the same time, the artillery went through a reorganization. Each of the three army corps was assigned a division of artillery comprising five battalions, the commanders of which were responsible to the corps' chief of artillery. The army's general reserve was abolished, thus diminishing the possibility of large masses of artillery being unused during battle as had often happened before. Nelson's Battalion, of which Kirkpatrick's Battery was a part, and which had been up to this point with the general reserve, was now placed with Ewell's Second Corps whose chief of artillery was Colonel John Thompson Brown.

No sooner had the reorganization of the Army of Northern Virginia taken place than it began its ill-fated invasion of Pennsylvania. Berkeley reached Gettysburg on the afternoon of July 1, after the enemy had been pushed beyond Gettysburg, and the day's action was concluded.

Upon awakening in the morning of July 2, Robin saw a sight that sickened even the veteran of battle he had by now become. Not far from where he had slept that night was a portion of Iverson's Brigade, consisting of "seventy-nine (79) North Carolinians laying dead in a straight line." Looking down the line Robin saw that "It was perfectly dressed . . . the feet of all these men were in a perfectly straight line." He could only reflect, "Great God! When will this horrid war stop?" He then added, "I turned from this sight with a sickened heart and tried to eat my breakfast, but had to return it to my haversack untouched." During the severest part of the battle on that second day of Gettysburg, Robin was stationed atop a building of Pennsylvania (now Gettysburg) College as a lookout, and from this vantage point he viewed the "grand, fierce, and awful conflict."

On July 3, the final day of Gettysburg, Berkeley's guns were in position on the extreme left of the Confederate line and were unused through-

[4] For Major Kirkpatrick, see the biographical sketch in Hotchkiss, *Virginia*, pp. 983-84; obituary in the *Daily Advance* (Lynchburg, Va.), October 18, 1897. Correspondence with Mr. Thomas S. Kirkpatrick was also very helpful.

out the day. "A great battle has been fought and lost, and our battery has *not* fired a single shot." The organization formed shortly before the biggest and perhaps most crucial battle of the war was not yet functioning properly.

Except for the battle at Mine Run at the end of November, he was not in any major action following Gettysburg until the beginning of the campaign in the spring of 1864 in the Wilderness. From this point on, Berkeley was in action almost continually until the end of the war. On the morning after that first terrible day in the Wilderness, Berkeley arose to find a "big pile of amputated arms, hands, legs and fingers within a foot or two of me."

Although Robin reported the action on May 12 at Spotsylvania Court House, "the most terrible day I have ever lived," June 3, at Cold Harbor, was to be far worse. At 6 A.M. on that day, his gun was ordered into position under severe artillery fire. So heavy was the fire under which they advanced that the first of the guns to reach its position had nearly all its crew disabled, "three men being killed and some eight or ten wounded," before the guns behind it were placed. Of the six messmates who went into action that day, Robin was the only one who was not killed or wounded.

Shortly after that fearful day at Cold Harbor, the Second Corps, now under Jubal A. Early, who replaced the ailing Ewell, was sent to the Valley to thwart the advancing Yankee marauder, General David Hunter, and to advance on Washington if possible. In a period of just one month, Berkeley and his comrades took part in a march which Early could describe without exaggeration as being "for its length and rapidity . . . without parallel in this or any other modern war." From June 20, when Berkeley's battery left Lynchburg with the Second Corps in pursuit of the fleeing Hunter, until July 20, when it reached Winchester after having been at the gates of Washington, D.C., the battery had traveled more than four hundred miles. During this march, in addition to several skirmishes, a major engagement with enemy forces under General Lew Wallace took place at the Monocacy River. Wallace was handed a decisive defeat, and the artillery played a significant part in the victory.

On the very day that Berkeley returned to Winchester, July 20, he was in a brief but severe action in which Dodson Ramseur's Division was surprised and badly handled by the enemy. In this engagement at Rutherford's Farm, to the north of Winchester, Berkeley's company "lost our entire battery, bringing out only one limber and a caisson." Four men of his company were killed, one mortally wounded, and twenty-five horses were lost. Since the spring campaign began, all four of the company's lieutenants were lost to service. "Our sergeants were acting as lieutenants, and privates as corporals and sergeants." It was not until the end of August that Kirkpatrick's Battery received their new guns.

The next month Berkeley was in one of the hardest days of action he experienced during the war. The battle at Winchester on September 19 spelled the beginning of the end for Early's army. Although the Second Corps was overwhelmed by General Philip Sheridan's superior force, Robin could justly claim that "the artillery covered itself with honor and glory." Again and again during that day the artillery saved the infantry from annihilation. Robin's battery "was engaged from sunrise until 9 P.M. with short intervals of cessation between fierce engagements at close quarters. We in our company fired about 1600 rounds of ammunition, about four times as much as we have ever used in a fight before." So severe was the company's loss in manpower that Berkeley acted as gunner, sergeant, and lieutenant during the battle.

The aftermath of Winchester held defeat for Early's small army. Fisher's Hill, a brief Indian summer in the early morning hours at Cedar Creek, a distressing winter with severe shortages of food for both man and beast, and, finally, utter defeat at Waynesboro on March 2, 1865, was all that was left for the sad remnant of the once proud army that only months before had approached the gates of the enemy capital. While fleeing across the railroad bridge in an attempt to reach safety in the mountains, Robin was captured.

Because of the absence of records of the army in those final days of the war, little is known of the activities of the remnants of Kirkpatrick's Battery or Nelson's Battalion. Colonel Nelson was in Lynchburg in the latter part of March, so presumably after the defeat at Waynesboro he was assigned to the defense of Lynchburg. Kirkpatrick probably went with him, for the legend persists in the families of both these men that rather than allow their guns to fall into the hands of the victor, they dumped them into the Staunton River. This legend is also preserved in Thomas Nelson Page's "Burial of the Guns," which was mentioned earlier.

After his capture, Robin was sent to Fort Delaware, located on Pea Patch Island in Delaware Bay. Here he remained until June 20, when he signed the oath of allegiance and boarded a boat for home. On June 24, "four years, one month and seven days" after he joined the Hanover Artillery, he returned home to face the uncertain peace.

Apparently Berkeley stayed at "White House" with his parents for some time after the war. By the fall of 1866, however, he had located himself in Loudoun County, Virginia. Here he tutored for various families, remaining for the longest time with William Beverley, of "Selma." Between the years 1873 and 1876, he taught at the Loudoun School at Leesburg, after which he returned to private tutoring. In 1882 he removed to Orange County, where he tutored for three years in the home of C. J. Stovin.[5]

It was while he was with the Stovins that he at last was able to marry his cousin, Anna Louisa Berkeley. The marriage ceremony took place in Richmond on August 8, 1883. It is not entirely clear why Robin and Nannie waited so many years to marry, for they had been courting since before the war. The reasons were undoubtedly to a great extent economic. Family records show that Berkeley and several of his sisters and brothers were married in the years immediately following their mother's death in 1882, suggesting that they felt responsible for her support during her lifetime.

In 1886, the Berkeleys purchased a small farm near Orange Court House, and there Berkeley established his own school. He continued the operation of this school until 1900, when he took a position teaching at the Locust Dale Academy in Madison County. In March of 1898, not long before he moved to the Locust Dale Academy, his wife Nannie died, leaving to Berkeley's care their only child, Landon Robinson. Berkeley retired from teaching in 1904. About 1914 he sold his farm and purchased a house in the town of Orange, where he lived until his death on January 16, 1918.

Although a very serious-minded young man, Robin Berkeley had a modest sense of humor, which is noticeable occasionally in the diary. One instance occurs in his account of the battle at Winchester on September 19, 1864, where at one point in the battle a shell exploded near a horse in Berkeley's limber and took off its head, "cut off the hind legs of the saddle horse in front of him and the front legs of the horse just behind him." The driver of the horse that had its head taken off was "left unhurt holding the reins and bit in his right hand, but covered from his face to his knees with the brains and blood of the horse." Berkeley added apologetically, "I could not help being amused at his appearance, yet it was an awful gruesome place to be amused."

[5] An account book kept by the author of the diary covering the years 1866-92 was used for information concerning his activities for these years. It is in the possession of Landon R. Berkeley.

Berkeley was a deeply religious person, a characteristic which is apparent from the diary and from the few of his letters that have survived. Throughout his life he was active in the Episcopal Church. For many years he was a vestryman of St. Thomas' Church in Orange. A bookish man, Berkeley was intensely interested in world affairs and an avid reader of newspapers. He was modest, and in later years talked little of his war experiences. Although he called attention to a job well done a few times in his diary, we must remember that this account was preserved for his son to read, and not for publication, and that in the main, the diary attests to his humility and lack of pretension. When some members of his company petitioned to have the battery transferred to Manassas at the time of the first battle there in the summer of 1861, Berkeley made it clear that he would not seek the glory of battle. He plainly stated, "I, being well satisfied, declined to sign this petition, at which some of the boys became indignant."

He was not reckless or bold; but he never refused to do his duty, no matter how onerous or dangerous. His diary attests to his own quiet bravery and to that of his comrades in arms.

There are few good diaries, published or in manuscript, by the men in the ranks of the Confederate Army covering the full period of the war, and such accounts by artillerymen are even scarcer. Because Robin Berkeley's account embraces the entire war, and because he was a private in the artillery, it is an unusually valuable and interesting contribution to Confederate literature. Another element that adds considerably to its value lies in the fullness of its account of Early's Valley Campaign of 1864, adequate documentation of which is exceedingly rare. Berkeley's diary not only gives an intimate picture of the life of the plain soldier; it gives also some idea of the increasing effectiveness of the artillery as the war progressed.

The text used for this publication is contained in three bound note books ten and three-eighths inches by eight inches. Each notebook contains forty-eight leaves (ninety-six pages). The first two notebooks are filled with text, while the text in the third occupies fifty-one pages. Pages fifty-two, fifty-three, and fifty-four contain the names of some of his fellow prisoners and the Federal officers at Fort Delaware. Pasted in on the following four leaves are five letters addressed to Berkeley, a manuscript copy of a letter from General Early to Colonel Carter or Colonel Nelson, and a broadside containing General Lee's farewell address. With the exception of Lee's farewell address, this material is included in the Appendices to this volume.

The text of the diary was written in these three notebooks by Berkeley some time after 1890, for on the cover of each of the notebooks is printed the date, Jan. 21, 1890, on which the trademark was registered. The text used here, then, is a late copy. A clue to the earlier history of the text of the diary is contained in a notebook of Latin exercises written by Berkeley while a student at Hanover Academy. Fifty pages of this notebook contain another version of the diary that was obviously written at a much earlier date than the one published here. This earlier account begins with his enlistment in the Hanover Artillery on May 16, 1861, and concludes with the entry on March 3, 1864. Although the entries in the earlier version are in general briefer, they contain some details not found in the later one.

On the second page of the earlier version, after the entry for May 27, 1861, appears the following statement: "I have lost my book in which I took down my notes after leaving the barn and will now have to write from memory." The period covered by the lost book must have extended well on into the winter and early spring of 1862, for it is not until Berkeley rejoined his company in March, 1862, following his long illness, that the day by day entries again begin.

From an examination of the two copies of the diary, it seems almost certain that Berkeley used his "notes," which were evidently compiled daily, not only for the earlier copy, but also for the later version of the diary. Unhappily, these notes cannot be found. From the phraseology of the text here published, however, it seems clear that many entries are taken almost verbatim from the notes, not only because so many of the phrases in the two extant versions are the same, but also because so much of the style of the later version is hardly that which Berkeley would have used in his later and more mature years.

The text as published appears largely as it does in manuscript except for spelling, which has been corrected. In cases where the spelling seemed to indicate an unorthodox pronunciation, the original spelling is called to the attention of the reader in the notes. In a very few cases where a sentence was extremely awkward, the order of the sentence has been changed to improve its readability without changing the meaning of the sentence. In phrases concerning the time of day the word *o'clock* has been either added or deleted, for the sake of clarity or to avoid repetition. Numbers have been spelled out or put in arabic numerals to lessen confusion in

Berkeley's usage in surrounding material. Punctuation has been added only where it was thought necessary for clarity, and paragraphs have been introduced for each daily entry. Names of estates have been placed within quotation marks. Words omitted in the original have been inserted in brackets, and when the diarist inadvertently repeated a word, it has been deleted without calling attention to the fact.

*FOUR YEARS IN THE CONFEDERATE ARTILLERY*
THE DIARY OF PRIVATE HENRY ROBINSON BERKELEY

# CHAPTER I

# ENLISTED IN THE HANOVER ARTILLERY

## *The Peninsula, 1861-1862*

When the Confederate War began in the spring of 1861, I was a pupil at the Hanover Academy[1] in my second year there, doing my very best to fit myself for the duties of life. My aunt, Mary B. Latané[2] of Essex County, was kindly paying my way at school. We had some seventy-five pupils, many being from the Southern states. Mr. H. P. Jones[3] was principal of the school. He was assisted by Mr. W. M. Fontaine, James M. Boyd and Alexander Mathews.[4] The entire faculty were M.A.'s of [the] University

---

[1] Hanover Academy, located on the Ridge Road (Virginia Route 738) in Hanover County, was founded in 1850 by Lewis Minor Coleman, and operated by him until 1859, when he accepted the Chair of Latin at the University of Virginia. Hilary P. Jones, one of Coleman's assistants, took Coleman's place as principal. The school was closed during the war years, but was reopened by Jones afterwards and continued in operation until 1886 or later. (John Wesley Boitnott, "Secondary Education in Virginia, 1845-1870" [Doctoral dissertation, University of Virginia, 1935], pp. 73-77; Rosewell Page, *Hanover County: Its History and Legends* [Richmond, 1926], p. 56.)

[2] Mary Barrett Berkeley, sister of the father of Henry Robinson Berkeley. (Berkeley will be referred to in the footnotes as HRB hereafter.) She married Thomas Latané of Essex County, Virginia. (Frances Berkeley Young, *The Berkeleys of Barn Elms* [New Haven, 1954], p. 111.)

[3] Hilary P. Jones was born in 1833 at Union Mills, Fluvanna County, Virginia. He attended the University of Virginia from 1852 to 1855, when he received his M.A. degree. After teaching at Hanover Academy for several years, he succeeded Lewis Minor Coleman as principal of the Academy. Jones joined the Hanover Artillery upon its organization in the spring of 1861, and was elected an officer of the Company. When not re-elected to his rank during the elections in the spring of 1862, he was given command of an artillery battalion. He had reached the rank of lieutenant-colonel by the end of the war. His son was the renowned naval officer of World War I, Admiral Hilary P. Jones. (*Students of the University of Virginia: A Semi-Centennial Catalogue . . .* [Baltimore, 1878]—the pages of this volume are not numbered, but the students' names are in an approximate alphabetical order; Page, *Hanover County*, p. 56.)

[4] William Morris Fontaine was born in Hanover County in 1835. He attended the University of Virginia from 1856 to 1858 and served as an officer of artillery during the Civil War. After the war he became a member of the faculty of West Virginia University. James M. Boyd was born in Lynchburg, Virginia, in 1839, and attended the University of Virginia from 1857 to 1860 and in 1867. He was later on the faculty of the Louisiana State Seminary.

of Virginia. It was a first-rate school and I had every reason to believe that my progress was satisfactory. My life there was happy and bright, when I was suddenly called away from my books to take part in all the trials, hardships, dangers and duties of a great and bloody civil war. This little diary will tell my boy of a few, only a few, of the dangers, trials, hardships, deaths and bloody scenes through which his father passed, as a private in the artillery.

*May 16, 1861. Friday.* I left school at the Hanover Academy, going up home in the afternoon, B. B. Turner,[5] a schoolmate, going with me.

*May 17. Saturday.* There was a big rally of the Hanover Artillery, a company formed about a month before, at the Hanover Junction [now Doswell]. We all went down to the rally and the dinner. A big Irishman, named Jim Gibson, took breakfast at the "White House"[6] this morning. I enlisted in the Hanover Artillery today. The following are its commissioned officers: Capt. William Nelson; 1st Lieut. Charles Cooke; 2nd Lieut. Frank Terrill; and 3rd Lieut. W. M. Fontaine.[7]

*May 18. Sunday.* We all attended Fork Church.[8] A very large and

Alexander F. Mathews, born in Greenbrier County, Virginia, in 1838, attended the University of Virginia from 1854 to 1858. After the war, he practiced law in Lewisburg, West Virginia. *(Students of the University of Virginia.)*

[5] Beverley B. Turner, son of Edward Turner of Fauquier County, Virginia, entered Hanover Academy in the same year as HRB. *(Catalogue of Hanover Academy* [Richmond, 1860], p. 15.)

[6] HRB's home. It was located in Hanover County on the Ridge Road (Va. Rt. 738) a short distance west of Fork Church, which still stands. "White House" burned after the war. (Historical Map of Hanover County," Manuscript Division, University of Virginia Library. This map, drawn for Hanover County's 300th anniversary, has pencil notations giving the locations of many old Hanover County homes. The map seems to be accurate, and its accuracy is supported by interviews with Rosewell Page, Jr., Landon R. Berkeley, and Harrison C. Berkeley. All future identifications and locations of Hanover County places are from these sources unless otherwise noted.)

[7] Of these, Capt. William Nelson, born in 1807, was the son of Capt. Thomas Nelson of "Oakland," Hanover County, and Judith Nelson (daughter of Governor Thomas Nelson). A bachelor, he lived at "Oakland," the birthplace of Thomas Nelson Page, throughout his life. Nelson was a colonel commanding an artillery battalion at the end of the war. He died in 1892. (Richard Channing Moore Page, *Genealogy of the Page Family in Virginia . . .* [New York, 1883], p. 165.) Nelson is discussed at greater length in the Introduction. Charles Cooke, born at "Dewberry," Hanover County, was the son of the Rev. John Cooke and Edmonia Churchill, whose first husband was Nelson Berkeley of "Airwell." Frank Terrill lived in Hanover County near Terrill's Mill on Taylor's Creek. An interview with Rosewell Page, Jr., resulted in information concerning all persons discussed in this note; William Morris Fontaine has been identified in note 4 above.

[8] The Fork Church, so called because it was located in the area between the forks of the Pamunkey River (North Anna and South Anna rivers), in St. Martin's Parish, Hanover County, is still standing on the Ridge Road (Va. Rt. 738). (Robert A. Lancaster, Jr., *Historic Virginia Homes and Churches* [Philadelphia, 1915], p. 278.)

serious-looking congregation. Doubtless they were thinking of the war and its unknown dangers and hardships. A good sermon by our pastor, Mr. [Horace] Stringfellow.

*May 19. Monday.* A wet and gloomy day. Parents and sisters tried hard to be bright and cheerful for their soldier-boys' sakes, but it was impossible for them to hide their deep anxiety. I went up to Beaver Dam Depot and got my uniform. Got back to dinner. We all went up to "Montout"[9] to take supper and bid them good-by. Sad and anxious-looking faces greeted us; but warm and tender hearts bade us good-by, doubtless praying that God would watch over us and soon bring us back in peace and safety. I gave my Literary Badge[10] to Nannie[11] with the request that she would keep it and wear it for my sake, and if I never came back, to keep it always in remembrance of me. Tears came into her eyes, and she said, *"You know I will do it."* We, i.e., Bev Turner, John Hill[12] and myself, came back to the "White House" about 10 P.M. Uncle Landon's[13] company, the Patrick Henry Riflemen [of Hanover County], are now in camp at the Fair Ground[14] at Richmond and being drilled.

*May 20.* I left home this afternoon with my company for Richmond, taking the train at Anderson's Crossing. We reached the city about 4 P.M. and were quartered in Trinity Church near the Exchange Hotel.[15] We took our meals, breakfast and supper, at the Columbia Hotel,[16] our officers paying for them. We had to look out for our dinner ourselves.

[9] "Montout," the home of Landon Carter Berkeley and HRB's future wife Nannie, was located next to HRB's home, "White House," on the Ridge Road (Va. Rt. 738).

[10] His badge as a member of the Hanover Literary Society at Hanover Academy. See *Catalogue of Hanover Academy*, p. 21, for the Academy societies.

[11] Anna Louisa Berkeley, daughter of Landon Carter Berkeley (1817-92), was HRB's first cousin, whom he married in 1883. (Young, *Berkeleys*, p. 121.)

[12] John Hill Berkeley, HRB's older brother. (*Ibid.*, p. 121.)

[13] Landon Carter Berkeley (1817-92) of "Montout," brother of HRB's mother, and his future wife's father. (*Ibid.*, p. 122.)

[14] The Fair Ground was located on West Broad Street in the area that is now Monroe Park. (Alfred Hoyt Bill, *The Beleaguered City: Richmond, 1861-1865.* [New York, 1946]. p. 47; Frank Earle Lutz, *A Richmond Album. A Pictorial Chronicle of an Historic City's Outstanding Events and Places* [Richmond, 1937]. p. 116; William A. Christian, *Richmond, Her Past and Present* [Richmond, 1932], p. 220.

[15] Located at the corner of Fourteenth and Franklin Streets. The Exchange Hotel, opened in 1841, was one of the centers of political and social circles of Richmond before the war. It was closed on March 16, 1896. (Christian, *Richmond*, pp. 139, 143, 452; Alexander Wilbourne Weddell, *et al.*, *Richmond, Virginia In Old Prints: 1737-1887* [Richmond, 1932], pp. 116, 227, 228, 230.) The Trinity Methodist Church, built in 1827, was located at the corner of Fifteenth and Franklin Streets, next to the Exchange Hotel. (Christian, *Richmond*, p. 130; Weddell, *Richmond*, map facing p. 116.)

[16] The Columbia Hotel was located at the southeast corner of Cary and Thirteenth Streets. (Weddell, *Richmond*, p. 116; John P. Little, *History of Richmond* [Richmond, 1933], p. 174; Christian, *Richmond*, p. 204.)

*May 21.* We were enrolled in the service of Virginia by John B. Baldwin,[17] to serve one year, if not sooner discharged. Soon after, we received orders to go to Jamestown by boat the next day. We, John Hill and I, went with Bev Turner to the Custom House to see Col. John A. Washington,[18] who was just from Bev's home. We saw Col. Washington, and also Gen. R. E. Lee, who was in Col. Washington's office at the time. Both of these are splendid-looking men.

*May 22.* *Thursday.* We remained in Richmond. In the evening, I went out to the Fair Ground with Uncle Landon, whose company is quartered out there. I saw many companies from all parts of the state. Many of our men got on a spree this P.M.

*May 23.* *Friday.* We went down to Jamestown Island, on the old Curtispect [Curtis Peck] steamboat, getting our breakfast on the boat. We got there about midday. We did not get any dinner. We were quartered in a large barn on the mainland, not having gotten our tents. We got Capt. Allen's[19] negroes to cook us some supper. We formed our mess today. It consists of the following members: John Hill Berkeley, Henry Robinson Berkeley, John McP. Cooke, Frank Hall, George Washington Nelson, Henry Martin Stringfellow, Beverley B. Turner and Dabney Williamson. During the next month Edmund M. Anderson, R. R. Stringfellow, John Hall and L. Points became members of our mess.[20]

17 John B. Baldwin, of Augusta County, was at this time Inspector General of Virginia Troops. After the Virginia Troops were officially turned over to the Confederate States, he was commissioned colonel of the 52nd Virginia Infantry. Subsequently, when illness forced his resignation from the army, Baldwin was elected to the Confederate States Congress. He was prominent in Virginia politics both before and after the war. (Jennings C. Wise, *The Long Arm of Lee or the History of the Artillery of the Army of Northern Virginia* [Lynchburg, Va., 1915], I, 116; Jed Hotchkiss, *Virginia* [Atlanta, 1899], pp. 708-9, Vol. III of *Confederate Military History*, Clement G. Evans, editor.)

18 The United States Custom House, located on Fifteenth Street between Main and Cary Streets, was used by various agencies of the Confederate government. President Davis had his office there. (Christian, *Richmond*, pp. 216, 223; Weddell, *Richmond*, maps opposite p. 116, p. 182. Col. John Augustine Washington, great grandnephew of George Washington, was commissioned aide-de-camp on Gen. Robert E. Lee's personal staff, but soon was acting as assistant adjutant general. He accompanied Lee on the West Virginia campaign where he was killed on September 13, 1861, while on a reconnoitering expedition. (Douglas Southall Freeman, *R. E. Lee: A Biography* [New York, 1935], I, 568-69, 639-40.)

19 Captain (or Colonel, as HRB later termed him) Allen owned a farm on the James River just east of College Creek, which is just below Jamestown Island. One of the many batteries along the James River was located on Jamestown Island. (*Atlas to Accompany the Official Records of the Union and Confederate Armies* [Washington, D. C., 1891-95], Plates XX, XIX, XVIII, XXVII.)

20 With the exception of Beverley B. Turner, who was from Fauquier County, all mentioned were from Hanover County. John Hill Berkeley has already been identified as HRB's older brother. George Washington Nelson was born in 1840 and attended the University of Virginia in 1858 and 1859. In the spring of 1862 he was elected Captain of the Hanover

*May 24. Saturday.* We went over to the battery on the [James] river front[21] this morning and helped unload some plank from a boat, having for our dinner some of the meanest bread and meat I ever saw. We returned to the barn about dark. Tonight our officers kindly invited us to take supper with them. We accepted and had a very good supper. The officers have two servants.

*May 25. Sunday.* We were compelled to try our hand at cooking some breakfast. Jack Cooke boiled some dumplings and made some coffee. I drank the coffee, but no one could go Jack's dumplings. They would have killed old Nick [Berkeley family horse] had he eaten them. Martin Stringfellow had services, after which we carried our rations to some of Col. Allen's negro quarters, bought some eggs and got the negroes to cook our dinner, which is the best meal I have eaten since we left Richmond.

*May 26. Monday.* We went over to the battery. I was put on guard for the first time today. It was very hot. The sun burnt all the skin off my ears. A little military cap does not suit a soldier who has to be out such a day.

*May 27. Tuesday.* We remained in the barn on the mainland [until] about the last of the week, when we were moved bag and baggage over to the [Jamestown] island and went into tents. We fixed up a tent and also built us two plank shanties. Jack Cooke sent home for a cook and in a short time we got ourselves fixed up very comfortably and got on very well. We learned each day something new and found out many things and ways to take care of ourselves and add to our comfort. Everything went on quietly and comfortably until June 10, 1861, when the battle of Bethel[22] was fought and caused some excitement, but things soon quieted

Artillery, and when that company was disbanded the following fall, he became an inspector general of artillery. After the war he was a prominent Episcopal clergyman. (Page, *Genealogy of the Page Family,* p. 183; *Students of the University of Virginia;* Rev. William A. R. Goodwin, *History of the Theological Seminary in Virginia* [New York, 1923], II, 59, 92, 128, 159.) John McP. Cooke was the son of the Rev. John Cooke of "Dewberry," and the brother of Charles Cooke, first lieutenant of the Hanover Artillery. (See note 7 above.) Leonidas Points came from Staunton. After the war he was on the staff of the School for the Blind in Staunton. His sister married the Rev. Robert Nelson, Capt. William Nelson's brother. (Interviews with Rosewell Page, Jr., and Mrs. Rosewell Page, Sr.) Henry Martin Stringfellow is probably the Henry Martyn Stringfellow mentioned in Lizzie Stringfellow Watkins, *The Life of Horace Stringfellow* [Montgomery, Alabama, 1931], pp. 73, 135. As later entries in the diary will relate, Stringfellow left the Hanover Artillery under unpleasant conditions and served in Texas during the latter part of the war. He was a horticulturist after the war. HRB's spelling of Martin is retained in the text.

21 The same battery referred to in note 19 above.

22 The battle at Big Bethel, located about eight miles northwest of Newport News, was intended as a surprise attack on the Confederate outpost there by a portion of the command of Brig. Gen. Benjamin F. Butler. The surprise element was lost, however, when one of the

down and we had nothing to change the dullness of camp life, except to drill, to do guard duty, work on our fortifications and have dress parade every evening. We enjoyed fishing and bathing. Edmund Anderson made a kite and sent [it] up by a mile of string, which excited the wonder of the ignorant. The 21st of July brought us the great battle of Manassas. The papers were full of wonderful accounts of this great battle and they excited our company so very much that there was a petition gotten up by some of the officers and men, asking the Secretary of War[23] to transfer our company to Manassas. I, being very well satisfied, declined to sign this petition, at which some of the boys became very indignant. They, however, very soon became reconciled and everything went on quietly and smoothly. About the last of September, Dr. Starke,[24] our surgeon, came to our mess and asked for volunteers to nurse the sick of the 14th Virginia Regiment, who had been left in his charge without nurses. Frank Hall, Dabney Williamson, Martin Stringfellow and I volunteered to sit up and nurse them every other night. We kept up this duty for about three weeks. A great many of these poor fellows died. Those that were left, Dr. Starke sent home as soon as they were able to go.

*October 1.* About this time a petition was gotten up asking Capt. Nelson to resign. This petition was signed by nearly all the company. We thought the Captain rather too strict and exacting; but most of us, later on in the war, learned to know him better and to love and admire his stern courage and noble qualities of head and heart, and were ready to follow him wherever he might lead. In reply to the petition asking him to resign, he said that he could not *conscientiously* do it. Things soon became quiet and worked on very smoothly.

*October 5.* I was taken sick with typhoid fever and gradually grew worse each day for a week or more.

*October 14.* I got a sick-furlough of ten days and Capt. Nelson took charge of me and carried me up to Richmond. We did not get to Richmond until about sunrise the next morning. I was delirious several times

Federal regiments fired into their own ranks and thus warned the Confederates. Brig. Gen. Ebenezer W. Peirce commanded Butler's forces at Bethel, while the Confederate force was commanded by Brig. Gen. D. H. Hill of Brig. Gen. John B. Magruder's army. (Freeman, *R. E. Lee,* I, 527-28; Robert U. Johnson and C. C. Buell, editors, *Battles and Leaders of the Civil War* [New York, 1887-88], II, 148-51.)

[23] Leroy Pope Walker of Alabama was appointed the first Confederate Secretary of War on February 21, 1861. He resigned on September 16, 1861.

[24] Dr. G. C. Starke was assistant surgeon in hospitals at Jamestown and the second Congressional District. (Wyndham B. Blanton, *Medicine in Virginia in the Nineteenth Century* [Richmond, 1933], p. 416.)

on the trip. The boat was delayed by a heavy fog on the river, having frequently to stop and wait for the fog to lift. Capt. Nelson carried me to the Powhatan House.[25] I tried to eat some breakfast, but could only drink a little milk. The Captain then carried me to a room, where I went to bed. I had a high fever. About midday, someone knocked at my room door, and when I told them to walk in, Uncle Dick[26] opened the door and came in. I was very glad to see him, but I saw at once, from his face, that he thought me a very sick boy. I remained at the hotel until the afternoon of October 15th when Uncle Dick and Capt. Nelson put me on the train, under the charge of Dr. P. Harrison,[27] who brought me up to Taylorsville and then took me home in his buggy. I have always thought of him kindly ever since. They were at supper when I got home and very much surprised to see me. Nannie, Ellen and Lizzie spent the night at the "White House." Papa had gone up to "Dewberry"[28] to sit up with Capt. John Harrison,[29] the doctor's brother; but when the doctor got there and told him he had brought me home sick Papa came immediately home. I went immediately to bed after getting a little supper. I was very ill for a month and it was thought for a long time that I would not recover; but by the goodness and mercy of God I was spared, and after being confined to my bed for nearly six weeks, I began to get a little better. I gradually improved and gained my strength very slowly. I remained at home until January 13, 1862, when Sister Bettie[30] and I went in the buggy with old Fannie horse on a visit to Aunt Mary Latané's in Essex County. We spent a most pleasant month with relations and friends; but all the time I thought of the war cloud, which would be sure to burst on us when spring opened. On our way home, we were caught in a snow and rain storm and took refuge in [the home of] Mr. Boggs,[31] where we were kindly and hos-

[25] One of Richmond's more exclusive hotels, the Powhatan House, was located on the east side of Eleventh Street between Broad and Capitol. When A. J. Ford became its proprietor after the war, it became known as Ford's Hotel, and continued in use until 1908. (Weddell, *Richmond*, pp. 116, 198; Lutz, *Richmond Album*, p. 102.)

[26] Richard Berkeley. There is confusion among members of the Berkeley family as to the identification of Uncle Dick. Internal evidence indicates that his last name is Berkeley, but Young, *Berkeley's*, does not list a Richard Berkeley who could be HRB's uncle.

[27] Dr. Prosser Harrison of Richmond. (Interview, Rosewell Page, Jr.)

[28] "Dewberry" was the home of the widow of the Rev. John Cooke. It still stands on the Ridge Road west of Fork Church.

[29] John Poe Harrison of Richmond. He married Ann Cooke, a daughter of the Rev. John Cooke of "Dewberry," and was a captain of artillery in the Confederate Army. Captain Harrison died not long after this entry in HRB's diary was made. (*Students of the University of Virginia;* interview, Rosewell Page, Jr.)

[30] Elizabeth Berkeley, HRB's older sister.

[31] The Rev. William (?) Boggs, a native of Pennsylvania, came to Virginia before the Civil

pitably entertained for two days. We reached "The Nut Shell," Uncle Phil Winston's,[32] on Sunday afternoon, February 16. Soon after getting there, we heard of the death of Dick Winston, Uncle Phil's half brother. We remained at "The Nut Shell" until February 20, when we, Bettie, Fan and I, came up home. We got badly stuck in the mud a mile below the dry bridge; but after much trouble succeeded in getting out with the help of some negroes, to whom I gave 50 cents for helping us out of the mud.

*February 21, 1862. Friday.* I walked up to "Montout" and spent the day. John Lewis[33] persuaded me to go with him the next day to Richmond to the inaugural of President Davis.

*February 22. Saturday.* John Lewis and I rode down to Ashland early this morning and went to Richmond on the accommodation train to witness the inauguration, leaving our horses at Ashland until our return. It was a wet and gloomy morning. Old man Dick Fox was on the train, and being right much in whiskey, he talked much and loudly about temperance. By the time we reached the city, it was raining very hard and the first thing we did was to go and buy an umbrella a piece. The crowd was very large, but orderly, and in the best of humor. I saw some of my company as tight as bricks. The President delivered his inaugural from the equestrian statue of Washington. It was short, ornate and hopeful, and was delivered in a pouring rain to which an attentive audience listened as if it had been beautiful spring weather. One old gentleman tried to keep up his umbrella; but the crowd forced him to put it down by hollering at him, "Put down that umbrella. Put down that *blue* umbrella!" We managed after the inaugural to get some dinner, but only after trying at several places and a long delay. We came up home that evening and had to ride up from Ashland in a heavy rain. We reached home about 6 P.M., the rain stopping about the time we got home.

*February 23. Sunday.* Remained quietly at home. It being too unlikely to venture up to Trinity Church, I remained at home after this,

War began and married an aunt of "Nannie," who became the wife of HRB. (Interview, Landon R. Berkeley.)

[32] Philip Henry Winston of Hanover County. He married Catherine Robinson Berkeley, sister of HRB's father. (Young, *Berkeleys*, pp. 111-12; Clayton Torrence, *Winston of Virginia and Allied Families* [Richmond, 1927], p. 47.) "The Nut Shell," located about a quarter of a mile east of Hanover Court House, still stands. (Interview, Rosewell Page, Jr.)

[33] John Lewis Berkeley, born in 1842, was the oldest son of Landon Carter Berkeley of "Montout," and HRB's cousin. He was wounded at Cold Harbor in June, 1864, the wound making him unfit for further service. After the war he entered the teaching profession and ultimately became principal of a public school in Danville, Virginia. (Hotchkiss, *Virginia*, pp. 723-24.)

until March 8, 1862, when I went to Richmond and re-enlisted for the war in the Hanover Artillery. I had two photographs taken of myself on this trip.[34]

[34] The photograph reproduced as the frontispiece of this book was undoubtedly taken at this time. A photograph in the possession of Landon R. Berkeley is probably the other mentioned here.

# CHAPTER II

# THE FIRST TIME I WAS UNDER FIRE

## *Yorktown to Seven Days, 1862*

*March 14 [i.e., 13], 1862.* John Lewis [Berkeley], Amos [Negro serv-ant] and myself went down to Richmond on our way to join my company, then stationed one mile below Yorktown. We stayed at the American Hotel[1] that night.

*March 13 [i.e., 14].* We went via the York River Railroad to West Point and thence by boat to Yorktown. A good many furloughed boys went down with us. Everyone on the boat today was talking about the great naval fight which had taken place in Hampton Roads on March 8 between the *Virginia* and the Yankee boats.[2] We reached camp about 2 P.M. and found only a small guard in charge, the company having gone down to Bethel on a scouting expedition.[3] We remained six days in camp before the company got back. When I was taken sick with typhoid fever last fall at Jamestown, my company was in charge of a water battery on

[1] The American Hotel occupied the southwest corner of Main and Eleventh Streets. It burned on Evacuation Day, April 3, 1865. (Alexander Wilbourne Weddell, *et al.*, *Richmond, Virginia In Old Prints: 1737-1887* [Richmond, 1932], p. 123; Frank Earle Lutz, *A Richmond Album: A Pictorial Chronicle of an Historic City's Outstanding Events and Places* [Richmond, 1937], p. 40.)

[2] On March 8, 1862, the Confederate ironclad, *Virginia [Merrimac]*, destroyed the *Cumberland* and the *Congress*, two Federal wooden men-of-war. The next day, March 9, the *Virginia*, sailing out to destroy the rest of the Union ships in Hampton Roads, met with the Northern ironclad, the *Monitor*, in an indecisive but historic battle.

[3] Maj. Gen. John B. Magruder felt that the *Virginia* could safeguard the James River from penetration by enemy ships and that his right flank, therefore, was safe from being turned. With this fact in mind, he decided to move the larger part of his command from the Warwick River line forward to the Bethel area. This he did about March 19. The scouting expedition mentioned here was one of the many sent out to reconnoiter Federal positions. (*The War of the Rebellion: A Compilation of the Official Records of the Union and Confederate Armies* [Washington, D. C., 1880-1901], Series I, Volume XI, part 3, pp. 386-88. All citations will be from Series I unless otherwise noted.)

the river front at that place, consisting of four sixty-four-pound guns, and we had been drilled to use these heavy guns. In November last my company had been ordered to Yorktown and given six field guns and horses with other necessary equipment. In my absence, the company had also gone on an expedition to Mathews Court House, but had remained there only a short time, and had then returned to Yorktown and gone into winter quarters about a mile below the town in a piece of woods. It was here that I found my company in March, 1862.

*March 28.* We moved bag and baggage within the fortifications of Yorktown. The town has been surrounded by a ditch 15 feet deep and 15 feet broad and has a big embankment on [the] inner side. This embankment is defended by many heavy mortars and siege guns, while many field guns are stationed between the heavy siege pieces. Nearly every framed house along the [York] river front has been pulled down because, if they should take fire during a fight, their burning might drive our men from their guns. Our guns were put in position on the breastworks and our horses picketed just outside the town. Here we remained until April 2, 1862, when we were ordered down to Dam No. 1 on [the] Warwick River.[4] We remained here until the evening of April 4, 1862, when we were ordered to Fort Magruder,[5] near Yorktown.

*April 5. Saturday.* The Yanks appeared in our front early this morning at Fort Magruder and began shelling us.[6] The shelling lasted two

[4] There were five dams on Magruder's Warwick River line. One was at Lee's Mill and one at Wynn's Mill. The remaining three were temporary dams built by the Confederates to keep the river flooded and thereby make a crossing by the enemy more difficult. These temporary dams were numbered for identification. The dams themselves offered crossings that had to be defended. In reporting of actions on April 16, Lt. Col. H. C. Cabell, Maj. Gen. D. H. Hill's chief of artillery, stated that Dam No. 1 was one of the weakest points in the Confederate line. There was but a small clearing at this point, which allowed space for only a few guns. It was a point "of great danger and commensurate importance to us . . . a 24 lb. Howitzer of Capt. Nelson's Battery [Hanover Artillery] occupied the front and most exposed position immediately at Dam No. 1." Although there are discrepancies in accounts concerning the location of Dam No. 1, it was located apparently about a mile below Wynn's Mill. (*Atlas to Accompany the Official Records of the Union and Confederate Armies* [Washington, D. C., 1891-95], Plates XV, XIX; *Official Records*, Vol. XI, pt. 1, pp. 412-13; John C. Palfrey, "The Siege of Yorktown," in *The Peninsular Campaign of General McClellan in 1862* [Military Historical Society of Massachusetts, Boston, 1881], I, 48; William Allan, *The Army of Northern Virginia in 1862* [Boston, 1892], p. 12.)

[5] Not to be confused with the Fort Magruder about a mile east of Williamsburg at which the Battle of Williamsburg took place on May 4 and 5. The Fort Magruder referred to here was about nine hundred yards south-southwest of the outer defenses of Yorktown, and was, at times, referred to as "White Redoubt." (*Official Records Atlas*, Plates XIV, XV.)

[6] April 5 is usually taken as the beginning of the siege of Yorktown. Maj. Gen. George B. McClellan had arrived at Fort Monroe on April 2, and immediately planned for an advance up the Peninsula. His army (*ca.* 60,000 men) began to move in two columns. One, Maj. Gen.

hours. This was the first time I was under fire and I thought we would all be killed; however, no one was hurt, not even a horse. We did not reply to the Yanks, and their small rifle shells did us no harm, bursting harmlessly above our heads and the fragments going far in our rear. This was the first time I saw Yankee soldiers and my first battle. In the afternoon, just before sunset, the Yanks sent up a balloon and threw a few shells, which did no harm. After dark, we were ordered back to Dam No. 1, which place we had left the evening before. We found [that] a large house, which stood about 300 yards beyond the east end of Dam No. 1, was on fire when we got there. I don't [know] why or by whom this house and several others in the neighborhood were burned. It seemed to me a useless and causeless destruction of private property. But such is war.

*April 6. Sunday.* The Yanks appeared in our front about eleven o'clock and a Yankee cavalryman captured one of our pickets within 200 yards of our lines. We did not know it was a Yankee until late that evening when John Hill [Berkeley] and old man Mosby[7] went out by permission and found the picket's musket and brought it in our lines; the musket was still loaded. We got a shot at a party of Yankee horsemen a little later in the day, and two men and a horse were seen to fall at the bursting of this twenty-four-pound howitzer shell.

*April 7. Monday.* We had quite a sharp skirmish this evening with a Vermont regiment,[8] which had crept up in a piece of very thick pines and opened on us. We fired some five or six shells into these thick pines, which caused the Vermont boys to retire.

*April 8, 9, 10, 11.* We remained at Dam No. 1, firing occasionally at

Erasmus D. Keyes's Fourth Corps, formed the left by taking the road through Warwick Court House. The other, consisting of Maj. Gen. Samuel P. Heintzelman's Third Corps and Maj. Gen. John Sedgwick's Division of the Second Corps, formed the right, which approached Yorktown directly. These columns reached the Yorktown-Warwick River line on April 5 and immediately attacked. The enemy found the Confederate fortifications too strong and decided to abandon frontal attack and rely on engineering methods and artillery to take Yorktown. (Palfrey, "The Siege of Yorktown," pp. 37, 45-46; *Official Records*, Vol. XI, pt. 3, pp. 63-71. For reports concerning actions on the Yorktown-Warwick River line, see *Official Records*, Vol. XI, pt. 1, pp. 277-422.)

[7] Phil Sam Mosby, a company member from Rockeville, Hanover County. (Interview, Rosewell Page, Jr.)

[8] This could have been the 2nd, 3rd, 4th, 5th, or 6th Vermont Regiment. These units formed Brig. Gen. W. T. H. Brooks's Second Brigade of Brig. Gen. William F. Smith's Division. Smith's Division, Keyes's Fourth Corps, was in the area of Dam No. 1 at this time, and apparently no other Vermont troops were on the Yorktown-Warwick River line. See *Official Records*, Vol. XI, pt. 1, pp. 279-84, for organization of the Federal army at Williamsburg, which was essentially the same as at Yorktown. For the location of Smith's Division headquarters, see *Official Records Atlas,* Plate XV.

the Yanks. All this time, I was very unwell, suffering terribly with diarrhea, our drinking water being very poor. We had no surgeon with us at this time.

*April 12.* We returned to Yorktown and placed our guns in position at different points on the breastworks, on the line running at right angles from the [York] river. We remained in Yorktown under an almost daily shelling from the Yankee gunboats until May 1, 1862. No one was hurt. I do not see how we escaped, for we were cooped up here for over three weeks and the place was crowded with men. Every night during this siege, the Yanks would throw a dozen or two of their big shells into the town between 9 and 10 P.M. These shells weighed 120 pounds, and when they exploded, it seemed as if they would destroy all of us. They frequently failed to explode and would go from 10 to 15 feet into the soft ground. The boys call these big shells "lamp posts," from their resemblance to the butt end of city gas lamp posts. One of these big shells fell diagonally under one of our tents, in which Shelbourne[9] was sleeping, and, after going down under the tent some 10 or 12 feet, it exploded and blew Shelbourne some dozen feet into the air, knocking him senseless. The boy soon, however, came to himself and in a few hours was all right again. This was the only accident in my company during the three weeks' siege. There was a dog or two killed. Thousands of dogs had collected at Yorktown during the previous winter to get scraps, bones, meat and bread, which our soldiers threw away in large quantities, rations then being very plentiful.

About the last of April, 1862, our company was reorganized and the following officers elected, viz. Capt. G. W. Nelson, 1st Lieut. W. M. Fontaine, 2nd Lieut. H. M. Stringfellow, 3rd Lieut. William Basye.[10] Our noncommissioned officers were also elected and the old ones were nearly all dropped. Our battery at this time was attached to Gen. Rains's Brigade

---

9 H. Shelbourne, a company member from Hanover County.

10 General Order No. 30, April 28, 1862, Adjutant and Inspector General's Office, issued in accordance with an act of Congress, ordered all units of twelve month volunteers to re-enlist and reorganize within forty days from April 16, 1862, or be drafted. (*Official Records*, Ser. IV, Vol. I, pp. 1094-1100.) In the election held by the men of the Hanover Artillery, Capt. William Nelson, a rather severe disciplinarian, lost his post as company commander to G. W. Nelson, a less exacting and more genial person. This happened often in the Confederate Army, and resulted in incompetent officers in many units. George Washington Nelson, of Hanover County, was born in 1840. He attended the University of Virginia in 1858 and 1859. Nelson remained the company commander until October, 1862, when it was mustered out. He then became an inspector general of artillery. After the war he attended the Theological Seminary in Virginia at Alexandria and became an Episcopal clergyman in Virginia. (William A. R. Goodwin, *History of the Theological Seminary in Virginia and Its Historical Background* [New York, 1923], II, 128, 154.) William Basye was a native of Hanover County.

and put directly under Gen. Rains's command.[11] The brigade was composed of the following regiments: viz. the 6th Georgia, 27th Georgia, 23rd Georgia, 13th Alabama and 26th Alabama.[12] It was a large, strong and splendid brigade.

*May 2.* Our forces began to evacuate Yorktown about dark. Our brigade started out about 8 P.M., and my battery was ordered to follow the 6th Georgia. We had hardly gotten out of the town on the Williamsburg Road when we were ordered back to the positions which we had left an hour before. This was done because we found the road so blocked up and crowded with wagons and ambulances that the troops could not possibly get along. There was heavy shelling tonight by the Yanks, to which our boys replied quite actively, making things quite lively. We got some sleep about daybreak. About a month before this, Uncle Landon [Carter Berkeley], who had been dropped at the reorganization of his company, came by our camp on his way home and left Henry Lacy to cook for us. Henry was a very good and trusty negro boy of about sixteen, and had waited in the dining room at "Montout" and been in the army with Uncle Landon for ten months. After getting Henry, we had sent Amos home.

*May 3. Saturday.* We remained all day in position at Yorktown. We pulled out about dark, following closely our brigade, and after a hard and laborious march through mud and darkness, we reached Williamsburg, where we went into camp on the Richmond side of the town.

*May 5.* We started towards Richmond about sunrise. It was raining hard. We had not gone far when our brigade was sent back with two of our lightest guns to the battle, which had begun on the York side of Williamsburg. My gun being a twenty-four-pound howitzer, we did not go back, but remained on the roadside all day. It rained hard all day. I had a severe chill today, which shook me almost to pieces. The chill was followed by a very high fever. I got as wet as a rat. About sunset it stopped

[11] Brig. Gen. Gabriel J. Rains. General Rains gained questionable popularity when, on the retreat from Yorktown, he placed "land mines" in the roads so that the pursuing Federal forces detonated them and suffered some casualties. The use of these mines raised loud complaints from Northerners (as well as Southerners), who claimed that this was an improper method of warfare. Rains denied this, but Maj. Gen. James Longstreet forbade him to use the mines further. The Confederate War Department became interested in the use of these mines, and the Secretary of War, George Wythe Randolph, later assigned Rains to the War Department to work on the development of mines. (*Dictionary of American Biography*, XV, 328. For the controversy concerning the use of mines on land, see *Official Records*, Vol. XI, pt. 3, pp. 509 ff.)

[12] Cols. A. H. Colquitt, Levi B. Smith, Thomas Hutcherson, B. D. Fry, and E. A. O'Neal commanding respectively. Actually, Smith's 27th Georgia was in Featherstone's Brigade, and

raining, and the rest of my battery went back to the battlefield. I was, however, too sick to go with them and remained with our wagons. Henry, our cook, got me a cup of coffee and fixed up some blankets to keep off the rain, after which I succeeded in getting a little sleep.

*May 6. Tuesday.* We continued our march towards Richmond. I feel a good deal better today. It is a bright, sunny day. We had very little to eat, our commissary wagons being stuck in the mud and many being compelled to throw out the rations in order to get along. John Lewis and I got hold of some corn, and parched and ate it. Nuckols[13] gave me the leg of a rooster, which he had captured. I cut it up and put it in a frying pan with a pint of water and got Henry to cook it for me until about half the water was gone. I then begged a little salt to put on it, and then enjoyed eating it very much. We could get no bread.

*May 7. Wednesday.* We continued our march towards Richmond. I had another bad chill today, followed by a very high fever. I was so sick at one time that I thought I would not be able to go any farther, and would doubtless have been left behind to fall into the Yankee hands but for John Hill, who, hearing of my condition, came back and got me on a limber, and carried me in that way to our camp for the night. We drew some rations today for the first time since leaving York. After this, we continued to fall back on Richmond, reaching the city on Sunday morning, May 18, 1862. By the time we got to Richmond, I had gotten a good deal better, but was still weak and poorly. We encamped on the River Road [New Market Road] one mile below the city, E. M. Anderson being quite sick.

*May 22.* Got permission to go to Richmond today. I left John Lewis quite sick. I felt quite anxious about him. I saw Uncle Landon and dined with him; he tried to get a pass to go out to see John Lewis, but did not succeed. He went up home that day, promising to come back on next Saturday.

*May 23.* John Lewis gets no better but rather grows worse. We remained on the River Road until May 25, when we moved to a Mr. Davis's farm on the Charles City Road, getting quite pleasant quarters in a large barn. In the meantime, E. M. Anderson and John Lewis Berkeley had been sent to the hospital in Richmond with typhoid fever. I had two chills

there is no record of it having been assigned to Rains's command during the retreat from Yorktown.

13 Either Alpheus B. or Addison N. Nuckols, both sons of the Rev. Harden D. Nuckols, a Baptist clergyman of Hanover County, and both members of the company. Addison was later a Danville, Virginia, physician. (Jed Hotchkiss, *Virginia* [Atlanta, 1899], p. 1078.)

while at Davis's barn. We remained at this barn until May 31, 1862, when we were ordered with our brigade into the Battle of Seven Pines. When we got to the junction of the Williamsburg and Charles City roads, we were stopped there because our guns were too big and heavy to get through deep mud. We remained at the junction of these roads until the Battle of Seven Pines was over.

*June 2. Monday.* We went into camp near the junction of the Williamsburg and Charles City roads on the farm of Mr. John Poe.

*June 3.* We exchanged our heavy guns for some lighter ones, and were then ordered with our brigade about three miles down the Williamsburg Road, stopping for the night in an open field on the right of the road coming up towards Richmond. It rained all night very hard. We all got wet. We had no blankets, having left them at the camp we quitted that morning.

*June 4.* We moved this morning across a little branch into some oak woods. We fixed up ourselves here quite comfortably. We remained here until June 25. I was very sick and poorly almost the whole time that we remained in this camp, suffering with chills and fever. We had hard living here, too, until just before we left, when Arthur [Negro servant] came down and brought us some home eatings.

*June 25.* We were ordered down the Williamsburg Road and remained on the front lines until dark, when we returned to camp. I had a bad chill this evening and had to be sent back to camp before the battery came in. About twelve o'clock at night our company was ordered, with its brigade, around to Mechanicsville. I, being too sick to go, was left in camp.

*June 26. Thursday.* Jack Cooke, Martin Stringfellow and I had a very good dinner today, but I could not eat much, as Dr. Lawson,[14] our new surgeon, had dosed me with too many of his pills. Late this evening Claudy Anderson[15] came back to camp and told us that our battery was near Mechanicsville, expecting every minute to go into a fight. I sent the boys some rations by Claudy. About night we heard firing in the direction of Mechanicsville, and, going to the top of a hill near our camp, we could

[14] Dr. John W. Lawson. After the war he was a member of the Virginia House of Delegates, United States Congressman from Virginia, and president of the Board of Visitors of the College of William and Mary. (Wyndham B. Blanton, *Medicine in Virginia in the Nineteenth Century* [Richmond, 1933], p. 407; Hotchkiss, *Virginia*, pp. 993-94.)

[15] Claudius Montgomery Anderson, son of John T. and Frances Anderson, was born July 21, 1842, in Hanover County. (Anderson Family Bible, photostats in the Manuscripts Division, University of Virginia Library.)

see very plainly the flashing of the guns as it grew dark. The firing continued until a very late hour at night.[16]

*June 27.  Friday.*  This morning, as I felt a little better, I wanted to go and find my company; but Lieut. Stringfellow ordered me to carry some sick men to the hospital in Richmond. I took them to several hospitals but could not get them in, all the hospitals in the city having been cleared for the reception of the wounded, who were coming in very fast from a great battle which was raging near Cold Harbor. I left the sick at a private boarding house and then went to the Central Depot,[17] where large numbers of wounded were arriving and having their wounds dressed. The sight was truly heart-rending. Our surgeons were very busy dressing wounds and amputating limbs, while all kinds of groans and expressions of pain escaped from the lips of the sufferers. The ladies of Richmond, may God ever bless them, from the maiden of sixty to the young girl in her teens, moved like ministering angels among these sufferers, doing all in their power to relieve the soldiers' pains and sufferings. I looked among them to see if I could find any of my company, but seeing none, I was glad to leave this sad place.

*June 28.  Saturday.*  Today we moved our camp back to Mr. Poe's farm, and, after doing this, I went after some corn and hay for Tom Duke.[18] We then made preparations to join our company early the next morning. Dr. Lawson, our surgeon, came back to camp tonight, which I think very strange behavior, as he reports our company still moving on the front.

*June 29.  Sunday.*  We started early this morning with our wagon to go to our company, which we learned the night before was near Cold Harbor. We passed over the entire battlefields of Mechanicsville and Cold Harbor. I then saw for the first time one of the most awful sights of war. Our dead had not been buried and the corpses were swollen, as if

---

[16] The action at Mechanicsville on June 26 took place on the second of the Seven Days battles. General Lee began this movement, his first as commander of what he called the Army of Northern Virginia, to prevent a siege of Richmond by General McClellan. McClellan's army was astride the Chickahominy River, and Lee determined to execute a turning movement by striking at the Federal right wing, north of the Chickahominy. The battle at Mechanicsville was fought on June 26, Gaines Mill on June 27, Savage Station on June 29, Frayser's Farm on June 30, and Malvern Hill, a disastrous end to Lee's movement, on July 1. For the battles, see Douglas Southall Freeman, *Lee's Lieutenants: A Study In Command* (New York, 1942-44), I, 503-604; Douglas Southall Freeman, *R. E. Lee: A Biography* [New York, 1935], II, 123-219; for Lee's rather elaborate plan of battle, see Freeman, *R. E. Lee,* II, 110 *ff.*

[17] Virginia Central Railroad Depot, on Union Street between Broad and Grace. (Weddell, *Richmond,* map opposite p. 116.)

[18] A member and at one time third lieutenant of the Hanover Artillery.

they would burst, and had turned as black as soot. I cannot imagine why these poor fellows have not been buried. They were killed on Thursday evening and now it is midday Sunday. They are Georgians and North Carolinians. We found our company in a field below Cold Harbor. The Yankee dead were quite thick just about this place, while a great many blankets, overcoats, tents, wagons, muskets and plunder of all kinds lay scattered over the field in great quantities. I found all the boys very well and unhurt, although they had been engaged two days. I saw Berkeley Minor[19] this evening and was glad to find him well and unhurt. The battle of Savage Station was fought this evening just across the Chicka-hominy River from us by Gen. Magruder. The Yanks having burned the bridge, we could not cross. I saw Gen. Stonewall Jackson this evening for the first time. He is not a man whom I would take for a great general, if I had to judge from his looks.

*June 30. Monday.* The bridge across the Chickahominy having been rebuilt, our brigade passed over and we followed it. We went over the battlefield of yesterday evening, where knapsacks, haversacks, oil-cloths, blankets and plunder of every description lay thick. It seems to me there were enough blankets and tents to supply 100,000 men. I secured two oilcloths and a beautiful red blanket, but I did not care to load myself down with plunder, knowing that the chances were that we would soon go into a fight.[20] I was acting as a driver today, my team being the wheel horses. Just after passing the [York River] railroad and getting onto the Williamsburg Road, two of our guns (my gun in front) were put in front with the skirmishers of the 6th Georgia Regiment, Col. Colquitt[21] in command. We advanced slowly on the Yanks, taking hundreds of pris-oners all along the road, which was scattered over with muskets, cartridge boxes, bayonets, blankets and vast quantities of plunder of various descrip-

19 Carter Nelson Berkeley Minor (1842-1930) of "Aetna," Hanover County, a member of the Stonewall Battery. He was later a lieutenant in the Engineers Corps. Berkeley attended the University of Virginia in 1859 and 1860. After the war he taught at the Episcopal High School, Alexandria, Virginia, and later was, for thirty years, a member of the faculty of Stuart Hall in Staunton. For a biographical sketch, see *University of Virginia Alumni News*, XVIII (Feb-ruary, 1930), p. 136.

20 For Maj. Gen. T. J. Jackson's statement concerning the plunder left by the enemy, see *Official Records*, Vol. XI, pt. 2, pp. 556, wherein Jackson states, "Many other evidences of the hurried and disordered flight of the enemy were now visible—blankets, clothing, and other supplies had been recklessly abandoned. D. H. Hill . . . gathered up probably 1,000 stragglers and so many small-arms that it became necessary to detach two regiments to take charge of them and to see to the security of the prisoners."

21 Col. (later Brig. Gen.) A. H. Colquitt commanded Brig. Gen. Gabriel J. Rains's old brigade during the Seven Days' Battles, Rains having been assigned to the War Department on June 18. (Freeman, *Lee's Lieutenants*, I, 268-69.)

tions. On reaching the White Oak Swamp, we found the Yanks on the opposite side in line of battle, ready to dispute our passage. Our battery with four others, making about thirty cannon, were soon put in position on a hill to the right of the road.[22] We very soon opened on the Yanks and were very hotly engaged for about three hours. We lost no men but had four horses killed. I can't see how we escaped. Col. Carter,[23] on our right, had three men wounded, and Capt. Rhett,[24] on our left, had two men killed and three wounded. We retired from the field about 4 P.M., having used up all our ammunition, and fresh batteries took our places. Gen. Jackson's men are now passing us in battle order. It is sad to think what bloody work they will do before sunset. It is now 6 P.M.; the Yanks have been defeated and driven from their positions, but, oh, how many of our brave boys have fallen! We endeavored to get our limbers and caissons filled with ammunition but could find none to suit. We have only a few rounds of canister left.

*July 1. Tuesday.* We were ordered up to the Fair Oaks this morning, and reached there about midday and went into an old Yankee camp on the right of the road as you go towards Richmond.[25] I wrote home. The Battle of Malvern Hill was fought this evening.[26] A terrible thunder and rainstorm raged during the battle. We could hear distinctly the noise of the battle. Jack Cooke came very near killing Bob Winston accidentally. Jack was standing near Bob, who was seated at the root of a tree, writing home to his parents to tell of his safety, when a pistol, which Jack was very carelessly handling, went off, and the ball buried itself in the tree, at the foot of which Bob was seated, not three inches above Bob's head. Bob was leaning over writing. If he had been sitting up straight, the ball would certainly have killed him. I never saw as mad a man as Bob; and well he might be.

[22] The report of Col. Stapleton Crutchfield, chief of artillery for Jackson's command, states that seven batteries totaling twenty-three guns were in action at this point, which was east of Long Bridge (which the enemy had destroyed) at White Oak Swamp. Jackson's report states the presence of twenty-eight guns and D. H. Hill's thirty-one, including five from Whiting's Division. (*Official Records,* Vol. XI, pt. 2, pp. 557, 560-62, 627.)

[23] Capt. (later Col.) Thomas Hill Carter, commanding officer of the King William Artillery.

[24] Capt. (later Maj.) A. Burnett Rhett, commanding the South Carolina Battery, Maj. Hilary Jones's Battalion (temporarily attached to D. H. Hill's Division).

[25] "Next day [July 1] all the artillery of General Hill's division were ordered back to Seven Pines to rest, for they had been marching and fighting up to this time constantly in advance of General Jackson's army." (Report of Capt. A. Burnett Rhett, *Official Records,* Vol. XI, pt. 2, p. 655.)

[26] For the disastrous Battle at Malvern Hill, see Freeman, *R. E. Lee,* II, 200-19; Freeman, *Lee's Lieutenants,* I, 588-604.

CHAPTER III

# WE WERE LEFT IN VIRGINIA

*Second Manassas to Sharpsburg, 1862*

*July 2, 1862.  Wednesday.*  We remained in camp at Fair Oaks, our limbers and caissons going to Richmond for ammunition. It rained hard all day. Mr. Marcellus Anderson,[1] who went to Richmond with the boys, brought back an old black bottle, which the boys soon emptied.

*July 3.  Thursday.*  We went back to the front and joined our brigade, which we found on the Charles City Road, and encamped on a Mr. Brackett's[2] farm. His house was full of Yankee wounded and his barn filled with Yankee sick. We remained at this place from July 3 to July 8. Everything quiet. While here, Jack [John McP.] Cooke, Bob [Robert B.] Winston, John Hill [Berkeley] and I buried one poor Yank, giving him his full share of Virginia land. We also appropriated to our own use two pigs and an old sow, which we found wandering in the swamp. Not being able to get any rations, our captain gave us his permission to take them.

*July 8.*  We went, with our brigade and Hampton's Cavalry, down to a Mr. Gatewood's[3] farm near Malvern Hill. We remained there one day and then returned to our camp near Richmond, on Mr. [John] Poe's farm; here, we remained very quiet until August 18 except that the first section of our battery, consisting of two guns, went on picket down on White

1 Marcellus M. Anderson, a company member from Hanover County.
2 Probably J. Brackett's farm, which was on the north side of the Charles City Road about nine miles east of the junction of this road with the Williamsburg Road. (*Atlas to Accompany the official Records of the Union and Confederate Armies* [Washington, D. C., 1891-95], Plate XIX.) McClellan's forces had retired to Harrison's Landing on the James River after the battle at Malvern Hill on July 1. Lee advanced his forces with the hope of attacking McClellan, but nothing resulted. On July 9, the Confederate army began drawing in closer to Richmond. (Douglas Southall Freeman, *R. E. Lee: A Biography* [New York, 1935], II, 220-30.)
3 Probably the farm of G. W. Gatewood on Sam's Branch, which flows into Carter's Mill Pond just east of Malvern Hill. (*Official Records Atlas*, Plate XIX.)

• 22 •

Oak Swamp every other week. During this time, our horses died like anything for want of proper care. We also, during this same time, lost a good
many men, among them, Claudy Anderson.[4]

Capt. G. W. Nelson and his officers, with the exception of Lieut. William Basye, who were elected in the spring, have proved themselves totally
incompetent to command a battery. The company is going to the dogs,
and unless something is done, and done very soon, it will go all to pieces.
Wash is as brave a man as I ever saw and fears nothing, but bravery alone
will not keep up a battery. It requires a hard-working, industrious man of
good executive ability; one who never tires, and is always on the lookout
for his men and horses. All of these are wanting in him and his first and
second lieutenants. Lieut. Basye is a good man and a good officer, and
would, if he were captain, make us a splendid battery; but being the junior
officer, with three over him, he hesitates to act. My mess occupies itself
during its leisure time in abusing Wash and his lieutenants for their laziness and want of energy.[5] Several of us about this time asked to be transferred to the Hanover Cavalry,[6] but Wash refused to sign our petitions
and we had to give up the idea. However, Jack Cooke was transferred to
the Hanover Cavalry about this time and Frank Hall to Braxton's Battery.[7] Mr. Marcellus Anderson got a discharge. I was, during all this time,
very poorly and unwell, suffering with chills and fevers which our surgeon, Dr. [John W.] Lawson, seemed unable to stop. I think my sickness
was due to weakness caused by my attack of typhoid fever last fall, from
which I have not fully recovered even yet.

*August 15.* We were ordered to move with our brigade towards the
Hanover Junction, but our horses were in such a very bad condition that

---

[4] Claudius M. Anderson died of typhoid fever on July 28, 1862, at the home of F. Mat-
thews in Richmond. He was interred the next day in Hollywood Cemetery. (Anderson Family
Bible, photostats in the Manuscripts Division, University of Virginia Library.)

[5] When the Hanover Artillery was mustered out during the reorganization of the Artillery Corps of the Army of Northern Virginia in October, 1862, Brig. Gen. William N. Pendleton, chief of artillery, stated, "Capt. G. Washington Nelson's battery [should be mustered
out] the men and horses not being wisely managed although . . . Nelson has served with as
distinguished gallantry as any officer . . . and yet he is not, in some respects, adapted to
take care of a battery, nor are his lieutenants, though one of them (Lieutenant Fontaine)
is a good officer. . . ." (*The War of the Rebellion: A Compilation of the Official Records of
the Union and Confederate Armies* [Washington, D. C., 1880-1901], Series I, Volume XIX, part
2, pp. 649-50. All citations will be from Series I unless otherwise noted.)

[6] The old Hanover Troop of the Virginia Militia. It came into the Confederate Army
with Capt. Williams C. Wickham as its commanding officer, and was assigned to the Fourth
Virginia Cavalry as Company G. Wickham was later the commanding officer of the Fourth
Cavalry.

[7] Capt. Carter M. Braxton's Fredericksburg Battery, attached to Maj. Gen. Ambrose P.
Hill's Division.

they were unable to pull our guns, so Channing Page,[8] who commanded the Morris Artillery, which battery was also from Hanover County, was ordered to take our place with Gen. [A. H.] Colquitt's Brigade and we were ordered to report to Maj. William Nelson.[9] After the Battle of Seven Pines, Gen. [Gabriel J.] Rains had been put in the ordnance department and Col. Colquitt of the 6th Georgia had been made a brigadier and put in command of our brigade.[10]

*August 18.* We moved this evening over to Maj. Nelson's artillery camp and reported to him for duty. Maj. Nelson's camp was about a mile from Oakwood Cemetery.[11] I am very much gratified at this change.

*August 19.* Wash Nelson made a little speech to his company at roll call this morning. He told them that he had *not* done his duty by them, acknowledged his faults, and promised, with God's help, to try and do better in the future, and prayed them to help and support him in his endeavor. He then had prayers, a thing which Maj. Nelson had always done as long as he was our captain, whenever it was possible to be done. This was a good beginning for Wash. I wonder if he will keep it up. Time will show. I doubt it.

*August 20.* We started early this morning for the Hanover Junction, going up the Old Telegraph Road. We encamped for the night near "Locust Level" spring about midnight.

*August 21.* Dabney Williamson sent Henry, our cook, early this morning to Mr. Edmund Winston's with a note, requesting his daughter, Miss Sally Barton Winston, to send him breakfast for himself and six messmates, but Henry, after much delay, came back with only a little buttermilk. John Hill, however, while Henry was gone to Mr. Winston's, had taken our flour, meat and coffee over to "Locust Level" house and gotten Jane Smith and her mother to get us up a breakfast, which these good and kind old family servants did with seemingly the greatest pleasure, adding some eggs and a little butter from their own scanty store. I never enjoyed a breakfast more and have always remembered the kindness of these old servants. We had hardly gotten through with our nice breakfast when we were ordered to pull out, which we promptly did. We only went as far

---

[8] Capt. Richard Channing Moore Page of Albemarle County, commanding the Morris Battery, Nelson's Third Battalion, reserve artillery.

[9] At this time commanding a battalion. It will be recalled that Nelson was the first commanding officer of the Hanover Artillery.

[10] As noted previously, Col. A. H. Colquitt succeeded General Rains on June 18. See Chapter II, note 21.

[11] Oakwood Cemetery, located east of Richmond, on Nine Mile Road. It is now within the city limits of Richmond.

as Hanover Junction and went into camp near that place. We immediately sent Henry home. Pa came down that evening and brought us some home eatings, spending several hours with us.

*August 22.   Friday.*   We remained at the Junction.

*August 23.   Saturday.*   All the ladies from our homes and neighborhood came down today to see us and spent the whole day with us. They brought us a great many nice home rations and then got us a royal dinner; we even had ice water and ice cream. Mrs. Winston, Bob Winston's mother, joined us about 1 P.M., on her way from Richmond. She was traveling in her carriage, with faithful old Dick, her driver. This was one of the most pleasant and happy days I ever spent in camp. These home people made heroes of us, yet we had only done our duty; at least, we had tried to do it. The day passed away very quickly and seemed very short.

*August 24.   Sunday.*   John Lewis [Berkeley] and I were detailed to go with our wagons after corn. We went up to Uncle Nelson's[12] for it. We had expected to hire some negroes at "White House" and "Montout," while we would have remained at home. When we got home, every negro was gone to the different camps to spend their Sunday, and we had to go on and load the wagons ourselves. We, however, came back by our homes and remained there until 9 P.M. and then returned to our camp at the [Hanover] Junction.

*August 25.   Monday.*   We moved from the Junction up to Mr. Edmund Anderson's gate, going into camp right in front of the gate. Mrs. Winston and Mrs. Aylett took dinner with us, remaining until nearly sunset. Uncle Nelson was over in camp, but did not come to our tent. The old gent was after the money for his corn. *He got it* and then got home.

*August 26.   Tuesday.*   Our camp was aroused about one o'clock last night and we were ordered to be ready to move at daybreak. All my clothes had been sent home to be washed and mended and I had to get permission to go over for them. It was about two miles from our camp over home; got there about three o'clock at night and found everyone asleep. All the family soon turned out and I remained with them for about an hour, when Papa brought me back to camp. I expected to find my battalion on the road, but they had not pulled out. We had to wait until Generals Hill's and McLaws' divisions[13] had passed and did not get off until 10 A.M. I do not see why our officers did not let us sleep until 7 A.M. We

---

[12] Nelson William Berkeley, older brother of HRB's mother.

[13] Maj. Gens. Daniel Harvey Hill and Lafayette McLaws, whose divisions had been ordered to march from the Richmond area (where they had been left to guard the capital city while the remainder of the army fought Gen. John Pope's Federal army at Manassas) to reinforce

marched very slowly today and encamped for the night at Greenbay.[14]

*August 27.*　We continued our march towards Culpeper Court House and encamped for the night near Louisa Court House.

*August 28.*　We continued our march towards Culpeper and encamped for the night near Orange Court House.

*August 29.*　We did not go far today, and encamped for the night near Rapidan Station on the Orange and Alexandria Railroad.

*August 30.*　We reached Culpeper today, which is quite a pretty village; but [it] has been very much pulled to pieces by the vile Yanks. We encamped for the night just north of the town on a creek.

*August 31. Sunday.*　We continued our march towards Manassas and were forced to remain in the road all night by attempting to cross the Rappahannock River, over which the bridge had been burned. It looked very much as if we were going to have rain, and Gen. Pendleton,[15] our chief of artillery, was anxious to get all his guns over for fear of a sudden rise in the river.

*September 1.*　We crossed the river early, and stopped at the Warrenton Springs, which are on the north bank of the river, to cook and feed our horses. After feeding and cooking, we continued our march, but after getting within a mile of Warrenton, our horses gave entirely out, and our company was left behind with orders to rest our horses one day and then to follow the command to Leesburg, Loudoun County, Virginia.

*September 2.*　We remained near Warrenton all day. Our horses were turned out to graze and a guard thrown around them. Some of our mess, I among the number, took breakfast at the hotel in Warrenton, but it was short rations. We, however, had genuine coffee in abundance, something unusual now.

*September 3.*　We continued our march towards Leesburg and encamped for the night at Gainesville on [the] Manassas Gap Railroad.

*September 4.*　We continued our march towards Leesburg, and encamped for the night a mile below Aldie, near Mt. Zion Church. Rations very short; nothing for breakfast but two ears of corn, boiled, i.e. *roasting ears.*

*September 5.*　We reached Leesburg, quite a pretty place, at 4 P.M. and found the army crossing into Maryland. We went into camp on the Winchester Pike, a mile west of Leesburg.

Lee's army, which was about to invade Maryland. (*Official Records,* Vol. XIX, pt. 1, p. 1019.)

[14] Located in Hanover County about three miles northwest of Beaverdam Station, at the junction of present Virginia routes 658 and 715.

[15] Brig. Gen. William N. Pendleton.

*September 6.* We remained in camp near Leesburg, watching our army crossing into Maryland. Dabney Williamson and I rode out to try and find some meal, but did not succeed. We came back through town and saw some pretty girls there.

*September 7. Sunday.* All our best horses were taken from us and given to the batteries which were going over into Maryland, and we were left in Virginia with a Maj. Richardson[16] and a big lot of broken-down horses to carry some guns, wagons and other plunder to Winchester. This state of things has been brought about by the laziness and incompetency of our company officers.

*September 8.* Bob Winston and I went out early this morning to look for some grub. We went to a Mrs. Clarke's,[17] who lived on the north of the Winchester Pike. She gave us a very nice breakfast and refused to let us pay for it. We came back by a Mrs. Heath's and saw there a Mrs. Adie and her daughter. We had a long and pleasant talk with the mother. The daughter, not over twelve, was very pretty, but had little to say. Our conversation related to the war and the great battles recently fought and the sad and great loss of the South in these battles. We got back to camp about ten in the day and found our battalion getting ready to move towards Winchester. We started about sunset. It was a bright moonlight night, and after going about twelve miles, we encamped on the south of the pike, on the farm of a Mr. Adams, who was quite an old man.[18] My health had greatly improved since leaving Richmond and I had fattened up several pounds.

*September 9.* I went back to Leesburg with all the drivers and sergeants of Major Richardson's command, to bring up a lot of extra guns. We came back with these extra guns to our camp at the Adams farm this afternoon about three.

*September 10.* We remained here all day. While here, we bought everything from the farmers remarkably cheap; chickens for 16 cents;

[16] Maj. (later Lieut. Col.) Charles Richardson, a Virginian, later was second field officer of Lieut. Col. John J. Garnett's Battalion, and succeeded Garnett when he was transferred out of the artillery. (Jennings C. Wise, *The Long Arm of Lee or The History of the Artillery of the Army of Northern Virginia* [Lynchburg, Va., 1915], I, 279, 327, 419, 720.) Artillery units in poor condition were ordered to remain at Leesburg under Major Richardson who was to attempt to strengthen them. The remainder of the artillery went into Maryland with the army and fought the Battle of Sharpsburg. Serviceable matériel and good horses were distributed among those units going to the battlefield. (Wise, *Long Arm*, I, 279; *Official Records*, Vol. XIX, pt. 2, pp. 592, 595.)

[17] There is a home of an A. H. Clarke located on maps of the period about a mile and a quarter north of the Pike. (*Official Records Atlas*, Plate VII.)

[18] Several Adams farms were located west of Purcellville.

butter 12½ cents; milk, at 25 cents per gallon and everything in the same proportion.

*September 11.*   We continued our march towards Winchester, and after crossing the Blue Ridge at Snicker's Gap, we encamped on the west side of the Shenandoah River. It was raining. All the drivers were immediately sent back to bring up the extra guns. We got these extra guns and got as far as the foot of the mountain (the rain in the meantime increasing very much) where our horses gave out completely. I wanted [to] leave the gun and go on to camp without it, but our sergeant would not consent to do this. Ours was the only team which had broken down; all the others, some sixty in number, had gone on to camp. We worked on these poor horses for four hours and got only some two miles. We then ungeared and turned them in a field of twenty acres with good grass and went to look for something to eat for ourselves. After going about a mile, we got a good, nice and plentiful supper from a farmer. I wanted to stay in this farmer's barn all night, as it was raining hard and promised to rain all night, and I could see no good in our going back to the field in which we had left our horses, as the field had a good stone fence all around it and the horses could not possibly get out. Our sergeant, however, did not agree with me, and we had to return to our horses. I slept that night on a pile of rocks in a fence corner, with my saddle cloth stretched on two slanting rails so as to protect my head a little, and with the cape of my overcoat turned over my head. It rained all night, but I was so tired that I slept soundly all night. A few rocks formed my pillow. I used to think Jacob's pillow was pretty rough, but I have changed my mind since this war began.

*September 12.*   I got up from my rock bed about sunrise. It had stopped raining and was clearing off. We had *no* breakfast. We got up our horses, geared them and put them to the gun. We succeeded in going only a mile or two; then we were obliged to give up the effort and to leave the gun and return to camp, a thing I wanted to do the evening before. Some fresh mules were sent for the abandoned gun and soon had it in camp. Henry, our cook, had fixed up for our dinner a very savory and promising hash; but John Hill, who had gotten hold of some beautiful *looking* beets, put some of his beets in the hash and made it so bitter that he about ruined it and we had to eat our bread dry. The boys of our mess, after this incident, dubbed this camp "The Beet-Slush-Camp," to John Hill's disgust.

*September 13.*   We continued our march towards Winchester and encamped at the Spout Spring on the Opequon Creek about seven miles from Winchester.

*September 14.   Sunday.*   The drivers and sergeants, I among them, went back to the Shenandoah River to bring up our extra guns. As we came back through Berryville, the congregations from the different churches were just coming out of Church. It was then that I first realized it was Sunday. We saw two very pretty ladies.

*September 15.*   We drivers carried all the extra guns to Winchester this morning and turned them over to Maj. Harman,[19] our corps quartermaster. I am very glad that we have finally gotten rid of these extra guns. A young lady at Winchester today gave us some very nice grapes. We returned to our camp at the Spout Spring on the Opequon, where we remained for about a week, and then we moved out on the Staunton Pike and encamped just beyond Kernstown on the east of the pike. We remained at this camp for some time, everything passing off very quietly until October 5, 1862.

19 Major John A. Harman, quartermaster for Stonewall Jackson's command.

# CHAPTER IV

# HANOVER ARTILLERY . . . BROKEN UP

## *Fredericksburg, 1862*

*October 5, 1862. Sunday.* Today we hear that our company, the Hanover Artillery, with many other batteries, is to be broken up and our men to be divided out between Capt. Woolfolk's[1] and Capt. Kirkpatrick's[2] batteries. This news caused a great excitement in our company, some of our men swearing that it was a great injustice and that they meant to go home; and some did go home. Wash [George Washington] Nelson, our captain, went over to Gen. [William N.] Pendleton's headquarters to see if this news was true. He learned that the company had already been broken up and that the men had the choice of going either to Capt. Woolfolk or to Capt. Kirkpatrick. Capt. Woolfolk's company is from Hanover and Capt. Kirkpatrick's from Amherst [County], Lynchburg and Bedford [County].[3] Most of our men seem to favor Woolfolk. Wash Nelson came

---

[1] Capt. Pichegru Woolfolk's Ashland (Hanover County) Battery.

[2] Capt. Thomas J. Kirkpatrick's Amherst Battery.

[3] Acting on instructions from General Lee, General Pendleton prepared a report containing recommendations for reducing the number and increasing the efficiency of the artillery organizations in the Army of Northern Virginia. This was necessitated by a reduced number of men and horses, and by incompetence of officers. In his report to Lee, Pendleton recommended disbanding about twenty-one batteries, the men and horses to be assigned to batteries of better quality but of reduced strength. Pendleton forwarded this report to Lee on October 2, 1862. As a result of this report, Lee issued Order No. 209 on October 4, which placed in effect Pendleton's recommendations. One of the batteries mustered out by this order was the Hanover Artillery, whose officers were to be relieved. Twenty of the battery's men were to be assigned to Kirkpatrick's Company, Nelson's Battalion, and forty to Woolfolk's Battery, S. D. Lee's Battalion. Pendleton's reasons for requesting the break-up of Nelson's Battery were that the men and horses were not "wisely managed," although, the report continued, "Captain Nelson has served with as distinguished gallantry as any officer in the Confederate Army. For cool intrepidity and heroic daring . . . Capt. Wash. Nelson is unsurpassed . . . and yet he is not, in some respects, adapted to take care of a battery." The report continued, "Nor are his [Nelson's] lieutenants, though one of them (Lieutenant Fontaine) is a good officer to be provided for." (*The War of the Rebellion: A Compilation of the Official*

back from Gen. Pendleton's headquarters very well satisfied, having been promised a very soft place on the General's staff.[4] He does not seem to care one cent as to what becomes of his men. But his men deserve no sympathy, for they were the men who elected him. I do feel very sorry that the old Hanover Artillery should have met such an untimely end. It was a splendid body of men, was the first artillery company from the County in the field, and deserved a better fate; [the company] erred in electing a man who had nothing but his personal bravery to recommend him.

*October 6. Monday.* This morning I handed Martin Stringfellow a communication signed by every man present, asking him to resign. This communication had been gotten up and signed before we knew our company was to be broken up. Martin became very indignant at finding certain names to this communication. He and John Hill had [a] fierce quarrel, and then he (Martin) shifted the quarrel to Sam Mills.[5] Sam abused him like a dog, told him that he had skulked out of *all* the battles around Richmond except White Oak Swamp, and that when wanted in that battle, had been found hiding in a gully in [the] rear of his guns. Sam wound up by telling him that he was a coward and a liar and that if he would lay aside his commission that [he] would lick him soundly. After this quarrel, Martin Stringfellow soon left the Army of Northern Virginia and went to Texas and got a place in Gen. [John Bankhead] Magruder's command as an ordnance officer. Many of his brother officers had witnessed this disgraceful behavior of his and he had to get out of Virginia.[6]

*October 7.* This morning, after a long debate, my mess decided to join Capt. Kirkpatrick's company, our old captain, Major William Nelson, advising us to go to that company. A good many of our men got drunk today; our company officers, having been relieved of duty, had no authority

*Records of the Union and Confederate Armies* [Washington, D. C., 1880-1901], Series I, Volume XIX, part 2, pp. 646-54. All citations will be from Series I unless otherwise noted.)

[4] After the reorganization, Nelson was considered an artillery officer unattached to a battery. At the Battle of Fredericksburg in December, 1862, Nelson commanded one of the two thirty-pound Parrott guns on the artillery line. Nelson's gun was the one to the left of the house of the Virginia historian R. R. Howison, and near Telegraph Road, where he "well performed his task." After this, Nelson was assigned as inspector of batteries for the First Corps and General Reserve. (*Official Records,* Vol. XXI, pp. 565, 567, and Vol. XXV, pt. 2, p. 613.)

[5] A company member, probably from Hanover County.

[6] The only record of Stringfellow's service found after this date is the Galveston, Texas, campaign where, according to Gen. John B. Magruder, Stringfellow, with two other artillery officers, "behaved with remarkable gallantry . . . volunteering to take charge of guns and personally directing the fire after the officers originally in charge of them had been wounded." As a result of this action, Magruder recommended Stringfellow for promotion to captain of artillery. (*Official Records,* Vol. XV, p. 218, and Vol. XXVI, pt. 2, pp. 65-66.)

over them. Five or six went home. About sunset we, who had been assigned to Kirkpatrick's company, were ordered to get ready and go over to
that company, which was encamped on the Front Royal Pike, near a little
church called Nineveh.[7] We got there that night about ten o'clock and
pitched our tent on the outskirts of Capt. Kirkpatrick's company, which
were all asleep.

*October 8.* Capt. Kirkpatrick[8] was introduced to us this morning
by Major Nelson. The Captain said that he felt deeply sorry for us that it
should have been found necessary to break up our company and to place
us in a company in whose organization we had had no part or lot; but that
he would try, with God's help, to make our lot a pleasant and agreeable
one; and that he knew that his lieutenants would aid him in this endeavor.
He wanted us to mix with his men; he did not want two or three parties
in his company and he wished every one of us to feel and to know that in
him we had a friend who stood ready to do all in his power for us. He said
a good deal more along this line. I have given enough to show the drift of
his remarks. I then went over to Major Nelson's headquarters to help him
and Nelson Meade[9] make out the payroll of the men who had come from
the Hanover Artillery and who had not been paid since March. About a
dozen or fifteen men came and join[ed] Kirkpatrick's Battery from Fleet's[10]
old company, which had also been broken up. Among these were John
and Andrew Hardy, two Bredens, and two Goods.

*October 9.* Edmund Anderson, who had been absent on sick furlough ever since May 23, 1862, got back to camp. He brought me $25 and
a letter from Papa. We remained at Camp Nineveh until November 1.
Nothing of interest happened during this time, except that there was a
great revival of religion in our camp. Some twenty-five or thirty men in
Kirkpatrick's Battery professed religion.[11] I became acquainted here with

[7] In Warren County, about three-quarters distant from Winchester to Front Royal.

[8] Thomas Jellis Kirkpatrick, born in Cumberland County, July 31, 1829, was educated at
Washington College (Washington and Lee University). He was a prominent Lynchburg lawyer
before and after the war, and was an ardent States' righter during the days before the outbreak
of war. He was promoted to major before the end of the war. Kirkpatrick is discussed more
fully in the Introduction. See the *Daily Advance* (Lynchburg, Va.), October 18, 1897, for an
obituary notice; Jed Hotchkiss, *Virginia* (Atlanta, 1899), pp. 983-84.

[9] Meade was probably from Clarke County. His father was the son of Bishop William
Meade, and his mother was a first cousin of Maj. William Nelson. (Interview, Rosewell
Page, Jr.)

[10] Capt. W. C. Fleet's Middlesex County Battery.

[11] After the return of the Army of Northern Virginia from Maryland, a widespread religious
revival took place. According to the Rev. J. William Jones, one of the "most powerful [revivals]
enjoyed in the army at this time" was in Kirkpatrick's company. Kirkpatrick stated that within

the Rev. Mr. Scott,[12] an Episcopal chaplain. It was also here that the Rev. W. T. [*sic*] Gilmer[13] became the chaplain of Maj. Nelson's Battalion.

*November 1. Saturday.* We were ordered to go to Culpeper Court House today.[14] We left camp at Nineveh today about midday and marched to Front Royal, encamping for the night near that town.

*November 2. Sunday.* We continued our march towards Culpeper Court House and after a hard day's march encamped for the night near Little Washington, the county seat of Rappahannock County.

*November 3. Monday.* We continued our march on Culpeper and after a hard and dusty day's march encamped for the night on Hazel River.

*November 4.* We reached Culpeper Court House and went into camp about midday on the Madison Court House Road, one mile from the town.

*November 5.* Edmund Anderson and myself were detailed to go with our battalion wagon train after corn. It was in charge of Sgts. Cunningham and Rucker.[15] The morning was clear and pleasant, but soon after we started it began to cloud up and look like rain. I very unwisely did not carry my overcoat. We took the Madison Court House Road. We did not find any corn until just about an hour before sunset and this corn was on the stalks in the field. Sgt. Cunningham went to the house and bargained with the ladies to get us a supper at one dollar each. It

three weeks between 40 and 50 of his company had been hopefully converted and that of the whole number (115) there was hardly a single man who was not in some way interested in the Christian faith. For a summary of the whole revival at this time, see J. William Jones, *Christ in Camp or Religion in Lee's Army* (Richmond, 1887), pp. 283-311; for statements on the revival in Kirkpatrick's company, see *ibid.*, pp. 286-93.

[12] The Rev. Hugh Roy Scott, a clergyman from King George County. (Jones, *Christ in Camp*, p. 286.)

[13] Actually Thomas Walker Gilmer. He was born in Charlottesville, Virginia, on July 26, 1834. He attended the University of Virginia, practiced law, and then attended the Union Theological Seminary in Virginia from which he graduated in 1860. In 1862, he was licensed by West Hanover Presbytery. On July 17, 1866, he was ordained and installed as pastor of the Fredericksburg Presbyterian Church, which he served until 1869, when he died. (*General Catalogue of the Trustees, Officers, Professors and Alumni of the Union Theological Seminary in Virginia, 1807-1924* [Richmond, 1924], p. 87.)

[14] In order to cover a possible Federal movement southward on the west side of the Blue Ridge Mountains, General Lee ordered General Longstreet to move his corps to Culpeper Court House on November 1. General Pendleton was directed to follow Longstreet's corps with the reserve artillery, of which Kirkpatrick's Battery was a part. (*Official Records*, Vol. XIX, pt. 2, pp. 686-87; Douglas Southall Freeman, *R. E. Lee: A Biography* [New York, 1935], II, 425-26.)

[15] Isaac W. Rucker, from Amherst County, a quartermaster sergeant for the battery. At Gettysburg he was taken prisoner and held at Fort Delaware. (Confederate War Service Records, XVIII, 402, Virginia State Library.) William Cunningham could not be further identified.

was at a Col. Early's and the detail consisted of about thirty-five men. The family consisted of a mother and some five or six daughters, some grown and the others in their teens. They gave us a good supper, the young ladies waiting on the table. By the time we had got the corn shucked and got through with our supper, it was dark and had begun to rain. Col. Early had a large barn and told us we might sleep in it and advised us not to try to get back to Culpeper Court House before daylight, that the road was very bad and that we would get into trouble if we attempted it [on] such a dark night. I tried hard to get Sgt. Cunningham to take this old farmer's advice and told him a good many of us had no overcoats, but he insisted on trying it. We had hardly gone a mile when three wagons in front not only turned over in a deep ditch, but actually turned upside down and spilt every ear of corn out in the ditch, with a mule to each wagon having its back in the ditch and its legs kicking in the air. Edmund Anderson and I went to a nearby farm house and got into a shuck stack and slept until about day when we awoke, and by taking a shortcut we succeeded in getting ahead of the wagons. Our sergeant, Ike Rucker, a splendid man, got after us for leaving when the wagons turned over and said he would have to report us. The penalty was [for us] to go on the next foraging expedition. We, however, never heard of the matter afterwards.

*November 6.* We reached camp with the corn just as the boys were about to go to breakfast. It is cold and cloudy; looks very much like snow.

*November 7.* It has been snowing briskly all day and is very cold. I paid Mayo two dollars to stand guard in my place for me.

*November 8 and 9.* We remained in camp. All quiet.

*November 10.* We remained quiet in camp all day. Heavy firing has been going on all day beyond the Rappahannock.[16] We remained at Culpeper until [the] 19th of November, and during this time Uncle Landon and Mrs. Winston came up to see us, bringing us clothes, shoes, blankets and home eatings. Mrs. Winston did not come out to camp as usual, but stayed at the Episcopal minister's in Culpeper, as the weather was very bad and it was snowing when she was here.

*November 19.* We got orders to go to Fredericksburg. Left Culpeper very late in the afternoon and went to Raccoon Ford, encamping for the night near that place.[17]

---

[16] Maj. Gen. Ambrose E. Burnside, who succeeded General McClellan as commanding officer of the Army of the Potomac on November 5, began moving his army towards the Rappahannock River. During this movement many skirmishes took place between the Confederate cavalry and the enemy forces. (*Official Records,* Vol. XIX, pt. 2, p. 706 *ff.*)

[17] Ascertaining that General Burnside was moving his army towards Fredericksburg, Gen-

*November 20.* We crossed the Rapidan and encamped for the night four miles beyond that river in the direction of Fredericksburg.

*November 21.* We waited a long time today for Maj. Moore's Battalion[18] to come up, and then continued our march towards Fredericksburg, encamping for the night somewhere in the woods west of Spotsylvania Court House, which the boys called "Camp Confusion," because the different companies of our battalion became very much mixed up in getting into camp that night.

*November 22.* We continued our march towards Fredericksburg and encamped for the night about ten miles from that city.

*November 23.* *Sunday.* We reached Fredericksburg and encamped on the east side of the old Telegraph Road, which leads from Fredericksburg to Richmond.

*November 24.* We fixed up our bed off the ground on some pine poles, putting little pine twigs a foot deep on top of the poles and some hen's nest grass on the top of the twigs. This made a very good and comfortable bed, and we slept first rate that night, a thing which we had not done for some time, owing to the ground being so damp and cold.

*November 25.* We built a chimney to our tent and fixed up a tent for Henry.

*November 26.* It began raining this morning and wound up with a snow. We remained quietly in this camp until December 11. The Yanks, in the meanwhile, had collected on the Stafford Heights on the north side of the [Rappahannock] river a very large army under the command of Gen. A. E. Burnside.[19]

*December 11.* We were aroused about 6 A.M. by the firing of two large signal guns.[20] We immediately got up and got some breakfast and made ready to go to the front, which we did by 8 A.M. The Yanks had begun to shell the old town and continued to do so until midday, burning

eral Lee issued orders that began the movement of the Army of Northern Virginia towards that city. General Pendleton was instructed to follow Longstreet's Corps with the reserve artillery. (*Official Records*, Vol. XXI, p. 1019.)

18 Major John W. Moore's Third North Carolina Battalion. (Jennings C. Wise, *The Long Arm of Lee or The History of the Artillery of the Army of Northern Virginia* [Lynchburg, 1915], p. 361; *Official Records*, Vol. XXI, pp. 929, 1027, 1028, 1039.)

19 General Burnside was preparing his army to cross the Rappahannock River, enter Fredericksburg, and attack Lee's army which was by this time entrenched on the heights behind the town.

20 Freeman states that the guns (which signalled that the enemy was attempting a crossing of the Rappahannock) were of Capt. John P. W. Read's Pulaski Artillery and were fired at about 4:45 A.M. (Freeman, *R. E. Lee*, II, 442-43.) For the Battle of Fredericksburg, see Freeman, *R. E. Lee*, II, 443-74, and Douglas Southall Freeman, *Lee's Lieutenants: A Study in Command* (New York, 1942-44), II, 325-76.

one entire square and many detached houses. Under cover of this shelling, they threw two pontoon bridges across the river at Fredericksburg and two lower down the river. Our company went down towards Hamilton's Crossing[21] this evening but soon came back to the Telegraph Road on the heights south of the town. We could see the old town burning in many places, while old men, women and children, and mothers with infants in their arms came in large numbers pouring out of their devoted city. It made our men very mad and indignant to see this sad and homeless procession. We returned to our camp after dark.

*December 12.* We left camp early this morning and went down the Telegraph Road towards Fredericksburg to within a mile of the city. A grand sight burst on our view. The whole army of Burnside had crossed the river and could be seen moving about like bees on the plain below us.[22] As far down the river as you could see, their line of battle extended, while their tents literally covered the hills on the opposite side of the river. A few shots were exchanged this evening by the artillery and there was some sharpshooting in our front. At dark, we returned to camp. I could but think of tomorrow, for those Yanks will have to fight tomorrow, *nolens volens,* and somebody will certainly get hurt.

*December 13. Saturday.* We went early this morning to the front and two of our guns, my gun being one of the two, were put in position on the heights south of Fredericksburg, just over, and very near, the home of Mr. Howison,[23] the historian. There was a large thirty-two-pound gun stationed on this hill and our two napoleons were put on either side of this large gun. Here, too, on this hill, Gens. Lee, McLaws, and Longstreet, with their staffs, had taken their stations, Gen. Longstreet commanding our left and Gen. McLaws' Division holding the line immediately in our front. We got [to] this position about 8 A.M. At this hour, we could hear

---

[21] Located at the southern end of the Confederate lines, at the point where the Richmond, Fredericksburg and Potomac Railroad crosses the Mine Road. (*Atlas to Accompany the Official Records of the Union and Confederate Armies* [Washington, D. C., 1891-95], Plate XXXI; Freeman, *R. E. Lee,* II, 453.)

[22] Federal forces spent the day of the twelfth entrenching on the south side of the Rappahannock and preparing for a major advance, which Lee was certain would come the next day. (Freeman, *R. E. Lee,* II, 451.)

[23] The Rev. Robert R. Howison (1820-1906), author of such works as *Fredericksburg: Past, Present, and Future* (Fredericksburg, 1890); *A History of the United States of America* (Richmond, 1892); and *A History of Virginia, From its Discovery and Settlement by Europeans to the Present Time* (2 vols.; Philadelphia, 1846-48). HRB's gun was on a hill termed Lee's Hill rather than on Howison's Hill, which was farther south on the high ground of the ridge and behind Howison's House. For the location of Lee's Hill, which was so named because Lee had established his field headquarters there, see Freeman, *R. E. Lee,* II, 443, 457-58.

plainly the Yanks at work on the plain below us, but we could see nothing, because a very heavy fog covered the plain. They seemed to be pulling down a building, judging by the noise. About 9 A.M. the Yanks assailed Marye's Hill and were driven back with great slaughter;[24] in falling back from Marye's Hill many took refuge in a railroad cut, right into which the heavy gun, where we were stationed, threw shell rapidly and accurately and made frightful slaughter among them. About ten o'clock the fog disappeared and we had a splendid view of the fight on our right, which was carried on by Jackson's Corps.[25] The battle raged fiercely all day and continued until dark. We did not fire a single shot, because at no time during the day did the Yanks get near enough to us for us to fire. We remained on the line of battle tonight. We were exposed all day to a heavy shelling from very large guns stationed on the Stafford Heights, but no one was hurt, being well protected by breastworks. When darkness came, we had the satisfaction of knowing that the Yanks had been repulsed at every point with very heavy loss. But alas, we, too, had lost some good men.

*December 14.* We expected the battle to be renewed this morning, but the Yanks don't seem inclined to try us again. It seems to me that we ought to go down on the plain and drive them into the river, or at least try to do it. A very bright and beautiful aurora was seen in the northern heavens tonight, which our men took as an omen of victory.[26]

*December 15.* All quiet today, except that the heavy guns exchanged a few shots. I don't see why our army doesn't assail the Yanks down on the plain. I fear they will get away from us.

*December 16. Tuesday.* At light this morning we saw plainly that Gen. Burnside had withdrawn his entire army to the north side of the

24 HRB is apparently in error with respect to time here. There is no recorded Federal attack in great force at this point until after 11:00 A.M.

25 Fighting on the thirteenth began shortly after the fog lifted, at about 10:30 A.M. The main Federal attack began on Jackson's front (the Confederate right), which extended from the vicinity of Deep Run southward to Hamilton's Crossing. The Confederate right bore the brunt of the attack until early afternoon when the main battle began shifting to the left, commanded by General Longstreet. The left extended from Deep Run northward to the heights opposite Beck's Island (Hunter's Island). See Freeman, *R. E. Lee*, II, 452-53, for the Confederate positions on December 13.

26 Freeman (*R. E. Lee*, II, 466) gives the date of the aurora borealis as December 13, using James H. Wood, *The War* (Cumberland, Md., 1910) as authority. Freeman notes also, however, that Gen. E. P. Alexander in "The Battle of Fredericksburg," *Southern Historical Society Papers*, Vol. X, Nos. 10 and 11 (October and November, 1882), gives December 14 as the date. For Lee's decision not to carry an offensive against the Federal army, see Freeman, *R. E. Lee*, II, 465-66.

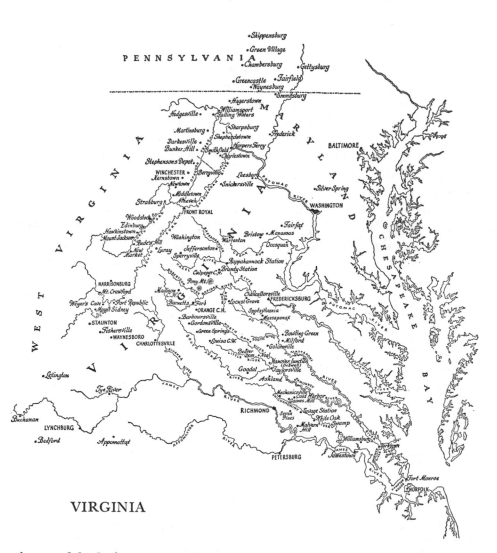

VIRGINIA

river and had given us the slip.[27] In a few hours we returned to our old camp. I took a good wash and put on some clean clothes.

*December 17.*  Remained in camp, very cold.

*December 18.*  Edmund Anderson, John Lewis Berkeley, Robert B.

[27] Under cover of darkness, Burnside had, on the night of December 15, removed his army to the other side of the Rappahannock and removed the pontoon bridges. (Freeman, *R. E. Lee,* II, 472-73.)

Winston and I went over the battlefield. We went to the extreme eastern end of the line and followed it up to Fredericksburg. We got some plunder; most of it had already been carried away. I got about a dozen pairs of good drawers and an oilcloth. There was a flag of truce in our lines and we met a Yankee lieutenant and four men, in charge of a Georgia sergeant, looking for dead Yanks. We had a long and pleasant chat with these Yankees, and told them where they would find four dead Yankees; but the Yankee lieutenant said, "Let the [dead] bury their dead and we will have a talk." Gen. Burnside had asked for a truce to bury his dead and we found the Yankee detail doing it at Marye's Hill. All the Yankee dead had been stripped of every rag of their clothing and looked like hogs which had been cleaned. The Yanks had collected several hundred of their dead on the brink of a deep pit which they were digging to bury them in, when we saw them. It was an awful sight. War is surely awful. I pitied these poor dead men. I could not help it. Yet these dead fellows were the *very* men, who, a few days ago, burned houses and drove old men, women and mothers with infants at the breast, and little children into a December night to die of hunger and cold.

*December 19. Friday.* Papa and Uncle Dick Berkeley got to camp on a visit to us. Quite cold.

*December 20.* John Hill and I rode with Pa and Uncle Dick over the battlefield, Sgt. Rickett, with Capt. Kirkpatrick's consent, lending me his horse. We went pretty much over the same ground, which I had gone over on December 18th, and we also visited Fredericksburg and Marye's Hill, which we had not done on the 18th of December. It was a very cold day and freezing all day. We called at Mr. Heart's in Fredericksburg and saw him. We got back to camp about 4 P.M. Had a very nice dinner, which Henry and John Hill had gotten up between them. We had a turkey that Papa had brought us.

*December 21. Sunday.* Papa and Uncle Dick went home. They had not been gone more than an hour, when Mrs. Winston and her faithful old driver, Dick, drove up with her carriage loaded with home eatings, clothes and comforts for "her boys" as she calls our mess. She always comes, if she and old Dick can reach us and sends when she cannot come herself, and always brings or sends us a large supply [of] rations and things useful to a soldier. Mrs. Winston, after remaining a few hours in camp with us, went over to a Mr. Garnett's and spent the night and returned home the next day.

*December 22, 23, 24, 25.* We remained in camp. All quiet.

# CHAPTER V

# ENJOYING OURSELVES IN MANY WAYS

## *Winter Quarters, 1862-1863*

*December 26, 1862. Friday.* We received orders to go and establish our winter quarters on the [Virginia] Central Railroad. We marched down the Telegraph Road and after going some twenty miles encamped for the night.

*December 27.* We reached old Dr. Tom Anderson's[1] farm about ten o'clock in the day. After much delay, our officers picked out a camp in a piece of pine woods on Dr. Tom Anderson's farm and quite near his house, which is known as "Providence." The camp was known to my mess as Pine Camp and was four miles from Hewlett's on the Virginia Central Railroad. As soon as we got into camp John Lewis Berkeley and I got permission to go home. We started, and were so fortunate as to be overtaken by Maj. [William] Nelson and Maj. Page[2] on horseback on their way home too. Maj. Nelson took me behind him, and the Major took John Lewis behind him on their horses and brought us out to old man Isaac Butler's gate. This was [a] very great help and saved us the disagreeable necessity of wading [the] North [Anna] River. When we got to Humanity Ford on Little River, we turned down the river and after going about a half a mile down the river, we found a small tree cut across it, by which we succeeded in crawling over coon-fashion. We got to "Montout" about 7 P.M., just as they were going to supper. Home people were

---

[1] Dr. Thomas Bates Anderson (1792-1872) of Caroline County. (Marshall Wingfield, *History of Caroline County, Virginia, From its Formation in 1727 to 1924.* [Richmond, 1924], p. 116.)

[2] Probably Maj. Thomas Jefferson Page, Jr., whose Yorktown "Magruder" Battery had been mustered out in October, 1862, and who was by this date second in command of Nelson's Battalion. (Jennings C. Wise, *The Long Arm of Lee or The History of the Artillery of the Army of Northern Virginia* [Lynchburg, Va., 1915], I, 422.)

very much surprised to see us. I took supper at "Montout" and went home about 9 P.M. There, too, they were surprised to see me.

*December 28. Sunday.* I went to Trinity Church with homefolks and took dinner at home and spent the evening at "Montout," leaving "Montout" about midnight for camp. We rode over to "Top and Castle"[3] and sent boy and horses back from there, we walking on to camp. John Hill got to "Montout" just as we left.

*December 29 and 30.* Worked on our chimney and fixed up our bed. On evening of [the] 30th we (our mess) were invited over to Dr. Anderson's to take tea. We had a very pleasant time with Miss Emma Anderson and her lady friends. It was nearly 4 A.M. when we got back to camp.

*December 31.* We worked on a kitchen for Henry and fixed up things generally.

*January 1, 1863.* New Year. What will it bring forth? Who of us will see the next New Year? We (my mess) took tea and spent the evening at Dr. Bob Nelson's.[4] A very pleasant time.

*January 2.* Spent the evening at Dr. Anderson's.

*January 3. Saturday.* Uncle P[hilip] H. Winston, Carter and Aunt Kate[5] with all the home folks came over and spent the day, bringing their dinner, and ours too, with more besides. We had a nice and pleasant time, and were excused by our officers from working on the stables, which were being put up for our horses. J. H. Berkeley and I returned home with them that evening.

*January 4. Sunday.* I attended Fork Church and dined at home and went back to camp that night.

*January 5 to 14.* We spent this time in camp, going out nearly every night to visit homefolks, friends and neighbors. The girls at "White House," "Montout" and Mr. [Horace?] Stringfellow's had gotten up a candy stew for us, which was to come off on [the] 15th.

*January 15. Friday.* This was the memorable day of the night when the candy stew was broken up by our company's being ordered up to Fredericksburg[6] very suddenly. John Lewis and I had gone over early in

3 HRB undoubtedly refers here to Topping Castle in Caroline County. (Interview, Rosewell Page, Jr.)

4 The Rev. Dr. Robert Nelson, who graduated from the Episcopal Theological Seminary in Alexandria in 1845, was for many years a missionary in China. Nelson was at home in Hanover County during the war. (William A. R. Goodwin, *History of the Theological Seminary in Virginia and Its Historical Background* [New York, 1923], II, 128, 276.)

5 Carter was HRB's sister, Louisa Carter; Aunt Kate was Catherine Robinson Berkeley Winston.

6 In the earlier version of the diary, HRB stated that they were ordered to Massaponax Church located on Telegraph Road several miles south of Fredericksburg.

the day. Everything was ready. It was nearly 8 P.M. The ladies, children and neighbors had assembled and we were expecting every moment the boys from camp to come in on us. The candy stew was at the "White House." Alas! The best laid plans of men and mice often fail, and of girls and soldier boys too. At 8 P.M., instead of the boys from camp, whom we were expecting, there came a note from Bob Winston informing us that our battery had been ordered up to Fredericksburg and had started, and that John Lewis and I must report at camp as soon as possible. I thought, at first, it was a joke which Bob Winston was trying to play off on us. But it proved no joke, but was one of war's stern realities. I shall always remember the sad gloom which this sudden interruption of our candy stew threw over that company, which had gathered at the old "White House," bent on having a pleasant evening and giving the soldier boys a good time. John Lewis and I remained until two o'clock at night and did our best to be cheerful, hopeful and happy and to cheer up these loved ones; but we left the young with sad and gloomy faces, and the old with thoughtful and prayerful looks. Ah! These good-bys in these bloody war times are truly heart-rending.[7]

*January 16.* We stopped at Pine Camp, put on our war-duds and then started to overtake our company. We overtook them, stuck in the mud, just beyond [the Caroline] County line. We sent back our servants, William Moore and George Lacy, who had brought us over from home, as soon as we came up with our company. It was only 8 A.M. when they turned back. We marched on and went into camp that night in a big oak woods a mile west of Massaponax Church. Here we remained until January 24, 1863, Saturday, when we were ordered back to Pine Camp, which we reached about two o'clock in the afternoon. I went over home on horseback, spent the night and came back Sunday morning, bringing three chickens to Capt. Kirkpatrick, which Uncle P. H. Winston had sent him.

*January 27. Tuesday.* The candy stew, which had been broken up on January 15th by our company's being ordered to Fredericksburg, came off tonight. Everything passed off very pleasantly and everyone seemed to enjoy themselves very much. Lieuts. [William] Basye and Latham and Sgt. Gillum were there and all my mess and also F. A. Kinckle,[8] who had

[7] There were indications of some movement of the Federal army, which was situated north of the Rappahannock River. General Lee, therefore, made moves to strengthen his Rappahannock line. (*The War of the Rebellion: A Compilation of the Official Records of the Union and Confederate Armies* [Washington, D. C., 1880-1901], Series I, Volume XXI, p. 1091 *ff.* All citations will be from Series I unless otherwise noted.)

[8] Frank A. Kinckle of Lynchburg, Virginia. He was the son of the Rev. William H. Kinckle, pastor of St. Paul's Church in Lynchburg.

recently joined our company and mess. It snowed tonight. We did not retire until nearly day.

*January 28.*   We had a very late breakfast. Bob Winston and Miss Agnes Stringfellow had a big snowball. Lieuts. Latham and Basye and Sgt. Gillum returned to camp, but gave our mess permission to remain until tomorrow. Some of the boys went up and dined at "Montout" and came back quite merry.

*January 29.*   Edmund Anderson, Frank Kinckle, John Lewis Berkeley, Dabney Williamson and I returned to camp today. We had to go up by Trinity Church bridge, the river being too high to ford.

We had built a bridge at Butler's Mill[9] over [the] North Anna River, when we first came to Pine Camp. About February 1st our mess planned to give the ladies, who had done so much for our pleasure, a dinner party, and this dinner party was fixed for February 5th. On February 4th, John Lewis Berkeley, Bob Winston and I dined at Uncle Dick's with the Misses Young and spent the night at home. J. H. Berkeley and Edmund Anderson came over this evening to carry some of the ladies over tomorrow to our camp dinner party.

*February 5.*   When we woke up this morning, it was snowing fast and it continued to snow fast all day. We had to put off our dinner party in camp for better weather. Edmund Anderson, J. L. and J. H. Berkeley and [I] returned to camp in the snow.

*February 8.*   Our camp dinner party which was to have been on [the] 5th instant and which was put off on account of the snow, took place today. It was a grand success. All the ladies from our Hanover [County] homes were there, with the old folks and the children. Our officers kindly lent us their double tent to set our dinner in and entered into it and enjoyed it as much as we boys did. Gen. [William Nelson] Pendleton, wife and daughter were there, and no one enjoyed the dinner, and the ladies, and the children more than the old General did. Mrs. Dr. Tom Anderson came with two servants, and brought her plates, knives, forks, etc., and did everything possible to make our camp dinner party a success. Our company remained with us until nearly dark. Gen. Pendleton had a cannon fired to let the ladies see the effects of a shell. We went home with the ladies.

*February 9.*   We returned to camp late tonight.

*February 10 to 12.*   Remained in camp.

---

[9] Located just north of Hewlett, Hanover County, at the approximate point where present Va. Rt. 601 crosses the North Anna River.

*February 13.*  A party given the "soldier boys" at Mr. Edmund Anderson's. A pleasant time. Girls from home and Nannie[10] [were] there. We crossed the North Anna River in a boat, when going over to the party, and got along very nicely; coming back, however, we grounded our boat on a rock, and Frank Kinckle, who got out on the rock to shove us off, got in the river and got wet up to his waist. We reached camp about sunrise and went to bed. We remained at Pine Camp until April 30th. We had gotten here on December 27, 1862, so that we were here about four months, a longer time than we have ever remained in any camp except at Jamestown, when we were holding a stationary river battery. During these four months, we visited our homes, friends and neighbors, enjoying ourselves in many ways, and our officers, from the highest to the lowest, indulging us in every way consistent with their duties. While here, I was confirmed by Bishop Johns,[11] at the Old Fork Church. Bob Winston was confirmed at the same time and place.

[10] Anna Louisa Berkeley, whom HRB later married.
[11] Bishop John Johns, who succeeded William Meade as Bishop of the Episcopal Church in Virginia. (Goodwin, *Theological Seminary*, II, 1-8.)

# CHAPTER VI

# SUCH BLOODY AND HELLISH WORK

## Chancellorsville to Gettysburg, 1863

*April 30, 1863.* We left Pine Camp this morning at six o'clock, and after a hard day's march over very muddy roads, encamped, about sunset, near Massaponax Church.[1]

*May 1.* We reached our lines south of Fredericksburg and put our guns into position near Hamilton's Crossing.

*May 2.* We were ordered back to the Po River, where we remained until May 7. While we were on the Po, Lee had fought the great Battle of Chancellorsville, and driven Gen. Hooker, who had taken Burnside's place, back across the Rappahannock River.[2] But Stonewall Jackson has been desperately wounded and lays in almost a hopeless condition at a Mr. [Thomas Coleman] Chandler's home, near Guiney's Station.

*May 7.* We were ordered on picket to Marye's Hill, where we re-

[1] During the early hours of April 29, under cover of fog, Gen. Joseph Hooker, who had succeeded Burnside after the Battle of Fredericksburg, had thrown down pontoons and was crossing the Rappahannock below the mouth of Deep Run. This and other movements indicated a general offensive by the Federals. Thus, Lee ordered his army to the front. HRB's company joined a large force of artillery, which was stationed at Fredericksburg with a limited force of infantry consisting of Maj. Gen. Jubal A. Early's Division and one brigade of Maj. Gen. Lafayette McLaws' Division. This Confederate force opposed the Union general, John Sedgwick, at Fredericksburg while the main portion of Lee's army was preparing to meet with Hooker's main force in the beginning stages of what was to become known as the Chancellorsville campaign. (Douglas Southall Freeman, *R. E. Lee: A Biography* [New York, 1935], III, 507-15.)

[2] Because of a confusion in the orders, Early evacuated Fredericksburg (except for a small detaining force), and most of the artillery were ordered to the rear to avoid capture. By the time Early had discovered that the orders were in error, the artillery was apparently too far to the rear to be brought up to the front again; at least General Pendleton made no effort to recall them. (Susan Pendleton Lee, *Memoirs of William Nelson Pendleton, D. D.* . . . [Philadelphia, 1893], p. 264; Douglas Southall Freeman, *Lee's Lieutenants: A Study in Command* [New York, 1942-44], II, 607-12.) Sedgwick, in command of the Sixth Corps at Fredericksburg, withdrew to the north side of the Rappahannock River during the night of May 4. Hooker's last troops retreated over the Rappahannock on the night of May 5. (Freeman, *Lee's Lieutenants*, II, 635, 644.)

mained very quietly until June 5th. During this time Gen. Lee divided his army into three Army Corps; [the] First Corps, commanded by Gen. [James] Longstreet; the Second Corps, commanded by [Gen. Richard S.] Ewell, and the Third Corps commanded by [Gen.] A. P. Hill. At the same time, all the artillery had been organized into battalions of three companies each, and attached to the army corps. Our battalion, which was commanded by Col. William Nelson, and composed of Kirkpatrick's, Milledge's and Massie's batteries,[3] was placed with the Second Corps.[4] In the meanwhile Stonewall Jackson had died. His death was not only a great loss to Lee, but to the entire Southern Confederacy.

*June 5.* We left our camp near Marye's [Hill] and followed our Corps in the direction of Culpeper Court House, encamping for the night near Spotsylvania Court House.[5] We started early this morning, but were soon stopped, and we remained in the road until Sunday morning, May [June] 7th, when we continued our march towards Culpeper, which place we reached on Monday, June 8th, about midday and encamped just north of town.

*June 9.* We remained at Culpeper Court House.[6] Today Lieut. Woodruff[7] attempted to arrange the gun crews and messes in our company to suit his notions. He suited no one, not even his own brother Pete. Lieut. Hobson[8] and the Captain [Kirkpatrick] came to our rescue and we all soon got back into our old places.

*June 10.* We marched from Culpeper to Little Washington, some twenty-three miles; a very hot and dusty day.[9]

[3] Capt. John Milledge's Regular Georgia and Capt. John L. Massie's Fluvanna (Virginia) batteries.

[4] For the reorganization of the Army of Northern Virginia after Chancellorsville, see Freeman, *Lee's Lieutenants*, II, 689-714; Freeman, *R. E. Lee*, III, 8-17. See *The War of the Rebellion: A Compilation of the Official Records of the Union and Confederate Armies* (Washington, D. C., 1880-1901), Series I, Volume XXV, part 2, pp. 840, 850-51 (All citations will be from Series I unless otherwise noted); Jennings C. Wise, *The Long Arm of Lee or The History of the Artillery of the Army of Northern Virginia* (Lynchburg, Va., 1915), II, 566 *ff.* for details concerning the reorganization of the artillery. Nelson's Battalion was made a part of the Second Corps reserve artillery.

[5] Having determined that an offensive in the East was essential to the fortunes of the Confederacy, Lee began moving his army from the Rappahannock line on June 3. On June 5, Lieut. Gen. Richard S. Ewell's Second Corps, to which HRB's battalion had been assigned, was ordered to move up the Rappahannock towards Culpeper Court House. Movements that led to the Gettysburg Campaign were beginning. (Freeman, *R. E. Lee*, III, 18-27.)

[6] General Ewell halted his march on the ninth to go to the support of the cavalry which, under Maj. Gen. J. E. B. Stuart, had engaged the enemy at Brandy Station. (*Official Records*, Vol. XXVII, pt. 2, pp. 439-40.)

[7] A. R. Woodruff, of Lynchburg, third lieutenant of Kirkpatrick's Battery.

[8] George W. Hobson, of Lynchburg, first lieutenant of Kirkpatrick's Battery.

[9] The Second Corps had been selected by Lee to lead the march into Pennsylvania by

*June 11.* We marched from Little Washington to Front Royal.

*June 12.* We reached Winchester about 10 A.M. Drove the Yanks into their fortifications, and by night had them closely invested.[10]

*June 13.* We closed in still nearer on the Yanks. We shelled them heavily just before sunset and captured their outer pickets.

*June 14. Sunday.* I was detailed to cook for the first detachment. Landon, Irvin and I got a nice dinner today. Landon was also on cook detail. He and I put our cooks to work and we enjoyed ourselves in the shade reading. We got back to the front with the cooked rations about two o'clock in the afternoon, where some lively skirmishing and shelling was going on in our front; but our boys were not in it.[11]

*June 15.* We were ordered at two o'clock last night to report to Gen. Jones,[12] whose brigade was just in our front. We promptly did so and found, at daybreak, that the Yankees had evacuated their fortifications and were trying to force their way out by the Harpers Ferry Road; but Gen. John Gordon had cut them off, and after a slight resistance they nearly all surrendered.[13] We passed through Winchester about sunrise, where the citizens seemed perfectly wild with joy, many old ladies and gentlemen rushing out on their porches in their night clothes, and waving flags, handkerchiefs and various other garments, while children and young girls shouted and hurrahed until their strength failed them. I saw a great deal of plunder, but got very little, some writing paper and envelopes being all. We encountered, in the streets of Winchester, over a hundred

crossing the Blue Ridge Mountains at Front Royal and moving through Winchester. This movement was begun at this point on June 10. (Freeman, *R. E. Lee,* III, 33-34.)

[10] It seems that HRB is in error here. There is no inference in the records that any of Nelson's batteries reached Winchester before midday of the thirteenth. See *Official Records,* Vol. XXVII, pt. 2, p. 440 *ff.* for various reports concerning the battle of "Second Winchester," which began the next day, June 13, and ended on June 15. The object of General Ewell's Second Corps was the Federal force under Maj. Gen. Robert H. Milroy.

[11] This was a diversionary action to cover Maj. Gen. Jubal A. Early's march to the Confederate left. After completely surprising the Federals, Early took the westernmost Federal fort at about sunset. For a discussion of this maneuver, see Freeman, *Lee's Lieutenants,* III, 20-23.

[12] Brig. Gen. John M. Jones of Maj. Gen. Edward "Allegheny" Johnson's Division, whose forces straddled the Front Royal Road. See Freeman, *Lee's Lieutenants,* III, map opposite p. 20.

[13] Brig. Gen. John B. Gordon was not involved in the defeat of Milroy's retreating force on the Martinsburg Pike. Actually the brigades of Francis T. Nicholls, George H. "Maryland" Stewart, and James A. Walker, all of Johnson's Division, were involved in this action. Gordon arrived after the victory had been obtained and aided only in rounding up prisoners and animals. Prisoners taken amounted to more than 2,300, Milroy having escaped with only a few hundred men. (Freeman, *Lee's Lieutenants,* III, 24-26; Allen P. Tankersley, *John B. Gordon: A Study In Gallantry* [Atlanta, 1955], p. 14.)

abandoned Yankee wagons. I went through a number of these, but saw nothing which I cared to take. I was on the lookout for a pair of new boots, but found none. Our battery, too, was moving rapidly towards Harpers Ferry and we had no time to explore Yankee wagons and Yankee quarters for plunder. The Yankee Gen. Milroy[14] and his cavalry escaped by going through some farms and byways. The Yankee prisoners abused him for everything mean and cowardly, but I could not see in what way Gen. Milroy was to blame. He could have done his men no possible good by remaining with them, and would only have been sent to Castle Thunder.[15] I think he acted right. We went on down the Harpers Ferry Road and encamped about six miles below Winchester. We captured about 3,000 men with all their baggage, wagons, arms, ammunition, commissary and quartermaster's stores. They succeeded in carrying off nearly all their mules and horses. We got, also, all their cannon and a large supply [of] uniforms and underclothes and blankets. The latter were all new and found in boxes packed just as they had come from the factory.

*June 16.* We remained near Winchester.

*June 17.* We marched to Martinsburg. Very hot and dusty. I came near giving out today. It was so very hot and I got so very tired that I had to throw away my overcoat, not having the strength to carry it. I fear I shall need it before I can get another. I got very far behind my company today, but later in the afternoon came up with them near Martinsburg, where we encamped for the night.

*June 18.* Came back and encamped near Darkesville.

*June 19.* Marched over to Shepherdstown on [the] Potomac.

*June 20.* We remained in camp. Frank, John Lewis, Bob and I got dinner at a farmer's, where we saw four nice ladies.

*June 21.* Edmund and I got a nice breakfast at a Union lady's. Andrew Hardy, who came in after us, had a spirited argument with her on the war. She said she felt very sorry for the soldiers on both sides and fed both alike.

[14] Maj. Gen. Robert H. Milroy. He had been in command of Federal forces in Winchester since December, 1862, had followed a harsh rule during his occupation, and was much disliked by residents there. (Oren Frederic Morton, *The Story of Winchester in Virginia, The Oldest Town in the Shenandoah Valley* (Strasburg, Va., 1925), pp. 185-86; See *Lee's Lieutenants*, III, 22-27, for Second Battle of Winchester.)

[15] Confederate prison in Richmond, which stood on the north side of Cary Street between Eighteenth and Nineteenth Streets. It was used for persons committed to imprisonment on heinous charges or as deserters from the Federal Army. (Frank Earle Lutz, *A Richmond Album: A Pictorial Chronicle of an Historic City's Outstanding Events and Places* [Richmond, 1937], p. 58; Alexander Wilbourne Weddell, *et al., Richmond, Virginia In Old Prints: 1737-1887* [Richmond, 1932], pp. 142-43.)

*June 22.* I made my exit into "My Maryland," wading the Potomac and getting my feet badly cut and bruised.[16] I shall never try to wade a river again barefooted. Encamped near Sharpsburg, Maryland.

*June 23.* We continued our march towards Harrisburg, Pennsylvania, passing through Hagerstown, Maryland. We encamped two miles from the Pennsylvania line. All the country through which we passed today is beautiful and rich, splendid wheat, hay and corn crops. Nearly all the people are Union.[17]

*June 24.* We crossed the Pennsylvania line at 8 A.M. We passed through Middletown and Greencastle, and encamped near Chambersburg. Beautiful country and splendid crops. I saw [a] great many young men in citizen clothes. People are not unfriendly seemingly. I have seen only two negroes since getting into Pennsylvania.

*June 25.* Remained near Chambersburg.

*June 26.* Marching through Chambersburg, we continued on towards Harrisburg, and encamped near Shippensburg. It rained all day. Wished for [my] abandoned overcoat. The country is beautiful. The people are Black Dutch.

*June 27.* We are now marching on Carlisle. A caisson box of the Third Richmond howitzers blew up just now, right in front of us. The top of the box was blown up almost out of sight. Two men had just gotten off the box. The wheel horses were badly burnt by the explosion. It was caused by bad packing. Encamped near Carlisle.

*June 28. Sunday.* We remained near Carlisle. Heard Mr. Gilmer preach. Got supper at an old Dutch farmer's.

*June 29.* We remained at Carlisle until midday and then came back towards Greenville [Green Village] for ten miles and encamped.[18]

*June 30.* We came back to Greensville [Green Village] and then took a left-hand road, and after going some three miles encamped for the night.

---

[16] After "Second Winchester," Ewell held his corps south of the Potomac to wait for the First and Third Corps to close up. On the afternoon of June 21, Ewell received orders from Lee to resume march and take Harrisburg, Pennsylvania. (*Official Records*, Vol. XXVII, pt. 2, p. 443.)

[17] During these few days prior to July 1 and Gettysburg, Ewell's force was busy foraging and collecting supplies for the hungry Confederate army. Lee hoped that his army could live off the riches of the Pennsylvania countryside for the better part of the summer without meeting the Federals in a major engagement. (Percy Gatling Hamlin, *"Old Bald Head"* [General *R. S. Ewell*] *The Portrait of a Soldier* [Strasburg, Va., 1940], pp. 140-43; Freeman, *R. E. Lee*, III, 18 ff.; Freeman, *Lee's Lieutenants*, III, 27-35.)

[18] Lee discovered on June 29, through one of Longstreet's spies, that the Federal forces had crossed the Potomac into Maryland and were in the vicinity. He had thus to recall Ewell southward and concentrate his forces. (Freeman, *Lee's Lieutenants*, III, 34-38, 48-50.)

*July 1.* Continued our march towards Gettysburg. On reaching the top of a mountain, we were hurried up very much and could hear plainly fighting in front of us. Our cannoneers mounted and we began a trot-march, which was kept up until we reached the battlefield just west of Gettysburg. The Yanks had been driven beyond the town.[19] Passed over a portion of the battlefield where the dead of both sides lay very thick and from which the Yankee wounded had not been moved. We encamped on the high hill west of the town.[20]

*July 2.* This morning on getting up, I saw a sight which was perfectly sickening and heart-rending in the extreme. It would have satiated the most blood-thirsty and cruel man on God's earth. There were, [with]in a few feet of us, by actual count, seventy-nine (79) North Carolinians laying dead in a straight line. I stood on their right and looked down their line. It was perfectly dressed. Three had fallen to the front, the rest had fallen backward; yet the feet of all these dead men were in a perfectly straight line. Great God! When will this horrid war stop? This regiment belonged to [Brig. Gen. Alfred] Iverson's Brigade, and had been pushed forward between two stone fences, behind which the Yanks were laying concealed. They had all evidently been killed by one volley of musketry and they had fallen in their tracks without a single struggle.[21] These seventy-nine North Carolinians were not the only dead on this hill; many others were scattered around, and in [a] wheat field at the foot of this hill were many dead blue coats. I turned from this sight with a sickened heart and tried to eat my breakfast, but had to return it to my haversack untouched. I received three letters this morning from home. At 9 A.M. I was sent with a detail of men to cut down some post and rail fencing around the Pennsylvania College and the town. I cut a great deal of this fencing down. In one place, I saw the body of a Yankee, which had been

[19] Lee had not planned a general engagement with the Federal forces in the area of Gettysburg. However, Henry Heth's division of Lt. Gen. A. P. Hill's Third Corps had, on their approach to Gettysburg, met with the enemy on the Chambersburg Pike northwest of the town during the morning of July 1. Heth was badly handled by the Federal forces, but at about three o'clock the van of Ewell's Second Corps, consisting of Rodes's Division, came from the north and relieved Heth. When Early's division of the Second Corps came up on Rodes's left, Lee ordered a general advance, and shortly thereafter the Confederates had pushed Federal forces to the hills south and east of Gettysburg and were in possession of the town. For the first day's battle, see Freeman, *R. E. Lee*, III, 68-85, and *Lee's Lieutenants*, III, 73-105.

[20] Located on Seminary Ridge.

[21] Iverson's Brigade, Rodes's Division, Second Corps, consisted of the 5th, 12th, 20th, and 23rd North Carolina Regiments. For statements and accounts concerning the tragic deployment of Iverson's Brigade, see Walter Clark, editor, *Histories of the Several Regiments and Battalions From North Carolina in the Great War, 1861-65* (Goldsboro, N. C., 1901), I, 632 *ff.*, II, 119, 235 *ff.; Official Records*, Vol. XXVII, pt. 2, pp. 553-54, 579-80.

cut in two. The head, arms and about one-half of his ribs had been thrown against a fence, and remained with his heart and entrails sticking to the top rail, while some 10 feet off the lower part of the body had been thrown into a mud hole in the road. It was very near a house, and there were three young men in the house. I asked these men why they did not bury this body and several others which were near their house, and they would give me no answer. About midday our battery was brought down to the town and stationed immediately behind the Pennsylvania College,[22] in order that we might go either to the right or left, as we might be needed. At 4 P.M. Gen. Longstreet opened on the enemy.[23] I was stationed on the top of the Pennsylvania College to keep a lookout for Yankee cavalry, and could see the advance of a greater part of Longstreet's Corps. It was grand, fierce and awful. By six o'clock all the atmosphere had become filled with smoke, like a thick fog, and I could only see the flash of the artillery through this thick smoke. After dark, the fighting appeared grand and sublime in the extreme. Surely darkness is the element, best suited, in which to carry on such bloody and hellish work as these two armies have been doing for the last two days. May God help the poor wounded on both sides. At 9 P.M. we moved back to where we came from that morning and remained there that night.

*June [July] 3. Friday.* A day ever to be remembered by the Army of Northern Virginia. Early this morning our battery was ordered around on our extreme left.[24] We were stationed under some hills, and ordered to hold ourselves in readiness to go into the fight at a minute's notice. Being under cover of the hills, we could see very little of what was going on, but could hear it all as we were very close up on the fighting line of battle. We were exposed the entire day to straggling shot, shell and bullets

[22] The College was located on Black's Turnpike just north of the town of Gettysburg. The cupola of the college building was used as an observation post. (Robert U. Johnson and C. C. Buell, editors, *Battles and Leaders of the Civil War* [New York, 1887-88], III, 267; *Atlas to Accompany the Official Records of the Union and Confederate Armies* [Washington, D. C., 1891-95], Plates XL and XLI.) It is now called Gettysburg College.

[23] Generally, Lee's plan of battle for July 2 was for Longstreet to deliver the main attack against the Federal left in the vicinity of a hill called Round Top at the southern end of Cemetery Ridge. Ewell was to keep the Federal right busy with a diversionary attack. See Freeman, *R. E. Lee*, III, 86-106, and *Lee's Lieutenants*, III, 106-40.

[24] Berkeley's company was apparently attached to Maj. Gen. Edward Johnson's Division which was located at the extreme left of the Confederate line at the foot of Culp's Hill. See Freeman, *Lee's Lieutenants*, III, 141-43, for discussion of the failure of Ewell to use properly his troops in this section of battle on July 3. Longstreet was to assume the main attack again on the third with a charge of the Federal center on Cemetery Ridge. Pickett's charge was the result. For the battle of July 3, see Freeman, *R. E. Lee*, III, 107-34, and *Lee's Lieutenants*, III, 145-67.

from the enemy's line. The fighting continued desperately all day, and every effort which we made to carry the Yankee works was repulsed with heavy loss on our part. Today about one o'clock the artillery fire surpassed any I have heard in the war. Its roar was as regular and constant as that of any musketry. There was a constant line of ambulances filing past us all day bringing out our wounded. At ten tonight, our entire army has fallen back to the hills west and southwest of Gettysburg, Pennsylvania. A great battle has been fought and lost, and our battery has *not* fired a single shot. We have been, however, exactly where our chief of artillery stationed us, and stood ready to try and do what he ordered us. We heard today Vicksburg had fallen.[25]

*July 4. Saturday.* We remained in position all day near Gettysburg. At 8 A.M. John Hawkins, my sergeant, gave me his horse and a dozen canteens and sent me to try and find some clear water, or as near clear as possible, for we had had no water fit to drink for two days. I strung the canteens about the horse, mounted and went out on the Shippensburg Road. I followed this road for five or six miles, going to every farmhouse in sight of the road. I visited a dozen or more farms. Every house, shed, barn and hut was filled with wounded, dying and dead men, both Yanks and Confederates. Blood everywhere. Dead and dying men everywhere. Can there be anything in this world more sad and gloomy than a battlefield. I think not. After going about six miles, I succeeded in getting some nice cool water, and after filling my canteens returned to my battery. The Yanks have not come down from the hills east of Gettysburg and have shown no desire to attack us at any time during the day. About 5 P.M. I counted ten or a dozen dwelling houses on fire between our line and the town. These houses were fired because Yankee sharpshooters had gotten into them and were annoying and killing some of our men. At 9 P.M. we left Gettysburg for Hagerstown. We did not go far that night, but we were on the road all night in a heavy rain.[26]

*July 5. Sunday.* We continued our march towards Hagerstown, the Yankees showing no desire to fight us. We encamped, for the night, near Fairfield. We have had nothing to eat, except wheat which we rubbed out of its heads in our hands and ate.

*July 6. Monday.* We came on slowly towards Hagerstown. We have had very little to eat since we left that ill-fated Gettysburg until tonight,

[25] This statement is, of course, in error. Vicksburg fell on July 4.
[26] Ewell's Corps was to be the rear guard during the first day (July 5) of the withdrawal from Gettysburg. For the order of the withdrawal of the Second Corps from Gettysburg to Virginia, see *Official Records*, Vol., XXVII, pt. 2, pp. 448-49.

when we encamped on a Dutchman's farm and went for his pigs, ducks and chickens. I don't think we left him a chick which was large enough to eat. The old man's wife, facetiously remarked to Frank [Kinckle], who had six old hens and a rooster in hand, that "he had overlooked six fat chickens in a coop and had better go back and get them." "With the greatest pleasure imaginable, Madam, I will go back and get them. It was entirely an oversight that we did not get them before, of this I can assure you." Frank then, handing me his old hens and rooster, went back and got the old lady's six fat chickens and brought them to camp. The old lady came out, and, making a big pile of the heads (the boys had cut off the chicken's heads as fast as they caught them), with tears in her eyes, exclaimed, "Oh de-heads, de-heads, de-heads." She told some of the boys, "It was a sin to take the big chicken from the little chicken." Some of our boys had taken the old hens and left the little chickens, because the latter were not large and old enough to eat. It was well for the old lady that this was the case, for had they been old and large enough to eat, we Rebs would certainly not have left her a feather. We found a little yellow cornmeal in the old man's big barn, out of which John Hawkins made a corn pone, very rough and rocky, but better than no bread. We made a big hash of our chickens and had an abundant, if not a royal, supper, at the old Dutchman's expense. This incident happened near Waynesboro, Pennsylvania, and it was the only time that we had free permission to help ourselves while in Pennsylvania. And even here, we were *not permitted* to go into the old farmer's house. We heard today, too, that our baggage and commissary wagons had been captured by the Yankee cavalry last night. I also learned today, that the four Berkeley brothers of the 8th Virginia Regiment were all wounded and had all been left at Gettysburg.[27] I also heard of Uncle Philip H. Winston's death from typhoid fever. Surely troubles come not single, at least not in war times.

*July 7.* We learned that our wagons had been certainly taken, and that we had lost everything, knapsacks, cooking utensils and worst of all, Henry, our cook, had been captured. We reached Hagerstown, Maryland, about an hour before sunset, and encamped north of the town.

*July 8.* We remained in the same place, and had a plenty to eat.

*July 9.* We still remained in the same camp. I received a letter from Papa.

27 The four brothers referred to here are Norborne, Edmund, William Noland, and Charles Fenton Berkeley of the 8th Virginia Regiment. All were wounded, but not all of them taken prisoners. Edmund was not wounded seriously and escaped. The three captured Berkeley

*July 10.*   About night we came through Hagerstown and encamped in a wheat field to the south of the town on the National Road.

*July 11.*   We went into line of battle parallel to the National Road, at our point, and remained so all day.[28]

*July 12.*   We continued in line of battle, the Yanks showing no desire to fight us.

*July 13.*   We remained in line of battle all day, the Yanks showing no disposition to attack. At 7 P.M. we started for Williamsport on [the] Potomac, but on reaching that place, we found the river too full to ford and had to go four miles below to Falling Waters, where a pontoon bridge had been put down. It rained hard all night and we had a very bad and terrible march. In passing a store, I sat down in a goods box and got a short nap. An infantryman awoke me and advised me to move on, if I did not wish to be captured. I immediately moved on.

brothers were later exchanged and returned to duty with their regiment. They were distant cousins of HRB. (Eppa Hunton, *Autobiography of Eppa Hunton* [Richmond, 1933], pp. 100-1.)

[28] Lee's engineers had selected a defensive line south of Hagerstown to cover the withdrawal in the event the Federals should vigorously pursue. (Freeman, *R. E. Lee,* III, 136.)

# SUCH IS HORRID WAR

## *Bristoe to Mine Run, 1863*

*July 14, 1863.* We crossed the Potomac into Virginia about 9 A.M. tired and worn out by our night's march in the heavy rain and over muddy roads. It had been three weeks since we crossed into Maryland. We went into camp about a mile below Falling Waters, cooked breakfast, and took a sleep and rested until 4 P.M., when [we] started out towards Martinsburg; but [we] only went two or three miles and then encamped on the right of the pike, as you come towards Martinsburg, for the night.

*July 15.* We continued our march and after passing through Martinsburg, went on to Darkesville and encamped to the west of the pike.

*July 16, 17, 18, 19.* We remained quietly in camp at Darkesville.

*July 20.* We came, this evening, up to within four miles of Winchester. I am quite sick tonight.

*July 21.* I feel better today. We passed through Winchester and went out to Spout Spring on the Berryville Road. We remained here only a few hours and then came back to within a mile of Winchester and encamped in a piece of oak woods.

*July 22.* We moved out on the Staunton Pike, and after stopping four hours to cook and feed and graze our horses, we marched to Newtown.

*July 23.* We started early this morning for Culpeper and after passing Front Royal and going about eight miles, we halted, fed and rested both men and horses for two hours, and then continued our march until nearly midnight.

*July 24.* We continued our march and encamped at the foot of the mountain west of Luray. It was a hot, dry and dusty march.

*July 25.* We crossed the Blue Ridge this morning, and after stopping at Sperryville until the evening, we pulled out and came two miles east of Woodville, and encamped for the night. Bob Winston and I got a nice breakfast at a little house on the side of the mountain near Sperryville, consisting of an abundance of nice hot biscuits, nice butter, rich milk and a plenty of nice strained honey. Paid a dollar a piece for it. I never enjoyed a breakfast more.

*July 26.* We came on to Culpeper Court House and encamped on a high hill west of town. It was Sunday. We have missed our cook, Henry, very much and get on poorly without him.

*July 27.* We remained at Culpeper. It rained in the evening.

*July 28 and 29.* We remained at Culpeper.

*July 30.* Mr. Jack Noel got to camp from our homes, bringing us home rations and clothing. We had lost all our clothes, when our cook and wagons were captured in Pennsylvania. It was an accident that our knapsacks happened to be in the wagons that night on which the wagons were taken. Capt. Frank Dean, our quartermaster, ever thoughtful of his men, had said to us the rainy night we left Gettysburg, "Boys, the wagon, which brings you your supper tonight, will be empty after you get your supper out of it, and you can put your knapsacks in that wagon. It will help you a little and you have a hard and wet night in front of you and need all the help you can get." We thanked him and threw our knapsacks in the wagon, expecting to get them the next day, but Mr. Yank scooped up that wagon that night and we never saw those knapsacks again. Hence, we welcomed Mr. Noel and his load. Mrs. Winston had sent him. Mr. Kinckle,[1] Frank Kinckle's father, also came to visit us today.

*July 31.* We remained at Culpeper. Mr. Kinckle and Mr. Noel went home.

*August 1.* Ordered to Orange Court House and marched nearly there. A very hot day.

*August 2.* Passing through Orange, we took the Plank Road and went west until we struck the pike leading from Gordonsville to Madison Court House. On reaching this pike we turned to our left, and after going two miles, we encamped in a piece of woods on the right of the road five miles from Gordonsville.

*August 3, 4, 5.* We remained quietly in camp at this place.

---

[1] The Rev. William H. Kinckle, pastor of St. Paul's Episcopal Church, Lynchburg, Virginia. See William Asbury Christian. *Lynchburg and Its People* (Lynchburg, Va., 1900), for references to the Rev. Mr. Kinckle. An Index to this volume was compiled separately by Lucille T. Dickerson (Madison Heights, Va., 1947).

*August 6.* We went back to within two miles of Orange, and encamped for the night.

*August 7.* We returned this morning to the camp on the Gordonsville and Madison Court House Pike, which we left yesterday morning.

*August 8 and 9.* We remained in camp.

*August 10.* I went to Mr. C. J. Stovin's today to see Miss Agnes Mayo. Spent the day and had a pleasant time and a good dinner. I returned to camp about dark.

*August 11 to 17.* We remained quietly in camp.

*August 18.* Mr. Winston, Bob's father, came up today, bringing us many good rations.

*August 19.* Mr. Winston went home. Mr. Edmund Anderson came up to Gordonsville and brought us a good many home rations. Edmund met his father at Gordonsville by appointment and brought the things out to camp. The old gent would not try our camp accommodations even for one night. Time passed, as usual, quietly in camp until August 30, Sunday, when I secured a leave of absence for twenty-four hours to go home.

*August 31. Monday.* I went home on the early train, leaving Gordonsville at 4 A.M. I got home about 7 A.M. just as the family were going to breakfast. I had a pleasant day at home.

*September 1.* I returned to camp. Saw Cousin Lucy Lewis and Josie at Gordonsville. We remained at this camp near Gordonsville until September 14th, when leaving early that morning we marched down to Raccoon Ford[2] and placed our guns in position on the high hill on the southern bank, overlooking the ford and the little hamlet just on the north bank of the river.

*September 15.* A regiment of Yankee cavalry had taken possession of the houses of the little hamlet and were annoying our people very much. My gun was ordered to drive them out of these houses. Bob Winston, our gunner, bolted a few shell through some of these buildings and the Yankee sharpshooters came out like bees from a hive and we soon had things very quiet.[3]

---

[2] On the Rapidan River northeast of Orange Court House. Advance units, chiefly cavalry, of Meade's army, crossed the Rappahannock in some force on September 13 and pushed the Confederate cavalry to the Rapidan River. Lee moved up Early's and Anderson's divisions and artillery to the Rapidan to stop further advance of Union forces. (*The War of the Rebellion: A Compilation of the Official Records of the Union and Confederate Armies* [Washington, D. C., 1880-1901], Series I, Volume XXIX, part 2, p. 720. All citations will be from Series I unless otherwise noted.)

[3] The Union cavalry force at Raccoon Ford was Brig. Gen. John Buford's First Cavalry Division. (*Official Records*, Vol. XXIX, pt. 1, p. 113.)

*September 16 to October 7.*  We continued on picket duty at Raccoon Ford. During this time things remained very quiet. One evening we
had a little excitement, which was very interesting to us. The Yanks had
gotten very indifferent and careless in the little village just across the Raccoon Ford and a Louisiana lieutenant of [Brig. Gen. Harry T.] Hays's
Brigade told his colonel that if he would give him twenty men he thought
he could bag them all. The colonel granted him permission and the young
lieutenant called for volunteers. He soon got his men. He took his men
down the river about two hundred yards to a shallow place in the river
where they waded over to the northern bank, unseen by the Yanks, and
creeping, half-bent in Indian file, up back of a garden fence, he and his
men got almost around the entire Yankee picket of at least fifty men before
they were seen. I tell you, there was lively work for about five minutes.
Many, in fact most of them, were unarmed, having taken off their swords
and pistols and laid aside their carbines. Our men rushed on them calling
on them to surrender, which most of them did at once, only some two or
three, who happened to be on their horses, getting away. The young lieutenant and his men brought over forty-seven prisoners back with them.
We on the southern bank of the river witnessed this whole movement. No
one of the men on either side was hurt. Gen. Lee, however, did not approve
of the action and the next morning issued a general order forbidding such
efforts. He complimented the young lieutenant and his men very highly
for what they had done; but said the wounding, or loss, of one of our men
would not have been compensated by the forty-seven prisoners and that
such deeds decided nothing and only made the enemy more careful and
watchful in [the] future. Bob Winston got a pair of brass spurs from one
of the Yankee lieutenants, who was captured on this occasion.[4]

*October 8.*  Late tonight we left our position at Raccoon Ford and
marched to within six miles of Orange Court House and went into camp.

*October 9.*  We passed through Orange Court House and after crossing the Rapidan at Barnett's Ford, we marched towards Madison Court
House, encamping within five miles of that place for the night. It was now
evident to me that Lee was trying to do for the whole Yankee army what
the Louisiana lieutenant had done a few days ago for the Yankee picket
at Raccoon Ford. God grant he may be as successful.[5]

---

[4] No record of the skirmish nor of Lee's order mentioned here could be found.

[5] His army diminished by the absence of Longstreet's First Corps, most of which had
been sent to Tennessee in early September to aid Bragg's campaign against Rosecrans, Lee
decided to take the offensive once again. Meade's army had also been decreased in size by

*October 10.*  Passing through Madison Court House we took the Culpeper Road and marched towards that place. We encamped, for the night, eight miles beyond Robinson River. Our cavalry, under Gen. Stuart, captured a hundred and forty Yanks.

*October 11.  Sunday.*  We marched five miles and encamped at Hazel River on Sperryville Road.

*October 12.*  We went to within five miles of Culpeper Court House and then turned off towards Warrenton, and after a hard day's march, encamped one mile from Warrenton Springs.

*October 13.*  We crossed the Rappahannock River, and marching a short distance we encamped near Warrenton.

*October 14.*  We passed through Warrenton and two miles north of the town came on the rear guard of the Yankees, who, having discovered Gen. Lee's plan, were retreating rapidly. Here we had an artillery duel with them and killed six Yanks, whom our sappers and miners buried in a freshly seeded wheat field in about five minutes from the time these poor fellows were alive and walking about. Such is war. We came up with the main body of the Yanks at Bristoe Station about five o'clock in the evening. A. P. Hill attacked them and was driven back, losing five guns in McIntosh's Battalion by bad management.[6] Such is war. The fighting continued late into the night. We encamped near Bristoe. We were not in the fight.

*October 15.*  We remained in camp near Bristoe all day. Capt. Kirkpatrick and Lieut. Craighill, our ordnance officer, had a personal fisticuff this morning, Capt. Kirkpatrick receiving a black face and a red eye. They very soon kissed and made up. Lieut. Craighill was taking Bill

---

the removal of the Eleventh and Twelfth Corps to Rosecrans, and thus the odds against Lee were not quite so great. Lee acted thus in an attempt to prevent the removal of additional members of Meade's army to the west and, by so doing, to give Bragg's offensive greater chance for success. Also, if Lee's advance were successful, and Meade could be held at the Potomac for the winter, the 1864 Campaign would open without undue exposure of Richmond. (Douglas Southall Freeman, *R. E. Lee: A Biography* [New York, 1935], III, 169-70.)

[6] Maj. (later Lt. Col.) David Gregg McIntosh's Battalion. From McIntosh's report of this battle (which is not wholly clear) it appears that the five guns lost consisted of three from Capt. William K. Donald's 2nd Rockbridge Battery, and two from Capt. William B. Hunt's Alabama Battery (formerly Robert A. Hardaway's). Freeman is apparently in error in stating that only four guns were taken. (*Official Records*, Vol. XXIX, pt. 1, pp. 427, 431, 436; Freeman, *R. E. Lee*, III, 183; Susan Pendleton Lee, *Memoirs of William Nelson Pendleton, D.D.* . . . [Philadelphia, 1893], p. 304.) The battle on this day was at Bristoe Station. Gen. A. P. Hill's Third Corps was engaged with and badly handled by the Federal Second Corps, which, concealed behind the bed of the Orange and Alexandria Railroad, completely surprised the Confederate force. For an account of the battle, see Douglas Southall Freeman, *Lee's Lieutenants: A Study in Command* (New York, 1942-44), III, 239-47.

Cunningham's part and the Captain was certainly in the wrong, which he candidly acknowledged and asked pardon.

*October 16.* We marched to Warrenton Junction and camped there for the night. A heavy rain in the morning. Infantry pulling up the railroad and cutting down telegraph poles, and cutting up the wire and burning ties and twisting rails.

*October 17.* We marched to near the Rappahannock Station and encamped.

*October 18. Sunday.* We moved down right on the river and encamped.

*October 19. Monday.* We crossed the Rappahannock early this morning in a heavy rainstorm on a pontoon bridge and then marched to Culpeper Court House and encamped near that place.

*October 20.* We remained in camp at Culpeper. All quiet.

*October 21.* We marched back to Brandy Station and encamped two miles southeast of that place near Stevensburg.

*October 22 to November 3.* We remained in this place. All quiet. Beautiful weather.

*November 1. Sunday.* Gen. Pendleton, an Episcopal minister and Gen. Lee's chief of artillery preached for us. I was on guard in the battery and the old General stood on a caisson box to preach.

*November 4.* We were ordered to Slaughter's Mountain[7] and marched there and went into camp near that place.

*November 5 and 6.* We remained near Slaughter's Mountain. All quiet.

*November 7.* We received orders at sunset to go immediately to Stevensburg. We started, at once, and after marching one mile north of Stevensburg, we were ordered back to Pony Mountain,[8] which place we reached about sunrise Sunday morning, tired and worn by our all night's march.

---

[7] In Culpeper County near Mitchell's Station on the Orange and Alexandria Railroad. (*Atlas to Accompany the Official Records of the Union and Confederate Armies* [Washington, D. C., 1891-95], Plate LXXXV.)

[8] In Culpeper County, just east of the Orange and Alexandria Railroad and south of Culpeper Court House. After the affair at Bristoe Station on October 14, the Army of Northern Virginia retired south of the Rappahannock River and formed a line. A *tête-de-pont* was maintained by the Confederates on the north side of the river. On November 7 the Federals attacked at this point and crossed the Rappahannock at Kelley's Ford. When the Confederates were forced to give up the *tête-de-pont* with considerable loss, Lee was compelled to retire his army to a line running from Pony Mountain across the Orange and Alexandria Railroad north of Culpeper to the vicinity of Chestnut Ford Church. (*Official Records*, Vol. XXIX, pt. 1, pp. 611-37.)

*November 8.* We remained in line of battle all day on the north side of Pony Mountain. At dark we started towards Rapidan Station, which place we reached at sunrise. This was one of the most disagreeable days and nights I ever spent, the weather being very cold and windy.

*November 9.* After stopping at Rapidan [Station] long enough to cook and feed our horses and rest a little, for both men and horses were very tired from two nights' march, we returned to our old position at Raccoon Ford, which we had left one month before.[9] It was very evident to me that Gen. Lee had not been as successful as the young Louisiana lieutenant had been. Our men put the blame on the slow movements of A. P. Hill's Corps on the two first days. Such is war.

*November 10.* All quiet.

*November 11.* The Yankees appeared in our front on the opposite side of the river. Their trains are running to Mitchell's Station. They have gotten new ties and new rails, and have relaid the track from Manassas to Mitchell's [Station] about as rapidly as our men tore it up, and I believe a little faster. They are very active in our front. They are evidently contemplating a move; maybe a big battle.

*November 12.* Our three-inch rifle gun took a few shots at some Yankee cavalry, which appeared in our front, on the north of the Rapidan River. Then all became quiet.

*November 13.* All quiet, all day. A few Yankee pickets in sight north of the river. The Yanks have moved their picket line a half a mile back from the [Rapidan] river.

*November 14.* We moved back to Mt. Pisgah Church[10] and went into camp right at the church. We were not permitted to use the church, although we were short on tents and clothing. I approve [of] this, because soldiers abuse churches very much when quartered in them.

*November 14 to November 18.* We remained at Mt. Pisgah Church. All quiet. The weather very cool and rainy.

*November 18.* We returned to Raccoon Ford. We had a big pot of nice bacon and cabbage for supper, gotten up by Abram, our cook, which we enjoyed very much. After our cook, Henry, had been captured at Gettysburg, Mrs. Winston had sent this boy Abram to take his place. I fear though, that we will have to send him home, because the government has stopped giving us rations for a cook, and seven men can hardly live on the

9 The line north of Culpeper being unfavorable, Lee retired his army south of the Rapidan River during the night of November 8.

10 A few miles southeast of Rapidan Station. (*Official Records Atlas*, Plate LXXXVII.)

rations which are issued for six. We all, however, had enough tonight and left an abundance for Abram.

*November 19.* We remained in camp about a mile back up on the hills from Raccoon Ford. All quiet.

*November 20.* We remained in same camp. All quiet.

*November 21.* We remained in same place. All quiet. It rained all day.

*November 22.* It cleared off before day. We remained in camp. All quiet.

*November 23.* Inspection of men, battery and horses by Col. [Thomas Hill] Carter, our chief of artillery for the Second Corps.[11] He found everything in good condition and ready for battle, on which he complimented men and officers.

*November 24 and 25.* We remained quiet, in camp.

*November 26.* The Yankee cavalry made some demonstrations at Raccoon Ford. Our battery was sent there, and taking its old position, we soon drove them off. Yanks are evidently feeling how strong we are. Landon C. Berkeley, Jr.,[12] got to our camp late tonight. He brought us some home rations, but left them nearly all at Orange Court House. I fear we shall lose them as the Yanks are certainly on the move, and we will certainly move tomorrow, if not sooner.

*November 27.* We left Raccoon Ford and marched towards Verdiersville, encamping near that place for the night. We heard that Gen. Bragg's army had been defeated and driven from Lookout Mountain. Our Southwestern armies seem to be always beaten. This evening old [Maj. Gen. Edward] "Allegheny" Johnson and his division licked the Yanks badly on Mine Run. He took them by surprise and handled them handsomely.[13]

*November 28.* We moved down to our line of battle, which had been formed along the west side of Mine Run, the Yankee line of battle having been formed on the east side. The Mine Run rises in [the] southeastern part of Orange County and flows north into the Rapidan River.

---

[11] Actually, Brig. Gen. Armistead L. Long was chief of artillery of the Second Corps. Colonel Carter acted as chief in Long's absence from the area as is the case here. (*Official Records,* Vol. XXIX, pt. 2, pp. 839-42.)

[12] Landon Carter Berkeley, Jr., HRB's first cousin who lived at "Montout" in Hanover County.

[13] If there were any element of surprise here, the Confederates were the ones surprised. Maj. Gen. William H. French's Third Corps of Meade's army attacked Johnson's Division on Payne's farm east of Mine Run and was repulsed. (Robert U. Johnson and C. C. Buell, editors, *Battles and Leaders of the Civil War* [New York, 1887-88], IV, 88; Freeman, *R. E. Lee,* III, 198. For the battle at Mine Run, see Freeman, *Lee's Lieutenants,* III, 269-79.)

*November 29.*   We remained very near our line of battle in a piece of oak woods near the Old Turnpike, only our three-inch rifle gun, Sgt. Rickett's, being placed in position.[14] We worked on fortifications tonight from 7 P.M. until midnight, and then went back to our company in the oak woods on the Old Turnpike. We had to work on the north side of a hill, exposed to a very cold north wind and a freezing temperature.

*November 30.*   A brisk cannonade was commenced this morning, but it failed to bring on the expected battle.

*December 1.*   Yanks show no desire to begin the battle. To me they seem to desire to get back to the north of the Rapidan River. We strengthened our fortifications along our entire line. The weather is cold, rainy and disagreeable.

*December 2.*   About daybreak, we were sent on the right of the Old Turnpike and placed our guns on a hill overlooking Mine Run. At sunrise, our advancing pickets found that the Yankee army was gone.[15] They captured all the Yankee pickets in our front, consisting of some three or four hundred men. We followed the Yanks to Wilderness Tavern. We had no fighting. The cavalry had a lively skirmish with the Yankee rear at Germanna Ford. We returned to our old camp east of Mine Run.

*December 3.*   A bright and frosty morning. We returned to our old camp at Mount Pisgah Church.

*December 4.*   All quiet. We built a chimney to our tent and fixed ourselves quite comfortable. I built a big fire and took a good and thorough bath down on a creek near camp. It was very cold work, for the weather was very cold.

*December 5, 6 and 7.*   We remained in camp. All quiet. Boys talking about winter quarters.

*December 8.*   We had to send our cook home on account of short rations.

*December 9.*   We remained in camp. All quiet.

*December 10.*   We went on picket duty at Raccoon Ford and remained there on picket, until December 16th, when we were sent back to our old camp at Mount Pisgah Church.

14 The guns of Nelson's Battalion were placed on the ridge occupied by Maj. Gen. Robert E. Rodes's Division and in the rear of his left near Zoar Church. This was to the north of the Old Turnpike, which ran from Orange Court House to Fredericksburg by way of Wilderness Church.

15 Persuaded that Lee's army was in an impregnable position, Meade began withdrawing his army north of the Rapidan River on the afternoon of December 1. Lee planned to attack on the morning of December 2, but to his surprise he found that the enemy was not there. The Mine Run affair ended operations for 1863. (Freeman, *R. E. Lee,* III, 202.)

*December 17.* A cold, rainy day. I was on guard. We stood four hours at a time, all of us who were on guard preferring to stand in this way. I was on from 8 to 12 both in the day and at night. At night, it rained hard and sleeted, and when relieved at 12 at night, I was so cold, wet and stiff that I could hardly move, and my oilcloth, which I had over my overcoat around my shoulders, and my hat were covered thick with ice. The poor horses, however, suffered more than I did. Such is war and its sufferings.

*December 18 to 24.* We remained at Mount Pisgah Church. All quiet. Weather cold. Ice three or four inches thick on a mill pond near camp. Boys play bandy on the frozen pond. At least a hundred on [the] ice, frequently at once.

*December 24.* Ground covered with snow, and very cold and clear. On guard.

*December 25.* Christmas Day. Camp very quiet. Our dinner consisted of some soldier-bread and black rice and a piece of salted beef about two inches square. The beef not being worth dividing, we cast lots for it. John Lewis Berkeley won and ate it. The rest of us, five in number, ate our rice and bread. The Hardy boys and George Bray got a little merry about dark. A little applejack had gotten into camp.

*December 26 to 29.* We remained at Mount Pisgah Church. All quiet.

*December 30.* We heard of poor Bob Nelson's death. He had been sick ever since April last. He died December 21st, 1863. He was nearly twenty-two. *Requiescat in pace.*

*December 31.* It rained hard towards evening. We drew some coffee, sugar and peaches today. Have not had any of these before for a long time. The old year will soon die. Let [it] die, with its bloody record of battles, deaths, devastated homes and vacant chairs! But such is horrid war.

# CHAPTER VIII

# CAMP CONFUSION

## *Winter Quarters, 1864*

*January 1, 1864.* We were encamped at [Mount] Pisgah Church, Orange County, Virginia. It had rained hard all the night before but early this morning it cleared off, turned cold and soon began freezing. About midday, we received orders to go to Fredericks Hall [Louisa County] on the Central Railroad and to go into winter quarters near that station. We went about ten miles that evening and encamped in a big woods, which the boys dubbed Camp Confusion, because we got much mixed up that night. Companies mixing up badly and wagons worse. Intensely cold that night.

*January 2.* Still very cold, freezing all day. Marched nearly to Fredericks Hall. Dabney Williamson and I got a supper from a Darkey and his wife tonight. It was ash cake and fried herring, [the] herring being fried with middling. Never enjoyed a supper more. Paid a dollar each for it.

*January 3. Sunday.* Reached Fredericks Hall early. Edmund Anderson and Bob Winston got nice boxes from home today, so we had enough to eat, once more in our lives.

*January 4. Monday.* We moved to our winter quarters 1 1/4 miles south of Fredericks Hall, on a Mr. Harris' farm.

*January 5.* Cleared off our camp ground, pitched our tents and began building our chimney.

*January 6 and 7.* Continued to work on our chimney, finishing it on afternoon of [the] 7th.

*January 8.* Slight snow. Saw a man shot today for desertion. Poor fellow! His crime was only going home to see after his wife and children. It was his third or fourth offense. His name was Martin. He was buried where he was executed. Did he not die for his country?

*January 9.* Began work on our stables.

*January 10. Sunday.* No preaching. Our chaplain, Mr. [Rev. Thomas Walker] Gilmer, being absent.

*January 11.* Mr. [Rev. William H.] Kinckle got to camp and brought us some saugum [sorghum]. He preached that night. A good sermon.

*January 12.* Mr. Kinckle went home. He always brings the boys a big lot of tobacco, both chewing and smoking. We worked on stables today.

*January 12 to 27.* Our whole time taken up in work on our stables. We built large pens out of large pine logs and covered them with plank. We had pressed a sawmill into use and got on quite rapidly.

*January 27.* I went home tonight on a seven days' furlough. I got home about ten that night.

*January 28.* On going down into the dining room the next morning, found Miss Millie Anderson and Cousin Mary Botts Berkeley.[1] The latter is teaching for Uncle Dick Berkeley. I walked over home with her that morning. Sam Anderson came for his sister that morning.

*January 29.* Took supper at "Krishnanagar."[2] Cousin Mary Botts came home with us on her way to the Rectory.

*January 30.* Remained at home all day, Cousin Mary having such a bad headache that she was unable to go to the Rectory.

*January 31. Sunday.* Carried Cousin Mary home this evening. I saw Cousin Kate Igleheart,[3] Cousin Mary's sister. I went to "Locust Level," (where Aunt Kate [Catherine Robinson Berkeley] Winston was then living), that evening, expecting to go to Richmond the next day.

*February 1. Monday.* Got left by the cars. Went up to see A. Morris about the assessment of damages done by [Maj. Gen. James Lawson] Kemper's Brigade on the "Locust Level" farm, one-third of which belongs to me. Spent rest of day at "Locust Level" with Aunts Kate and Sally, and with Sister [Louisa] Carter.

*February 2.* Went to Richmond and returned that night. The city looks sad and war-worn. What is to be its fate? Would that this horrid war might be stopped.

*February 3.* Came up home from "Locust Level." All well at home.

[1] Mary Botts Berkeley (d. 1908) was the daughter of Dr. Edmund Berkeley and Mary Randolph Spotswood Brooke. (Frances Berkeley Young, *The Berkeleys of Barn Elms* [New Haven, 1954], p. 115.)

[2] The home of Richard Ferrell Berkeley, located on the Ridge Road not far west of "White House."

[3] Catherine Spotswood Berkeley, daughter of Dr. Edmund Berkeley, married William T. Iglehart of Annapolis, Maryland. (Young, *Berkeleys*, p 113.)

Uncle Dick and Aunt Bettie spent the evening with us. John Lewis Berkeley walked in about dark, accompanied by his cousin Phil Mayo.

*February 4. Thursday.* I walked up to "Montout" in the afternoon and went with John Lewis and P. Mayo over to "Krishnanagar" and took supper, and returned home late that night.

*February 5.* Returned to camp at Fredericks Hall, being twelve hours behind time. Met Frank Kinckle and Bob Winston at depot. Got put on broom squad for four days, for staying over time. Lieut. George Hobson put me on. He is a good fellow, a brave man and a conscientious Christian. He said that he hated to do it, but was compelled to take some notice of the delay. I told him it was "O.K." I would be perfectly willing to sweep camp a dozen mornings for one more day at home.

*February 6.* Swept camp this morning. There is always a detail of six men every morning while in winter quarters to sweep the huts of our camp and carry off all dirt and refuse. We received orders at 8 P.M. to go immediately to Morton's Ford, on [the] Rapidan River in Orange County, Virginia. Begged Maj. [Thomas] Jefferson Page, who was in command of our battalion in Col. Nelson's absence, to let us remain in our comfortable quarters until daybreak and get a good night's rest; but, he, having no practical knowledge, ordered us to be ready to start at ten o'clock that night. We started in wind, rain and utter darkness, and men and horses were floundering in mud, rain and darkness the whole of that night, and when daylight came we had only gotten about a mile or two from camp, while men and horses were worn out and little fit for a hard day's march over a heavy and muddy road.

*February 7. Sunday.* Continued our hard march towards Morton's Ford. Col. Nelson, who had been down to his home, "Oakland," in Hanover, came up with us about sunset, and the first thing he said to Maj. Page was, "Jeff, had you let these poor men and horses remain in their comfortable camp last night, you would be ten miles nearer Morton's Ford than you are now." Behold the difference between a practical and theoretical officer! Encamped tonight at our old "Camp Confusion."

*February 8.* Passed Verdiersville and encamped three miles beyond that place on the Plank Road between Orange and Fredericksburg. Bad news in regard to our camp at Fredericks Hall and all of our baggage, which had been left there. We were entirely without tents on this trip.

*February 9.* Ordered to remain up here all the winter, which caused some swearing. Moved up Plank Road towards Orange Court House and encamped for the night.

*February 10.*   Moved within four miles of Orange Court House. Picked out a camp in a big oak woods. Began the chimney for our tent and sent to Fredericks Hall for our baggage. We had done a great deal of hard work at our camp at Fredericks Hall and were ordered away before the poor horses could enjoy their comfortable stables, or the men their quarters. But such is the fate of soldiers in war.

*February 11.*   Finished our chimney. Fixed up a sort of a shelter and slept very comfortably.

*February 12.*   Ed Anderson and John L. Berkeley went home. They walked to Louisa Court House where Major John Page[4] gave them a dinner and got Gen. Pendleton to sign their pass for three days' leave.

*February 13.*   Went to Orange Court House today with Frank Kinckle.

*February 14. Sunday.*   Our baggage and tents, which had been left at our old camp at Fredericks Hall, got to us by rail. We put up our large tent and got fixed up very comfortably. Frank Kinckle went home today on a thirty-day furlough, because he had secured a recruit. John Hill, Bob Winston and myself got, late tonight, a forty-eight-hour leave of absence to go to our homes. This pass gives three days at home, as our officers always kindly date them the day after we start.

*February 15.*   J. H. Berkeley, Bob Winston and I walked over to Melton's Crossing, on [the] Central Railroad today on our way home, in three hours, a distance of 15 miles; being left by the mail train, we walked on down to Trevilian's Depot. Got a supper from the railroad hands (negroes). Paid a dollar each for it. It was while here for a night freight that John Hill lost his pocketbook, containing about a hundred dollars of Confederate money. John remained there that night, hoping to find his money. He, however, heard nothing of it and came down on the accommodation train the next morning and went on to "Locust Level." Bob Winston and I went on to Hanover that night, getting home about two o'clock at night. Found all at home well and glad to see me.

*February 16.*   Went up to "Airwell" to see Sister Bettie, who is now teaching Cousin Mary's children and took supper at "Montout."

*February 17.*   Took dinner at "Krishnanagar."

*February 18.*   Returned to camp at Orange Court House. It took the train all day to run from Richmond to Gordonsville. It was crowded with

---

4 Chief quartermaster for the Artillery Corps, Army of Northern Virginia. (Jennings C. Wise, *The Long Arm of Lee or The History of the Artillery of the Army of Northern Virginia* [Lynchburg, Va., 1915], I, 427.)

soldiers and the engine had nothing but green pine wood to make steam. Col. Bob Mayo[5] was on board. He came from "Montout" that morning. We got to camp about 12 P.M.

*February 19 to 27 [i.e., 26].*   Was in camp on the Plank Road, east of Orange Court House.

*February 26.*   Dabney Williamson and I went home on a forty-eight-hour leave, walking over to Trevilian's Depot and taking the train there about 2 P.M. and getting home about 4:30 P.M.

*February 27.*   Went up to "Dewberry" to prayer meeting with some of my sisters, seeing nearly all the good people there in the neighborhood.

*February 28.  Sunday.*   Went to Trinity Church and heard Mr. [Horace] Stringfellow preach. I walked up to "Montout" after dinner. Had a long war talk with Uncle Landon. I fear that our loved ones are rather in the dark about our present condition and the great uncertainty of how this horrid and bloody war will end. It looks dark and very doubtful at present. I mean our future. I walked out with Nannie in the evening, having a long talk with her, and then went home to supper.

*February 29.*   Returned to camp near Orange Court House on Plank Road. Chances are I may never see home again. This horrid war is getting so bloody and so desperate.

*March 1.*   Remained in camp.

*March 2.*   Ordered with Gen. Johnson's Division[6] to Chancellorsville.

*March 3.*   Arrived at Chancellorsville at 9 A.M. and remained there until the morning of March 5th, [when] we came back to our camp on Plank Road near Orange Court House.

*March 5 to March 23.*   We remained in same camp near Orange Court House.

*March 24.*   Heard Dr. Reid[7] of Richmond, who paid us a visit about this time, preach both morning and night. Splendid sermons.

*March 25.  Good Friday.  On guard.  Rained.*

*March 26.*   Heard Dr. Reid preach morning and night.

*March 27.*   My birthday.  Easter Sunday.  Dr. Reid preached and administered the Communion.

*March 28.*   Beautiful day.  Mr. Reid preached. Wrote home. Bob Winston got back off a ten-day furlough.

5 Probably Robert M. Mayo, commanding the 47th Virginia Regiment.
6 Maj. Gen. Edward "Alleghemy" Johnson's Division, Second Corps.
7 Probably Dr. Charles H. Read of the United Presbyterian Church of Richmond.

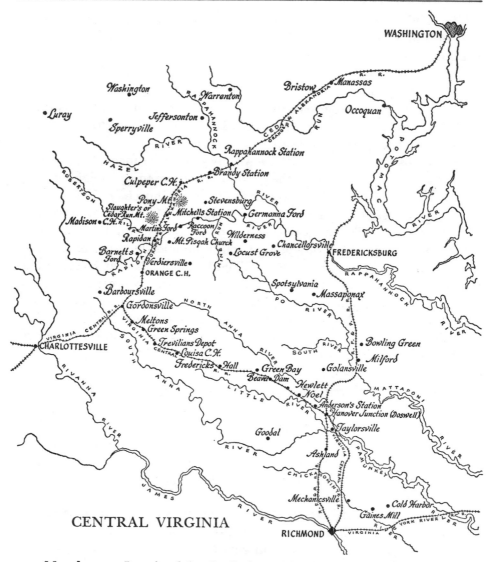

CENTRAL VIRGINIA

*March 29.* It rained hard all day and night. About 9 P.M. a bold spring "busted" out in our fireplace, putting out all our fire, and compelling us to go to bed.

*March 30.* Had hard time getting breakfast this morning, owing to spring being in our fireplace. Had to cut ditch, draw off the water, bring in about two feet of dirt and ram it down in the fireplace and then make our fire on this pile of dirt. After doing this, we succeeded in getting a comfortable breakfast. It cleared off brightly this morning.

*March 31.* Remained in camp. Everything quiet. The war storm must soon be on us. Sent two April fools.

*April 1.* My messmates at this time were: E. M. Anderson, J. H. Berkeley, J. L. Berkeley, Dabney Williamson, W. H. Hoge, F. A. Kinckle, R. B. Winston and myself. All these men were my friends; I loved them. They requited honorably my regards; we served and fought; we smiled and wept in concert. We reveled or we sorrowed side by side. All quiet in camp, expecting the war storm to break upon us every day. Our anxiety is intense.

*April 2.* Rain and snow. This bad weather delays the opening of the campaign.

*April 3.* On guard.

*April 4.* Rained all day.

*April 5.* Rained and hailed all day. This day two years ago, I first met the Yankees in arms at Fort Magruder, near Yorktown, Virginia.

*April 6.* Cleared off about ten; all quiet in camp.

*April 7.* Beautiful bright day. All quiet in camp.

*April 8.* Day of fasting and prayer, appointed by President Davis. My whole mess kept it very strictly.

*March [i.e., April] 9.* Rained all day.

*April 10.* On guard; rained all day.

*April 11 and 12.* All quiet. When will the war storm come?

*April 13.* Worked at sawmill all day, carrying off heavy oak planks; got back to camp that night very tired.

*April 14.* Wrote to Nannie. Heard Dr. Ramsey[8] preach.

*March [i.e., April] 15.* Wrote home and got a letter that evening from Mollie.

*April 16.* Rained all day.

*April 17. Sunday.* Heard a good sermon from our chaplain, Mr. Gilmer.

*April 19, 20 and 21.* Remained in camp; all quiet; a clear day. Got a letter from home. At night boys had a grand concert to the new and old Corporals. A bright and beautiful night.

*March [i.e., April] 22.* Went to Orange Court House and sent money from there [for] three pieces of music. Received orders tonight to move to the front at 9 o'clock tomorrow morning. The spring campaign is about to open.

---

[8] Probably Dr. James B. Ramsey of the First Presbyterian Church of Lynchburg.

# CHAPTER IX

# CAN WE DO IT?

## Wilderness to Cold Harbor, 1864

*April 23, 1864.* Moved from our camp near Orange Court House to Summerville Ford and put our guns in position on southern bank of the Rapidan River. The Culpeper side of the river is covered with Yankee tents as far as the eye can reach. What a mighty host to keep back! Can we do it? We will try. Who of us will be left when peace comes?

*April 24.* On guard. It rained very hard at night. It was Sunday.

*April 25.* Bright and clear day, after a rainy night. Got a letter from Sudy that evening.

*April 26.* Answered Sudy's letter. Still on the front with guns in position. Mr. Bowles began to cook for us today.

*April 27.* It turned very cool.

*April 28.* Still very cool. Received letters from Bettie and Nannie.

*April 29.* Answered Nannie's letter and received one from Nannie Carter.

*April 30.* Put on my new pants today and threw old ones away. It is one year today since we left Pine Camp in Caroline County, four miles from Hewletts on [the] Central Railroad.

*May 1.* Heard two good sermons today from Mr. Leps,[1] chaplain of the 31st Virginia. It was Sunday. Wrote to Mother.

---

[1] James Henry Leps (1823-89) was a native of Hampshire County, Virginia (now West Virginia). After graduating from the College of New Jersey (now Princeton University) and Princeton Theological Seminary, he became a Presbyterian minister being ordained by Greenbrier Presbytery on July 19, 1853. He was pastor of the Presbyterian Church at Parkersburg, Virginia (now West Virginia), at the outbreak of the Civil War. From 1862 to 1865 he was a chaplain in the Confederate Army. Immediately after the war he served the Presbyterian churches at Frankford and Falling Spring, West Virginia. He died in Roanoke, Virginia. (E. C. Scott, *Ministerial Directory of the Presbyterian Church, U. S. 1861-1941* [Austin, Texas, 1942], pp. 401-2.)

*May 2.* Received two letters from home.

*May 3.* Great activity in the Yankee camp. They are certainly on the move.

*May 4.* This morning, on getting up, we found that all the Yankees had disappeared from our front. Received orders to be ready to move at a moment's warning. Moved in the afternoon down to Mine Run.[2]

*May 5.* Moved early this morning towards Chancellorsville. We came suddenly on the Yanks in thick woods on the Orange side of Wilderness Tavern.[3] Not being able to get positions for our guns, we went back a short distance into a field on the right of the pike. The infantry fighting very soon became heavy and desperate. The doctors established the field hospital of the 1st and 2nd divisions at a spring near us and very soon they began to bring out the wounded very rapidly. It is a beautiful spring day on which all this bloody work is being done. About 1 P.M. our boys brought out an entire Yankee regiment they had bagged. Gen. "Allegheny" Johnson reported killed; Gens. [John B.] Gordon and [Leroy A.] Stafford mortally wounded.[4] The first section of our battery has been ordered into the fight. Capt. [John] Milledge of our battalion has been engaged and has had one man wounded. At 5 P.M. we had driven the Yankees nearly three miles and taken many prisoners.[5] Gen. Walker of [the] Stonewall Brigade is reported killed.[6] All night, our surgeons, some twenty in number, have been cutting off arms, legs, etc., and dressing their wounds. This morning when I got up about 4 A.M. there was a big pile of

[2] By the morning of May 4, Lee determined that the enemy's movements, first noticed on May 2, were towards Germanna and Ely's Fords on the Rapidan River. This meant that Grant was moving towards Fredericksburg, thus the orders for the movements of the Confederate forces to the right. At dawn the soldiers were ordered to prepare three day's rations. Ewell's Corps, to which HRB's artillery was attached, advanced by the Old Turnpike. (Douglas Southall Freeman, *Lee's Lieutenants: A Study in Command* [New York, 1942-44], III, 343-46.)

[3] The van of Ewell's Second Corps (Brig. Gen. John M. Jones's Brigade of Johnson's Division) was ordered to halt at about 11:00 A.M. Federals were just ahead, crossing the Old Turnpike at Germanna Ford Road. (Freeman, *Lee's Lieutenants*, III, 349.)

[4] Of these, only Brig. Gen. Leroy A. Stafford was mortally wounded. There is no record of the wounding of Johnson and Gordon. Of Ewell's command, in addition to Stafford, Brig. Gen. John M. Jones was killed, and Brig. Gen. John Pegram received a leg wound. (Freeman, *Lee's Lieutenants*, III, 351.)

[5] For the account of the first day's fighting of the Wilderness Campaign, see Freeman, *Lee's Lieutenants*, III, 349-52. Berkeley is in error in stating that the Federals had been driven more than three miles. The lines at the end of the day were substantially the same as when the two armies first made contact. As the fighting died in the afternoon on Ewell's front, Lieut. Gen. A. P. Hill's Corps, advancing on the Orange Plank Road, met the Federals, and a fierce battle ensued until nightfall, both sides holding their own.

[6] Brig. Gen. James A. Walker was not killed. He was wounded severely several days later, on March 11 at Bloody Angle. (Freeman, *Lee's Lieutenants*, III, 407.) Walker was later a congressman and lieutenant governor of Virginia.

amputated arms, hands, legs and fingers within a foot or two of me. A
horrid sight.

*May 6.* This morning forty men of my company, I was among the
number, were given muskets and forty rounds of ammunition and sent
down on our extreme left to act as sharpshooters under Lieut. Basye, who
stationed us in a big woods, with orders for us to keep a sharp lookout
for Yankee scouts and cavalry. We remained there some four hours without seeing or hearing a single Yank and then reported to our company at
Locust Grove. The first gun of our battery was engaged late last night
and early this morning, but no one was hurt.[7]

*May 7.* We moved tonight about dark around to Verdiersville and
stopped just beyond that place on the Plank Road. Yanks on the move,
edging around towards our right.[8]

*May 8.* Marched to Shady Grove Meeting House.[9]

*May 9.* Marched to near Spotsylvania Court House.

*May 10.* We went into position early this morning, west of the
Court House. There have been several attempts made to carry our lines,
but all failed. About 4 P.M. the Yanks broke into our lines on our left.
This caused us to leave our position, after we had been engaged a short
time. It was only a small party of Yanks who broke in; they were all killed
or captured. We left the field and went into camp near the Court House
to feed and refresh men and horses.[10]

*May 11.* We returned this morning to our position, which we left
the night before and remained there until after dark, when we were or-

[7] The major fighting on May 6 was on Hill's front, to whose support Longstreet soon
came, and a rout of the Federal forces followed. Just as it seemed that a severe defeat might
be handed Meade's army, Longstreet was wounded, and thereafter the Confederate advances
came to a halt. For this day's action, see Freeman, *Lee's Lieutenants,* III, 354-66.

[8] On the seventh, Grant began to shift Meade's army to the left in what turned out to be
a move towards Spotsylvania Court House, in an attempt to establish a new supply line on
the Rappahannock River. The only fighting done on this day was chiefly between cavalry
units in the Spotsylvania Court House area. (Freeman, *Lee's Lieutenants,* III, 376-79.)

[9] On the eighth, the Confederate First Corps (now commanded by Maj. Gen. Richard
Heron Anderson) met the Federals at Spotsylvania Court House. Ewell's Corps arrived shortly
after 5:00 P.M. to save the day for the Confederates, the Federals having threatened to turn
Anderson's right. This day's action took place on a line between Brock Road and Shady Grove
Church Road, somewhat over a mile northwest of Spotsylvania Court House. (Freeman, *Lee's
Lieutenants,* III, 380-87.)

[10] Freeman (*Lee's Lieutenants,* III, 395-96) places the time of the beginning of this engagement as 6:10 P.M. Col. Emory Upton's Brigade broke through the western face of the portion
of Ewell's line called "Mule Shoe." Simultaneously, Brig. Gen. Gresham Mott's force was to
pierce the eastern face of the salient, but due to the concentrated artillery fire of Hardaway's
and Nelson's guns his attack failed. The breakthrough by Upton, though serious, was quickly
repaired, but not without considerable loss to the Confederates.

dered out to feed our horses and get ammunition. Went into our old camp, which we had left that morning.[11]

*May 12.* A great battle began early this morning, about 3 A.M. Our line of battle was broken right at the place which we had left the night before, our men being taken entirely by surprise.[12] A portion of Page's[13] and Cutshaw's[14] battalions, while on the road going in to take our position of the day before, together with nearly the entire division of Gen. "Allegheny" Johnson, was captured by the Yanks.[15] Re-enforcements were sent to this point and after long and desperate fighting the Yanks were driven back and our line was re-established. Our battery went into position near the [Spotsylvania] Court House and was under a heavy artillery fire all day without replying to [the] Yanks. This has been the most terrible day I have ever lived. At one time, it seemed as if by mere brute force and overpowering numbers that the Yanks would trample us into the mud. It rained hard during the first part of the day, but cleared off about 1 P.M. At 9 A.M. Gen. R. E. Lee and staff, consisting of about forty men, rode into our battery, a little to the rear of my gun, and halted for a moment. Scarcely had they done so, when two Yankee scrapling shells came over and bursted right in among Gen. Lee and his staff, enveloping them with thick clouds of smoke. I could see that two horses were down

[11] Under the impression that the Federal army was withdrawing from the battle line, Lee ordered all guns removed from the front line so that they would be ready for quick pursuit of the Federals. Brig. Gen. A. L. Long had all of the guns on the Second Corps's front removed except for a few. See Freeman, *Lee's Lieutenants*, III, 398 *ff.*, and *R. E. Lee: A Biography* (New York, 1935), III, 315-16, for discussion of this movement, which proved to be a disastrous one during the hours following.

[12] Shortly after midnight, Maj. Gen. Edward Johnson concluded that the enemy was massing for an attack on his salient, which was the apex of Ewell's line called the "Mule Shoe," or "Bloody Angle," as it was called after the action which took place that night. Johnson quickly requested Ewell to have the artillery guns, which had been removed from the front only a few hours before, returned. The guns did not arrive in time to aid in repulsing the enemy attack, which began about 4:30 A.M., May 12, and Ewell's line was broken. Only through heroic efforts was the breach repaired. (Freeman, *Lee's Lieutenants*, III, 399-410; Freeman, *R. E. Lee*, III, 317-26.)

[13] Maj. Richard Channing Morris Page's Battalion, formerly commanded by Col. Thomas Hill Carter. Colonel Carter was placed in command of the Second Division of the Artillery of the Second Corps on April 7. Major Page succeeded Colonel Carter in command of the battalion. (*The War of the Rebellion: A Compilation of the Official Records of the Union and Confederate Armies* [Washington, D. C., 1880-1901], Series I, Volume XXXIII, pp. 1234-35. All citations will be from Series I unless otherwise noted.)

[14] Major (later Lieut. Col.) Wilfred Emmet Cutshaw.

[15] Two batteries of Cutshaw's Battalion had been left with Johnson on the night of May 11. Upon receiving orders to place more artillery back on Johnson's front, General Long sent R. C. M. Page's Battalion forward. This battalion arrived just in time to be captured except for two guns. In all, the enemy captured twenty guns; twelve from Page's and eight from Cutshaw's battalions. (*Official Records*, Vol. XXXVI, pt. 1, p. 1086.)

and their riders. A second after, Old Mas' Bob rode out of the smoke on Traveller, amid the loud shouts of A. P. Hill's Corps, which was just in our rear. The horses of two couriers had had their legs cut off; the front legs of one, the hind legs of the other. The horses were shot.[16]

I have often thought what might have been the result had Gen. Lee been killed then. The expression on his face as he rode out of that smoke has always remained firmly vised in my memory. At one time during this day, Capt. [John] Milledge came to our battery and asked for some volunteer cannoneers to help him out for a short time, he [his battery] having come up so very rapidly that his own cannoneers had been unable to keep up. J. L. Berkeley and W. H. Hoge of my mess with five or six others went over to help him. J. H. Berkeley's horse and also Col. Nelson's horse was killed. When Col. Nelson was told by his courier that his splendid horse had had one of its feet taken off by a cannon ball, his reply was, "Thank God it is not one of my men." About 2 P.M. Gen. Lane,[17] with two brigades of infantry, was sent into the woods, some distance to our right: he and his men made things very lively in those woods for about an hour or more; and when they came out, they brought some three thousand Yanks and three or four Yankee flags. These Yankee flags were sent down our line of battle by couriers on horseback and encouraged our men very much. We remained in position all that night on the line of battle. It was a bright moonlight night. The Rockbridge boys were on our right and gave us some songs, which the Yankee pickets encored.

*May 13.* We took a new position a half mile to the left of [the] Court House. Yanks were quiet all day.

*May 14.* We expected a fight today, but after a short shelling everything remained quiet.

*May 15.* The Yanks withdrew their pickets from our extreme left. We fired about forty rounds on them, after which all was quiet for the rest of the day.

*May 16.* We were relieved this morning and went into camp near [the] Court House to refresh men and horses.

*May 17.* Remained in [the] same place all day. Cooked three days' rations.

16 No record of an incident of this exact kind could be found. He was exposed to danger many times during this trying day. A similar one is reported in Freeman, *R. E. Lee,* III, 331.

17 Brig. Gen. James H. Lane, Wilcox's Division, Third Corps. Lee had ordered Lane's Brigade to advance on the Federal left from the rear of "Heth's Salient" (See Freeman, *R. E. Lee,* III, map on p. 323) and under cover of an oak wood, in an attempt to give relief to the hard-pressed Confederates at the "Bloody Angle." Brig. Gen. William Mahone's Brigade, under Col. Daniel A. Weisiger, was sent in support of Lane. (Freeman, *R. E. Lee,* III, 522-24.)

*May 18.* Early this morning [the] Yanks commenced to shell our line near [the] Court House, most of the shell falling in our camp. A. I. Hewitt was badly wounded by one of these shell. Our battery moved behind a piece of woods and after staying there a short time, went up behind the Court House on our left, and to the left of the road leading from [the] Court House towards Orange. We remained quietly for the rest of the day, the Yanks having stopped shelling us.

*May 19.* Remained in [the] same place all day. Second Section relieved Capt. [John L.] Massie last night. I wrote home.

*May 20.* Remained in the same place. Perfectly quiet all day. Received two letters from home. Yanks moving around on our right.

*May 21.* Received orders to follow [Maj. Gen. Robert E.] Rodes's Division to our right.[18] When we reached the Telegraph Road, we found that the Yanks were moving on Milford on [the] Richmond, Fredericksburg and Potomac Railroad and so we turned down the Telegraph Road, stopping for the night at Goldensville [Golansville, Caroline County].

*May 22.* Continued our march to Hanover Junction. Dabney Williamson carried me to his sister's, Mrs. Fox's. She gave us a nice breakfast up in her room, the entire lower floor of her house being taken up by officers. Coming on to Hanover Junction, [I] fell in with Uncle Dick and Cousin Ned Taylor. John Hill, John Lewis and myself got permission and went over to "Locust Level," where Aunt Kate Winston was then living, getting there about one o'clock in the day. We returned to our camp at Hanover Junction about sunset.

*May 23.* Moved to Taylorsville and afterwards went down to Garnett's Tobacco House, remaining there until 8 P.M. and returning to our old camp at Taylorsville.

*May 24.* Moved to [Hanover] Junction early this morning, [and] after being there a short time, went back to Taylorsville. Later in the afternoon we went back to the [Hanover] Junction, put our guns in position on [the] left of [the Richmond], Fredericksburg [and Potomac] Railroad and built good breastworks.

*May 25.* Went over to "Locust Level," [and] took supper there. Heard from home. Yanks had not been there up to 10 o'clock this morn-

[18] By early morning of the twenty-first, General Lee knew that the enemy was moving southward towards Milford. Lee determined to establish his line on the North Anna River and ordered his army to begin marching for Hanover Junction. (Freeman, *R. E. Lee*, III, 340-42.) For the route of the Second Corps in the march to Hanover Junction, see *Atlas to Accompany the Official Records of the Union and Confederate Armies* (Washington, D. C., 1891-95), Plate LXXXI.

ing. Yanks at Mr. Edmund Anderson's, Little River being the line of battle. Got back to camp late tonight.

*May 26.*   Rainy day. All quiet. Yanks on a move.

*May 27.*   Moved early this morning towards Ashland. I went by "Locust Level," got something to eat, and left John Hill there, Lieut. Basye having gotten permission for him to remain there a week or ten days, as he was quite sick and looking bad. I overtook my battery near Ashland, where it had halted to feed the horses. We then marched towards Atlee's Station on [the] Central Railroad and encamped a mile from the station.[19]

*May 28.*   Continued our march towards Richmond, edging our way around to the James River below the city. We encamped on Meadow Bridge Road three miles from Mechanicsville.

*May 29.   Sunday.*   All quiet. At 12 o'clock [noon], we went over to the Old Church Road and took position on the left of that road. We remained here until nearly night when my gun was ordered farther down the Old Church Road and unlimbered right in the middle of the road. At this point we met many wounded coming to the rear and there was considerable confusion, while just in front of us there was heavy fighting going on.[20] At this time, Col. Nelson came up, who soon restored order, and the firing just in front of us soon stopped. We remained down there in the road until dark and then returned to where we had left the rest of our battery and there we spent the night. Captains Massie and Milledge's batteries of my battalion were hotly engaged late this evening, and Lieut. Anslie [Benjamin F. Ancell] of Massie's Battery was killed and two of their men wounded.[21] Milledge had one man wounded.

*May 31.*   We returned to the position which we left last night and threw up breastworks. At night we moved about two miles to the right and took a position [at] the edge of some pines, the pines being immediately in our rear. We reached this position about daybreak. Thus ends the month of May, 1864. It has been a month of marching and fighting all the

[19] For events taking place from May 27 to the action at Cold Harbor, see Freeman, *R. E. Lee,* III, 360 *ff.* Gen. U. S. Grant was side-stepping his army to the left, and Lee moved with him to keep his army between the enemy and Richmond.

[20] The Confederate cavalry met in a vigorous action with General P. H. Sheridan's command near Haw's Shop, threw the enemy back, and captured prisoners from the Fifth and Sixth Corps. The Confederates were soon forced to withdraw, however. (Freeman, *R. E. Lee,* III, 365.)

[21] This action was carried on chiefly with Maj. Gen. Robert E. Rodes's Division near Bethesda Church. The attack which failed was under the direction of Maj. Gen. Jubal A. Early, who had succeeded the ailing Ewell to the command of the Second Corps on May 27. (Freeman, *R. E. Lee,* III, 369-71.)

time. My company has been very fortunate, not having yet had but one single man wounded.

*June 1.*   The Yankee sharpshooters have been very bad all day and several men have been killed near us.[22]

*June 2.*   We remained in position, under quite heavy shelling until 4 P.M., when we followed up the Yanks who had evacuated their works just in our front and to our left. We captured some two hundred or more of their sharpshooters, killing quite a number of them. These were the very fellows who had been worrying us all day. We got even with them this evening. We followed the Yanks about a mile down the road towards Cold Harbor and then encamped for the night right on the side of the road.[23]

*June 3.*   At 6 A.M. today we were ordered into position under a most tremendous artillery fire. We had to go through a very thick piece of pines and [had] to cut a road as we went along. Our company carried into the fight about 115 men and some 60 horses. The first gun and its crew were in front, and before the other guns, which immediately followed it, could get in position, the first gun's crew had been nearly all disabled, three men being killed and some eight or ten wounded, while every horse was either dead, or wounded. We carried in five guns. After heavy loss both in horses and men, we got into position and did good work. I am the only one of six messmates left who went into the fight this morning who has not been wounded. Poor Edmund Anderson, with whom I breakfasted, I am told is mortally wounded. I trust God that it may be better with him than I hear. I have not seen any of them, except Bob Winston, whose place I took when he fell. His is a flesh wound and thought not to be dangerous. We had eight men killed on the field and some forty wounded, and thirty-five horses killed. Yet, notwithstanding this heavy loss, we held our position and are still ready to do good work. It is now 5 P.M. and the heavy fighting seems to be over. The sharpshooters, however, are still at it. Our infantry lost hardly a man.[24] The Yankee loss was very heavy. Frank Kinckle was

[22] This was the first day of the Battle of Cold Harbor, which began on the First Corps's front. The Confederate attack was badly managed by Maj. Gen. Richard H. Anderson, commanding the Corps since the wounding of General Longstreet at Wilderness. Lee had hoped the attack would result in a rolling up of the Federal left. (Freeman, *Lee's Lieutenants*, III, 506-7.)

[23] In this action, General Early had moved General Rodes's Division forward "along the road from Hundley's Corner towards Old Church." The enemy retired from the entrenchments. Rodes was supported by the divisions of Maj. Gens. John B. Gordon and Henry Heth. (Jubal Anderson Early, *Lieutenant General Jubal Anderson Early, C.S.A. Autobiographical Sketch and Narrative of the War Between the States. With Notes by R. H. Early* [Philadelphia and London, 1912], p. 363.)

[24] For the action that day at Cold Harbor, see Freeman, *R. E. Lee*, III, 388-91; Freeman,

knocked down by a fragment of a shell and very badly hurt, but refused to leave the field until the fighting was over. Late at night we went back to the position we left yesterday evening. I stumbled on Col. Robert Mayo and Bedell Berkeley that night in the dark. Had to go on guard that night, although I had been on guard the night before. About 3 A.M., Lieut. Basye, a brave and good man and a warm friend of my mess, came and took my place on guard to let me go back to our field hospital to see Edmund Anderson. I started, but met McDaniel, who told me Edmund was dead. Alas, my noble friend and bosom companion. I little thought, when we separated this morning, that it was for the last time on earth. Such is war. No nobler soul or braver man ever died for his country.

*June 4.* Our company was relieved this morning and went back to near Gaines Mill to recruit in men and horses. I went by our field hospital and saw Edmund Anderson's body. He looked perfectly natural. His friends in Richmond have been notified of his death and will come for his body today.

Chris Harris was killed yesterday. A noble and a brave boy; one of our best soldiers. His father got to camp today only to find his boy dead on his country's altar. It is truly pitiful to see the old man with his dead boy; and yet this dead boy has to be carried to his poor mother. God have mercy on the poor mothers whose boys this cruel war is taking from them. We have lost fourteen men killed from yesterday's battle; eight died on the field and six since of their wounds. Col. Nelson came to my tent this morning and insisted on my writing to father. I could see no use, for all the bridges are burnt and the railroads torn up. I wrote, however, as he thought it was my duty to do it. He made the mail boy wait for my letter. The Colonel (Nelson) is a good and brave man, and a high-toned Christian gentleman. In that terrible battle yesterday both he and Lieut. Hobson of our battery walked up and down on the top of our breastworks and gave their orders calmly and deliberately, while the death storm raged around them. The tears trickled down Hobson's cheeks as he saw one after another of his brave men go down before this terrible iron hail. Among the bravest of our battery, who fell yesterday, was Christian,[25] a boy of fifteen, who came to us six weeks ago. Poor boy, a shell took off his head while he was bravely doing his duty like an old vet.

*Lee's Lieutenants,* III, 508. The enemy made a series of onslaughts all along the Confederate front but was repulsed. The Confederate losses amounted to 1,500 killed and wounded. The Federal losses amounted to 7,000. The enemy now retired to rest during the days following.

[25] Probably John Christian, of Lynchburg, Virginia. (William Asbury Christian, *Lynchburg and Its People* [Lynchburg, Va., 1900], p. 459.)

*June 5.  Sunday.*  Remained in camp. Frank Kinckle and I are all [that is] left of our mess. John Hill still absent on sick leave. Edmund Anderson's remains were carried to Richmond and buried in Hollywood. The bodies of our other dead boys, who were killed on the 3rd of June, have been taken home by the Lynchburg committee.

*June 6.*  Formed a mess today with John McCary and John McCausland; they are from Lynchburg. They are good men. Bathed and put on some clean clothes. Very much refreshed by it.

*June 7.*  Uncle Lewis Berkeley stopped for a few moments at my tent. He is now surgeon in Gen. Corse's[26] Brigade and was on his way to Richmond with a number of ambulances filled with sick and wounded men, whom he was carrying to the hospitals.

*June 8.*  Remained in Camp. A prayer meeting in Capt. Massie's camp at night.

*June 9.*  John Hill returned to the Company today from "Locust Level." Heard from our wounded boys; all doing very well.

*June 10 and 11.*  Remained in camp. All quiet.

[26] Brig. Gen. Montgomery D. Corse's Brigade, Pickett's Division.

# CHAPTER X

# TO THE VALLEY

## Lynchburg to Kernstown, 1864

*June 12, 1864.* Uncle Lewis Berkeley came by again on his way to Richmond. Preparations made for a big march somewhere. Boys think to the Valley.[1] Gen. Pendleton preached in the evening.

*June 13.* Started this morning before day.[2] Struck the Brook Pike and then the Mountain Road and after a long day's march encamped for the night two miles west of Goodall's in Hanover County. Our corps now commanded by Gen. [Jubal A.] Early.[3] Cooked a day's rations.

*June 14.* Continued our march towards Louisa Court House and encamped ten miles east of it, near Dr. Philip Pendleton's.[4]

*June 15.* Started just at sunrise, and after a hot and dusty day's

---

[1] Maj. Gen. David Hunter, now commanding Federal forces in the Shenandoah Valley, was rapidly advancing up the Valley, and on June 11 entered Lexington, Virginia. To attempt to push Hunter out of the Valley, and if successful to advance on Washington, D. C., Gen. Lee assigned Lt. Gen. Jubal A. Early (Early having been promoted to temporary lieutenant general on May 31 to replace R. S. Ewell, now on indefinite sick-leave) and the Second Corps. Early was told to take two battalions of artillery with him (Nelson's and Braxton's were selected) and Brig. Gen. A. L. Long was to accompany him as chief of artillery. The orders came to General Early on June 12. (*Lieutenant General Jubal Anderson Early, C.S.A. Autobiographical Sketch and Narrative of the War Between the States. With Notes by R. H. Early* [Philadelphia and London, 1912], p. 371; Douglas Southall Freeman, *Lee's Lieutenants: A Study in Command* [New York, 1942-44], III, 524; *The War of the Rebellion: A Compilation of the Official Records of the Union and Confederate Armies* [Washington, D. C., 1880-1901], Series I, Volume XXXVII, part 1, p. 346. All citations will be from Series I unless otherwise noted.) The reader should note that the term "up the Valley" means, in the Shanandoah Valley, south, the Shenandoah River flowing northwards into the Potomac River.

[2] For the route and camp sites of the Second Corps for the march to Lynchburg, see *Atlas to Accompany the Official Records of the Union and Confederate Armies* (Washington, D. C., 1891-95), Plate LXXXI. The Virginia Central Railroad could not be used for transporting troops because of the damage done by the enemy. (*Early*, p. 371.)

[3] See note 1 above.

[4] Dr. Philip Barbour Pendleton (d. ca. 1904) of Cuckoo, Louisa County. (Malcolm H. Harris, *History of Louisa County, Virginia* [Richmond, 1936], pp. 102, 237-38, 402, 404-5.)

march encamped to the south of Gordonsville on the Charlottesville Road near Mr. Henry Taylor's in [the] Green Spring neighborhood, which is one of the prettiest countries I ever saw. I was quite sick all night, getting very little sleep.

*June 16.* Marched to near Charlottesville. Quite sick all day. Rode some in our ambulance for the first time since I have been in the war. Felt a little better; but still quite poorly.

*June 17.* We passed through Charlottesville. I saw Miss Mattie Jones, but did not speak to her, because I was so very ragged and dirty. Took the Lynchburg Road and after marching about twenty miles from Charlottesville, encamped for the night near the Nelson [County] line. All our infantry were put on cars at Charlottesville this morning and hurried to Lynchburg to meet the Yankees under Gen. David Hunter, who has gotten almost into that city.[5]

*June 18.* Reached Tye River Station tonight about 7 P.M. It is twenty miles from Lynchburg.

*June 19.* Put our guns and caisson boxes on the cars and all [the] sick and [the] cannoneers, reaching Lynchburg about 9:30 A.M. We went home with our messmate, Frank Kinckle, whose father is the pastor of the [St. Paul's] Episcopal Church in Lynchburg. They gave us a nice breakfast. It being Sunday we attended church in morning and afternoon. We spent the night at Mr. Kinckle's, having pleasant time and getting a good night's rest.[6]

*June 20.* Our horses, drivers, wagons and carriages, which had come from Tye River by the county road, having arrived last night, we remounted our guns and boxes and afterwards, getting our breakfast at Mr. Kinckle's and taking leave of the good man, we rejoined our battery, which had taken the Salem Pike and after a long and hot day's march encamped for the night fifteen miles west of Lynchburg.[7]

*June 21.* Continued our march towards Salem and encamped for the night [at] Bedford Depot, on [the] Virginia and Tennessee Railroad.

*June 22.* Marched to within five miles of Salem, then turned to the

[5] Early could not muster enough rail transportation to take his corps to Lynchburg, towards which he learned on the sixteenth Hunter was rapidly approaching. Early ordered the infantry to be shuttled to Lynchburg by railroad. The artillery and wagon trains left Charlottesville by ordinary roads. (*Early*, p. 373.)

[6] During the night of June 18, the enemy withdrew from before Lynchburg and moved towards Liberty, Virginia. At daybreak Early began pursuing. Artillery personnel had to wait in Lynchburg for their horses, drivers, and equipment. (*Early*, p. 376.)

[7] For the route of Early's pursuit of the enemy until June 22, when pursuit was abandoned, see *Official Records Atlas*, Plate LXXXI. The artillery followed along the same route.

right and marched in the direction of Fincastle, which is the county seat of Botetourt County; encamped for the night near the county line between Botetourt and Roanoke [counties].[8]

*June 23.* We were allowed to sleep until sunrise for the first time since leaving Richmond. Marched to near Buchanan [Botetourt County], on the James River, and encamped for the night.

*June 24.* Crossed the James and continued our march towards Lexington, Virginia, encamping within nine miles of Lexington. We had run Hunter and his Yanks out into the mountains beyond Monroe.

*June 25. Saturday.* Passed through Lexington, all the infantry filing by Stonewall Jackson's grave. As I looked at his grave and thought of the future, my heart sank within me. I saw Frank Page, who pressed me to go to Gen. Pendleton's. I thought [it] best not to go. Went over the ruins of the Virginia Military Institute, which Hunter had burnt on his way against Lynchburg.[9] The people of Lexington were particularly kind to our soldiers. We encamped five miles north of Lexington on the Staunton Road.

*June 26.* Continued our march towards Staunton and encamped for the night within ten miles of it. Very hot and dusty.

*June 27.* Passed through Staunton and encamped on Port Republic Road two miles from town. Saw Brother Tommy[10] and Uncle Carter[11] for a short time. Both looked well and happy.

*June 28.* Remained near Staunton. Washed my clothes and mended them up. Went to see William Mead Berkeley, who took us to see Cousin James Latané, who is now pastor of the Episcopal Church in Staunton.

*June 29.* Marched to Harrisonburg, encamping within three miles of the town.[12]

*June 30.* We continued our march down the Valley Pike and encamped for the night on a high hill two miles from New Market.

*July 1.* Marched to near Woodstock.

[8] The artillery units were by now up with the main army. Early had stopped pursuit on the twenty-second (except for the cavalry which followed the enemy into West Virginia) in order to rest his weary troops and to allow the artillery to come up. (*Early,* p. 379.)

[9] General Hunter had burned the buildings of the Institute and Governor John Letcher's home on June 12. (*Official Records,* Vol. XXXVII, pt. 1, p. 97.)

[10] Younger brother of HRB.

[11] Evidently a brother of HRB's father. (Frances Berkeley Young, *The Berkeleys of Barn Elms* [New Haven, 1954], p. 111.)

[12] General Early had now determined to carry out Lee's plan of advancing down the Valley, invading Maryland, and threatening Washington if possible. He began marching on June 28. (*Early,* p. 382.)

*July 2.* Marched to near Newtown. Very hot, dry and dusty. Hard on men and horses.

*July 3.* Marched through Winchester and encamped at Bunker Hill, where a road crosses the pike at right angles.

*July 4.* Taking the right-hand road, we passed through Smithfield and Charlestown, Jefferson County, Virginia [West Virginia] and encamped on the Harpers Ferry Pike four miles south of Harpers Ferry. Here we remained all night. The Yanks who were in Harpers Ferry have retired to the Maryland Heights, leaving a good deal of plunder in the Ferry.[13] Some of our boys went into the town to plunder. They got quite a lot of sugar, coffee, hardtack, molasses, etc. John McCorkle[14] went in on a mule and undertook to bring out a water bucket of molasses on his mule. The Yanks were amusing themselves by throwing among our plundering boys a lot of shell. They did no harm and no one was hurt; but a lamp post (i.e. a nine-inch shell) whizzing from the Maryland Heights, "busted" about three yards in [the] rear of John's mule's tail, while John was on his way back to camp with his water bucket of molasses. This shell lighted up all the surroundings for a few seconds, and John's mule lighted out for camp; that mule made two-forty time to camp. John, however, clung bravely to his molasses, knowing full well that "lasses" was "lasses" in Dixie in those days, and finally arrived in camp covered completely with molasses, having about two quarts left in his bucket. He spent the rest of the night washing his clothes and his mule. Thus ended for us, The Glorious Fourth of July, 1864.

*July 5.* In the afternoon we marched over to Shepherdstown and encamped near the town for the night.

*July 6.* Left camp near Shepherdstown and, after crossing the Potomac River, which came a little above our waist, we encamped near Sharpsburg, Maryland. Had to examine my caisson boxes to see if the water had gotten into any of them, while crossing the Potomac. I found them O.K.

*July 7.* Remained in camp near Sharpsburg all day.

*July 8.* Marched to Frederick City, Maryland, and encamped near the town.[15]

13 The Federal force at Harpers Ferry was under the command of Brig. Gen. Max Weber, who retired from the town to Maryland Heights at about 7 P.M. on the evening of the fourth. (*Official Records*, Vol. XXXVII, pt. 1, pp. 184-86.)

14 John J. McCorkle, a company member from Lynchburg. (William Asbury Christian, *Lynchburg and Its People* [Lynchburg, Va., 1900], p. 495.)

15 Finding the enemy too strongly entrenched at the Maryland Heights, Early decided to abandon any frontal assault and advance toward Washington. (*Early*, p. 385.)

*July 9.* Passed through Frederick City and took the Washington, D. C., Pike [Georgetown Pike] and came upon the Yanks in line of battle on [the] Washington side of the Monocacy River; the latter is a small stream flowing into the Potomac.[16] We first took a position on the left of the Washington Pike and afterwards crossed over to [the] right and put our battery on a hill fronting a still higher hill held by the Yanks.[17] We got here about 1 P.M. We were ordered to open on the Yankees, as soon as we heard Gen. [John B.] Gordon's Division open on our right. Gordon was flanking the Yanks on our right.[18] About 3:45 P.M. we heard, on our right, some heavy fighting in a big field of big corn. We immediately opened on the Yanks in our front. I was acting as gunner, which position I had filled since R. B. Winston was wounded on June 3, 1864. We were hotly engaged only for about twenty minutes, the Yanks in our front giving away very soon; but, alas! We had three splendid men killed: viz., Gardner and Page were killed instantly by a shell and Lieut. George Hobson was killed by a sharpshooter after the enemy had been routed, and was retreating rapidly from the field. Hobson had had a wheel on his gun knocked to pieces by a cannon shot and could not go with us as we moved rapidly down the pike after the Yanks. While his men were putting a new wheel on his gun, he and J. H. Berkeley, being on their horses, rode to the brow of the hill in front of them (which hill overlooked the river), and halted their horses. Just at the moment they halted, two Minié balls whizzed over from beyond the river, one of which struck Lieut. Hobson on the right shoulder and, passing diagonally downward, stopped on his left hip. He sank from his horse and was caught by my brother and laid on the grass. He never spoke after being struck and breathed his last in about ten minutes. Just as he was shot, he was talking to my brother (J. H. Berkeley) of Gardner and Page, who had been killed a few moments be-

[16] The enemy force encountered was Maj. Gen. Lew Wallace's Eighth Corps, which had been supplemented with troops from the Richmond-Petersburg front. (*Official Records,* Vol. XXXVII, pt. 2, pp. 191-200.)

[17] For the position of Kirkpatrick's Battery, which was at the extreme left of the Confederate line, see *Official Records Atlas,* Plate LXXXIII.

[18] The main attack was made by Gordon's Division on the Confederate right just north of the point where Ballenger's Creek flows into the Monocacy River. The enemy forces opposing him were of Maj. Gen. James B. Rickett's Division, Sixth Corps, which had been transferred to Wallace's command from the Richmond-Petersburg front. By late afternoon the beaten enemy retired toward Baltimore. Early, realizing that enemy forces in the Washington area had already begun to be reinforced by troops from General U. S. Grant's front, did not press pursuit. For the next few days he must be cautious lest his small force be annihilated by superior numbers. (*Official Records,* Vol. XXXVII, pt. 2, p. 80; *ibid,* pt. 1, p. 191 *ff.,* 347-52; Douglas Southall Freeman, *Lee's Lieutenants: A Study in Command* [New York, 1942-44], III, 560-64; *Early,* pp. 387-88.)

ANNA LOUISA BERKELEY
*(Mrs. Henry Robinson Berkeley)*

EDMUND BERKELEY
*The Diarist's Father*

THREE BERKELEY WAR COMRADES
*John Hill, John Lewis, and Henry Robinson*

fore and whose bodies had been left unburied a short way behind us. And these were the last words on his lips, "Those poor boys must be buried and their graves marked, if I have to go back." As he reached the word, "back," the fatal ball struck him and he sank from his horse. Our chaplain, Mr. Gilmer, carried his body and those of Gardner and Page back to Frederick City and had them all three put into coffins, neatly buried and their graves marked. Lieut. [A. R.] Woodruff is missing tonight and has not been seen or heard of since one o'clock today. A cannon ball came very near taking my head off today. I think it was the same ball which killed Gardner and Page. I was leaning over aiming my cannon and it passed just over my head. If I had been standing up it would have struck me full in the face. We crossed the Monocacy River and after having followed the enemy for three miles we went into camp in a wheat field, which had just been cut. We found a wounded Yank in the fence corner near our campfire and carried him to our fire, gave him some water and after dressing his wound (he had been shot through the leg) and giving him some supper and a cup of coffee we fixed him a bed with some bundles of wheat and put him on it. He was very grateful and told us that he was a Marylander and was only about ten miles from his home. He said he was only eighteen. He looked very young. He said that he had been told that we were very cruel to our prisoners, and that when we first came to him, he thought we were going to kill him immediately.

*July 10.* The Yanks are falling back on Baltimore. We took the Washington Pike, and after a long and hot day's march encamped for the night twenty miles from that city. We gave our wounded Yankee some breakfast this morning and fixed up his blanket on four stakes to keep off the sun. We left him to his friends. I have no doubt that by this time he is at home. Lieut. Woodruff still missing. He is supposed to have been killed or captured. He was last seen in Capt. Carpenter's Battery,[19] asking for us and left there to find us. Some of our boys think he has deserted to the Yanks. I have very little confidence in him. I have just found, on going to bed, that it is Sunday. In times of marching and fighting, a soldier frequently forgets the days of the week, all being just alike.

*July 11.* We marched to within two miles of the corporate limits of Washington City and encamped at "Silver Spring," the home of Postmaster General [Montgomery] Blair.[20] We can see the dome of the capitol and

---

[19] Capt. John C. Carpenter's Allegheny Battery.

[20] "Silver Spring," located on the Seventh Street Pike, was the home of Francis P. Blair, the father of the Postmaster General. Montgomery Blair's home, "Falklands," was located next to "Silver Spring." (*Official Records Atlas*, Plate LXXXIX.)

a large part of the city. There has been some heavy picket fighting this evening. There is a rumor that we are to try and storm the fortifications at daybreak tomorrow.[21]

*July 12.*   Remained near Washington, D. C., all day on the farm of Francis P. Blair. It is called "Silver Spring." Is a beautiful place with a large lawn running down to a beautiful and cold spring fixed up with marble basins, etc. There was very heavy skirmishing this evening, but no attempt to take the strong fortifications in our front. We retreated after dark and marched all night towards Leesburg, Virginia.

*July 13.*   Continued to march towards Leesburg, marching all night, only stopping at 4 P.M. long enough for the men to cook and eat and for our horses to be fed. We reached the Potomac River, at Edwards' Ferry[22] about day[break].

*July 14.*   Crossed the Potomac about 7 A.M. and encamped at the Big Spring two miles north of Leesburg. The march from Washington to this place has been the most severe I have ever experienced. We marched two nights and two days consecutively and during that time only halted our march the second afternoon long enough for men and horses to get something to eat. This heavy marching was made necessary because three Yankee armies were after us, any one of which was as large as our army under Gen. Early. These Yankee armies were Canby's at Washington, D. C., Gen. Wallace's at Baltimore and Gen. Hunter's now at Frederick City, Maryland.[23] We marched out from between their converging lines. We got to the Big Spring about 9 A.M. I never had been so sleepy and tired before in all my life. I threw off my knapsack and blanket, crawled under an Osage orange hedge and in two minutes was fast asleep. We slept until 5 P.M. and then woke up and cooked and ate a hearty supper, feeling much refreshed after a bath.

[21] Early had planned to storm the enemy's fortification of the morning of the twelfth, but during the night he received reports that more reinforcements from Grant's army were at Baltimore ready to move to Washington. At daybreak he saw the enemy fortifications lined with troops and decided that an assault, even if successful, would incur such losses that his small army might not be able to escape. He remained before Washington all day of the twelfth, but ordered the Corps to retire after dark. (*Official Records*, Vol. XXXVII, pt. 1, p. 348; *Early*, pp. 389-95; Freeman, *Lee's Lieutenants*, III, 565-67.)

[22] Opposite Leesburg, Virginia. (*Official Records Atlas*, Plate LXXXI.)

[23] The pursuit by the enemy from Washington was made by units from the Sixth Corps under command of Maj. Gen. Horatio G. Wright. Gens. Franz Sigel, David Hunter, George Crook, and W. W. Averell had joined forces to attack Early in Loudoun and Frederick counties, Virginia. (*Official Records*, Vol. XXXVII, pt. 1, pp. 265 *ff.*) Maj. Gen. Edward R. S. Canby was at this time in command of forces in Alabama and Mississippi, and Maj. Gen. Lew Wallace did not engage in the pursuit.

*July 15.* Remained near Big Spring and washed our clothes.[24]

*July 16.* We pulled out this morning and taking the Winchester Pike marched to Snickersville and encamped for the night. The Yankee cavalry made a dash on our wagon train about 3 P.M. and burnt a few wagons. We fired a few rounds at them. Two Yankees were killed and a few captured.[25]

*July 17. Sunday.* We crossed the mountains by Snicker's Gap and continued our march towards Winchester and encamped near Berryville.

*July 18.* Remained near Berryville. Received six letters from home. Some of these letters had been following us ever since we left Richmond.

*July 20.* Moved last night from Berryville and marched three miles north of Winchester and there halted to get breakfast for men and horses. We remained in this place until 4 P.M. when we were ordered to follow Ramseur's[26] Division down the pike towards Martinsburg. The Yanks in the meanwhile had driven back our cavalry. After going about a mile down the pike, Ramseur ran into an ambush the Yanks had set for us. Just as we reached the farther edge of a piece of woods, and while our men were still in line of march; the Yanks opened on us from behind a stone fence at close quarters before our line of battle could be formed, or our men load their guns which were empty. Our men gave way and, [with] the Yanks charging when they saw our confusion, the whole thing soon became a panic.[27] We lost our entire battery, bringing out only one limber and a caisson. We had twenty-five horses killed and four men killed in our battery. The following men were wounded, viz., Lieut. [William] Basye, lost right foot, Lieut. Latham, believed to be mortally wounded, left at his aunt's in Winchester, Bolling Hewitt, John Hawkins, Frank Miller, Billy Good.[28] The last two were left on the battle field and fell into the hands

24 On the fourteenth and fifteenth Early rested his weary army. Early stated that the march by his small army from Cold Harbor to Washington "over the circuitous route . . . down the Valley and through the passes of the South Mountain . . . is, for its length and rapidity, I believe, without parallel in this or any other modern war—the unopposed excursion of Sherman through Georgia not excepted." (*Early*, p. 999.)

25 This attack was made by two regiments of the 21st New York Cavalry, Col. William B. Tibbits commanding. Fifty-four men and eighty wagons were taken by the Federals. Troops from Rodes's and Ramseur's divisions repulsed the attack. (*Official Records*, Vol. XXXVII, pt. 1, pp. 319-20; *Early*, p. 396.)

26 S. Dodson Ramseur, commanding Early's former division with temporary rank of major general since June 4, 1864. (*Official Records*, Vol. XXXVI, pt. 3, p. 874.)

27 This engagement was at Rutherford's farm (near Stephenson's Depot). Ramseur had expected to meet a smaller force. Instead he engaged a larger force under General Averell, and Averell's heavy flank attack caused panic in Ramseur's ranks. Averell did not follow up his victory. (*Official Records*, Vol. XXXVII, pt. 1, pp. 326-27, 353; *Early*, p. 397.)

28 Of these, A. Bolling Hewitt and Frank T. Miller were from Lynchburg, Virginia. (Christian, *Lynchburg*, p. 409.)

of the Yankees. Several other men were slightly hurt. Lieut. Basye's foot was cut off late tonight after we got back to Newtown, where we encamped for the night. Today's loss takes from our battery all four of our lieutenants, who started from winter quarters the first of April. Our sergeants are acting as lieutenants, and privates as corporals and sergeants.

*July 21.* We marched three miles towards Strasburg and then stopped and cooked, and fed the few horses we had left. We then went on to Strasburg and encamped there for the night.

*July 22.* Marched just beyond Strasburg and took the right-hand road; went out towards North Mountain for a mile and encamped there for the night.

*July 23. Saturday.* Remained here all day and washed our clothes.

*July 24.* We moved back towards Winchester early this morning and came on the Yanks at Kernstown. It is Sunday and I am riding Frank Kinckle's horse, Frank being sick and riding in our ambulance. Having lost our guns, and not having gotten others, we (I and my company) had the pleasure of looking on at this hot and successful little fight without taking part in it. After a short and hot fight our men drove the Yankees from all parts of the field, killing and capturing a good many. The Yankee cavalry at one time during the battle, charged the 61st and 2nd Virginia Regiments in an apple orchard. It was a very daring charge, and they did it to save their wagon train, but their loss was very heavy. It seemed to me, looking on from a distant hill, that every man was killed or captured and few horses went back, but most were without riders. I went to the spot when the fight was over. The wounded had been removed, but dead Yankees lay thick. Oh! How horrid is war. We ran the Yanks through Winchester and followed them, until night stopped us near Bunker Hill.[29] We found in Winchester this evening Lieut. Latham, and Frank Miller. William Good had died of his wounds and been buried by the good people of Winchester. I visited the place where we lost our battery and am fully convinced if Gen. Ramseur had not interfered with us, we would never have lost our guns or the battle. We had taken position on the right and were ready to fire, when Gen. Ramseur ordered us to limber up and come over on the left of the [Martinsburg] pike. We did limber up and started over and it was while we were crossing the pike that the Yankees charged us and our infantry gave way. We could have fired at least a dozen rounds

[29] The Battle of Kernstown was fought with the enemy under Bvt. Maj. Gen. George Crook, including units from Hunter's and Sigel's commands and Averell's Cavalry. The main Confederate attack was on the enemy's left flank and the Federals were routed. (*Early*, p. 399.)

of canister into the crowded ranks of the Yanks while we were limbering up and I believe the canister would have saved the day, because I have never seen them fail to run when you went for them with canister at close quarters. It is sad to think of that mistake which cost us at least a hundred men killed and two hundred wounded. I would not like to be a general having men killed by my errors and mistakes. Frank Miller's right leg has been amputated above the knee; this puts an end to his soldier life. He joined our company in March. He is only sixteen years old. He behaved in the fight like an old soldier. No doubt his mother will be glad to have her boy back home minus his leg. Alas! How many boys we have buried since we left our winter quarters in Orange. Who will be the next to fall?

*July 25. Monday.* It commenced to rain early this morning and continued to rain until eleven o'clock. We marched this evening to Bunker Hill and encamped there for the night.

*July 26.* We marched today to Martinsburg and encamped near that town, remaining in [the] same camp very quietly until Sunday, July 31, when we moved up to Bunker Hill and encamped on the Winchester side of that town. We remained at Bunker Hill until Thursday.

*August 4.* Down to near Falling Waters on [the] Potomac River.[30]

*August 5.* We crossed the Potomac, and marching to Hagerstown, [we] encamped near that place for the night. Rained hard that night.

*August 6.* We recrossed the Potomac and marched to near Hedgesville, through a rich and lovely country and there encamped for the night.

*August 7.* We returned to our old camp near Bunker Hill. Frank Kinckle, who had gone up to Staunton with Lieut. Basye, and some of our other wounded boys, got back to camp today, bringing the sad news of the death of Lieut. Basye and Bolling Hewitt. Both of these brave and good men lost their lives by trying to get to their homes after being wounded. Lieut. Basye died in Staunton of mere exhaustion, the very evening he got there, and brave Hewitt passed away in his mother's arms a few hours after getting to his home near Lynchburg, Virginia. Dr. Semple,[31] our surgeon, says these men would both have gotten well if they had remained in the hospital at Mount Jackson as he ordered them. In both cases their wounds were healing nicely. They died of exhaustion from their long hundred-mile trip in an ambulance over a rough pike. Frank begged Lieut. Basye to stop and not attempt the trip, but he would go on.

[30] The whole of the defeated enemy force retired to Harpers Ferry and Maryland Heights. (*Early*, p. 400.)

[31] Dr. James Semple, surgeon for Nelson's 31st Artillery Battalion. (Wyndham B. Blanton, *Medicine in Virginia in the Nineteenth Century* [Richmond, 1933], p. 415.)

# CHAPTER XI

# ARTILLERY COVERED ITSELF WITH HONOR AND GLORY

## Third Winchester, 1864

*August 8, 1864.* We remained quietly in camp at Bunker Hill until August 10, when we moved up to near Winchester and encamped for the night.[1]

*August 11.* Marched through Winchester and, after stopping in an apple orchard for three hours, we took the right-hand road and followed Maj. [John A.] Harman's wagon train over very rough and crooked road, which runs parallel to the Staunton Pike, and after a march of some fifteen miles, we were ordered to join our battalion near Middletown on the Staunton Pike, which we did about ten o'clock that night. We were put with the wagon train today because we were expecting a battle and we have yet no guns, my company not having been given any guns since losing its guns on July 20. We have, however, collected our horses and are in daily expectation of getting a new battery.

*August 12. Thursday [Friday].* We marched to Strasburg, where the army went into line of battle. We went four miles south of the town and encamped on the right of the [Valley] pike, where we remained quietly

1 On August 9, Early learned of a large enemy force being concentrated at Harpers Ferry, consisting of the Sixth and Nineteenth Corps, and Crook's forces under a new commander, who Early soon discovered was Maj. Gen. Philip H. Sheridan, just transferred from Grant's army before Richmond and Petersburg. Upon learning of this, Lee sent Maj. Gen. Fitzhugh Lee's Cavalry and Maj. Gen. Joseph B. Kershaw's Division under the command of Lieut. Gen. Richard H. Anderson. Anderson's command was to operate east of the Blue Ridge in cooperation with Early. On August 10, Early began a series of marches to deceive the enemy into thinking his force was larger than it was. (*Jubal Anderson Early C. S. A. Autobiographical Sketch and Narrative of the War Between the States. With Notes by R. H. Early* [Philadelphia and London, 1912], p. 406; Douglas Southall Freeman, *Lee's Lieutenants: A Study in Command* [New York, 1942-44], III, 574-75.)

until August 17, when, the Yanks falling back on Harpers Ferry, we followed them to Winchester, where our men took fifteen hundred prisoners and a Yankee battery of four guns.[2] My company encamped for the night near Kernstown.

*August 18. Thursday.* Our battalion moved to Winchester. We had a very good rain this morning.

*August 19. Friday.* We marched to Bunker Hill and occupied our old camp. We got a plenty of good apples. Frank Kinckle made orderly sergeant, in place of Sgt. Gillum, who was killed in that terrible battle on June 3rd at Cold Harbor, near Richmond.

*August 20. Saturday.* It rained all day. We remained in camp all day.

*August 21. Sunday.* The whole army marched towards Charlestown, coming on the Yankees, just beyond Smithfield [West Virginia], where hot and heavy skirmishing lasted until dark.[3]

*August 22.* The Yanks were found minus this morning, having retreated during the night to Harpers Ferry. Our battalion went on towards Charlestown and encamped on the left of the pike just before getting to town.

*August 23.* We remained in the same camp.

*August 24.* We moved our camp out on the Berryville Pike.

*August 25.* We marched to Smithfield and from there towards Shepherdstown. Some fighting five miles beyond Smithfield, which was soon over and we continued our march towards Shepherdstown, encamping near that place. A Mrs. Dr. Boutler, who was the wife of one of [the] surgeons and who had two pretty and sweet little daughters of eight and ten years of age, gave me two nice rolls for my supper, which I enjoyed very much. Her home had been burnt by the Yankees and she had been turned out of it at ten o'clock at night with her two little girls and had not been permitted to take a single piece of clothing, except what she and her children had on.[4] This act of barbarity had been done by the order of

[2] Upon learning that Early was being further reinforced, General Sheridan retired his forces to a defensive line at Halltown, Virginia, in front of Harpers Ferry. The enemy forces mentioned here were under Brig. Gen. Alfred T. A. Torbert. (*The War of the Rebellion: A Compilation of the Official Records of the Union and Confederate Armies* [Washington, D. C., 1880-1901], Series I, Volume XLIII, part 1, p. 424. All citations will be from Series I unless otherwise noted. See also *Early*, pp. 407-8.)

[3] This was the engagement at Welch's Spring, between Smithfield (now Middleway) and Charlestown, West Virginia. (*Atlas to Accompany the Official Records of the Union and Confederate Armies* [Washington, D. C., 1891-95], Plates LXIX, LXXXII.) There were several other engagements on this date. (*Official Records*, XLIII, pt. 1, p. 570.)

[4] On July 19, 1864, "Fountain Rock," the home of Col. Alexander R. Boteler (who was

Gen. David Hunter of the Yankee army, a man who was born and raised in this neighborhood, and who burnt many other beautiful homes. His own uncle's house, Mr. Andrew Hunter's among the rest, at whose home, he, David Hunter, had lived and been treated as a son.[5] When I saw Mrs. Boutler she was at her mother's in Shepherdstown. Her burnt home, which I visited later is a lovely place. When will this horrid and awful war have an end?

*August 26. Friday.*   We marched back towards Winchester and encamped for the night near Leetown. A rumor in camp that we are to go to Mt. Crawford for our new guns. At night we heard our new guns are in Winchester and that we would go for them tomorrow.

*August 27. Saturday.*   Ordered with eight drivers and eight gunners to go for our new guns, but the order was very soon countermanded and we only marched to Camp Crimm. Crimm is the name of the man on whose farm the camp is situated.

*August 28. Sunday.*   We remained at Camp Crimm.

*August 29.*   We went for our new guns, which had been brought to within two miles of us, and got them. We are very much pleased with them. They were made at the Tredegar Iron Works in Richmond.

*August 30.*   We remained in camp, but the other two companies belonging to our battalion went with some infantry down to Martinsburg.

*August 31.*   Remained in camp.

*September 1.*   Remained in camp. We are getting an abundance of nice and ripe apples now. I weigh more now than I ever did before in my life.

*September 2.*   We marched up to near Winchester and went into camp north of the town for the night.

*September 3.*   We marched back to near Bunker Hill. We met with some Yankee cavalry and had a running fight of three or four miles

not a doctor), was burned at the order of General Hunter. Mrs. Boteler was not at home at the time of the burning. Her daughter, Miss Helen Boteler and the Boteler's daughter, Mrs. David Shepherd, and Mrs. Shepherd's three children ages eighteen months to five years, were there on that day. This is undoubtedly the house to which HRB refers although his statements are not accurate. On the same date, the home of Edmund J. Lee was burned while his bedridden wife and two young children were at home alone. Perhaps HRB confused the names when he sat down to record the events of the day. (Millard K. Bushong, *A History of Jefferson County West Virginia* [Charlestown, W. Va., 1941], pp. 172-76.)

[5] At the order of Maj. Gen. David Hunter, Andrew Hunter's home in Charlestown was burned on July 17, 1864. Andrew Hunter was the General's first cousin, not his uncle. Statements made at the time, and since, that General Hunter had lived in his cousin's home as a child, and had been treated as one of the family while there, have been questioned by many. (*Ibid.,* pp. 172-73; *Official Records,* Vol. XXXVII, pt. 2, p. 367.)

with them. We fired some ten shots a piece. Gen. Bradley Johnson's Cavalry Brigade camp was surprised by the Yankee cavalry and some of his wagons were captured. The Yanks then ran into our rear and were then soon driven off by our guns and Gen. Rodes's Division, after which we went on up towards Winchester and encamped for the night near that town.[6]

*September 4. Sunday.* We marched out on the Berryville Pike and came on some Yankees about two miles east of Winchester. Some little skirmishing earlier in the day. Everything became quiet about night.[7]

*September 5.* We returned to our old camp on the Martinsburg Pike near Stephenson's Depot, which we left yesterday morning. On our march we met the most awful thunder and lightning storm that I have ever encountered in my life and I thought we would never get our fires started tonight. It rained so very hard just as we got into camp and everything was so wet and soggy we used up nearly all the matches which we had in the whole battery, before getting a fire started. But after one fire got started, we soon had many brightly burning. The storm finally, after lasting four hours, passed over, and about midnight we succeeded in getting some supper and then bunked on the wet ground in very wet clothes.

*September 6.* Rainy day. We remained in camp all day.

*September 7.* We moved our camp to the west of the Martinsburg Pike and encamped in a piece of woods. Got a plenty of nice apples today.

*September 8. Thursday.* We remained in camp all day. Heard of the fall of Atlanta.[8] The future looks dark and hopeless for the South.

*September 9.* We remained in camp all day; late at night we received orders to be ready to move at sunrise tomorrow morning.

*September 10. Saturday.* We moved early this morning in a heavy rain down to Bunker Hill, with Rodes's and Ramseur's divisions. We had

[6] Maj. Gen. Robert E. Rodes's Division left Stephenson's Depot for Bunker Hill on the morning of September 3 to support Lomax's Cavalry. On September 2, Maj. Gen. Averell, commanding the Second Division, U. S. Cavalry, had fallen upon Brig. Gen. John C. Vaughan's and Brig. Gen. Bradley T. Johnson's cavalry at Bunker Hill and routed them. Rodes drove Averell from Bunker Hill. (George E. Pond, *The Shenandoah Valley in 1864* [New York, 1883], p. 143, in *Campaigns of the Civil War,* Vol. XI; *Early,* p. 411; *Official Records,* Vol. XLIII, pt. 1, pp. 45, 497, 572, 1026; *ibid.,* pt. 2, p. 862.)

[7] Lt. Gen. R. H. Anderson had encountered Crook's Corps on September 8 while attempting to retire from the Valley by way of Berryville and Ashby's Gap. On the morning of September 4, General Early took three divisions to Berryville to support Anderson. Finding the enemy strongly entrenched, Early retired his command on the afternoon of the next day. Rodes's Division went to Stephenson's Depot. (*Official Records,* Vol. XLIII, pt. 1, p. 572; *Early,* pp. 411-12.)

[8] Lt. Gen. John B. Hood evacuated Atlanta on the morning of September 2.

a little skirmishing with Yankee cavalry[9] and then about dark we went into camp near Bunker Hill for the night.

*September 11.*   We returned to our old camp near Stephenson's Depot. We had a very hard rain last night. I have been wet for more than two days.

*September 12.   Monday.*   We remained quietly in camp all day.

*September 13.*   We had inspection of guns, men and horses today. We marched down the pike, after our inspection, a few miles, but returned to our old camp before night.

*September 14.   Wednesday.*   We remained in camp all day. I wrote to Papa.

*September 15.   Thursday.*   We came up to Winchester today and went into camp, near a Mr. Baker's, who lives on the Berryville Pike, on [the] left as you go towards Berryville, in a small brick house situated in an oak grove.[10]

*September 16.   Friday.*   We remained very quiet in camp at Mr. Baker's. Tom Henderson, who was wounded in that terrible battle on June 3rd at Cold Harbor, got back to camp.

*September 17.   Saturday.*   Received a letter from Nannie. All quiet.

*September 18.   Sunday.*   It was very quiet all day. Some of the boys went to Winchester to church at night. Got a letter from [Louisa] Carter [Berkeley] today.

*September 19.   Monday.*   This has been one the longest and hardest day's fighting that I have done since this awful war began.[11] The

---

[9] The enemy encountered were of Brig. Gen. W. W. Averell's command. (*Official Records*, Vol. XLIII, pt. 1, p. 573; *ibid.*, pt. 2, pp. 65, 66.)

[10] Nelson's Battalion was now attached to Maj. Gen. S. Dodson Ramseur's Division, Rodes's Division having returned to Stephenson's Depot. (*Early*, p. 413-14.) J. Baker's home was located less than a mile east of Winchester, north of the Berryville Pike. (*Official Records Atlas*, Plate XCIX.)

[11] This is the Third Battle of Winchester, or the Battle of the Opequon, as Sheridan called it. When the battle began before daybreak, Ramseur's Division with Nelson's Artillery battalion were on a line across the Berryville Pike about two miles east of Winchester. Ramseur's force, the artillery, and the cavalry, under Maj. Gens. Lunsford L. Lomax and Fitzhugh Lee, held the Federals for several hours although fighting against superior numbers. General Early summoned to the support of Ramseur the divisions of Generals Gordon and Rodes, who were stationed in the vicinity of Stephenson's Depot, north of Winchester. Gordon and Rodes arrived with their divisions between 10 and 11 A.M., by which time Ramseur's Division had been pushed back about a mile. Upon the arrival of Gordon and Rodes, a counterattack was made. But success was only temporary. In mid-afternoon the Federals massed for another attack, and in spite of the reinforcement of Early's force by Maj. Gen. John C. Breckenridge, the Confederates began to withdraw, and towards evening retreated through Winchester to Newtown. Praise of Nelson's Battalion for its part in the battle was high. Of the crucial morning hours General Early states, "Nelson's and Braxton's Battalion had performed wonders." Colonel Thomas Hill Carter, commanding officer of artillery, Second Corps, wrote,

Yankees attacked us before sunrise this morning on the Berryville Pike. Our battery has been engaged all day. We had, it seemed to me, not less than five or six to one against us. We kept them back the entire day, until about 5 P.M. when their cavalry, breaking into our wagon train, caused our left, composed of Vaughan's[12] cavalry, to give way, and our army was compelled to fall back. We came back in good order, even stopping to water our horses, and retreated towards Strasburg and going into camp for the night near Kernstown. We had some ten or twelve men wounded in my company. Capt. Massie, of our battalion, had four or five men killed and some ten or twelve wounded. Capt. Milledge, of our battalion, lost two men killed and some eight or ten wounded. This was a great artillery fight, and the artillery covered itself with honor and glory; but its loss has been very heavy. My battery was engaged from sunrise until 9 P.M. with short intervals of cessation between fierce engagements at close quarters. The Yanks would come at us frequently, with three heavy lines of infantry. When we would concentrate on the first a very heavy artillery fire, which never failed to break it, and this [first line] falling back on their second line made that line give way, and the two routed lines going back on their third line made that line also give way. The Yankee loss must have been very heavy in killed. Bluecoats, our infantry say, never laid thicker than they did today in front of Rodes's Division; but, alas, Gen. Rodes was killed.[13] We, in our company, fired about sixteen hundred rounds of ammunition, about four times as much as we have ever used in a fight before. All our wounded were left in Winchester and consequently

"Fortunately the Artillery was under perfect control to the last, and . . . fought with untiring courage. The guns retired from point to point, halting, unlimbering, and firing. . . ." It was indeed a great day for the Confederate artillery. Of this day's battle, General Early later wrote, "When I look back to this battle, I can but attribute my escape from utter annihilation to the incapacity of my opponent." (Early, pp. 420-28; Jennings C. Wise, The Long Arm of Lee or The History of the Artillery of the Army of Northern Virginia [Lynchburg, Va., 1915], II, 884-87; Official Records, Vol. XLIII, pt. 1, pp. 24-25, 46-47, 552; Freeman, Lee's Lieutenants, III, 577-81.)

12 Brig. Gen. John C. Vaughan commanded a Tennessee cavalry brigade under Maj. Gen. John C. Breckenridge. Vaughan was not solely responsible. Other Confederate units under Breckenridge were involved. When the Confederates were pushed back on the extreme left the Federals found themselves behind the Confederate line. Breckenridge had checked the Federal advance with fine artillery support. But at the minute when the Confederates had seemed to have fixed their lines, the men of Gordon, Ramseur, and Rodes, hearing the firing to their left rear, became uneasy and began to retire in some confusion. Early attempted to rally his men and hold back the enemy on a line nearer Winchester. He was not successful, however, and by nightfall his troops were moving south of Winchester, in retreat. (Early, pp. 424-26; Freeman, Lee's Lieutenants, III, 580.)

13 Maj. Gen. Robert E. Rodes, a native of Lynchburg and graduate of Virginia Military Institute (1848), was killed while directing his troops in the charge of enemy lines at about noon. (Early, p. 427.)

are in Yankee hands. Little George Ware acted bravely and gallantly to-day. He is our ambulance driver and he carried his ambulance frequently between the lines of battle, and under heavy fire, to bring out our wounded as bravely and as gallantly as anyone could possibly do, although he is a boy of only sixteen. I acted today as gunner, sergeant and lieutenant. Col. Nelson acted as chief of artillery, and our Capt. Kirkpatrick was commanding our battalion.[14] This left us with only one commissioned officer, Bill Harris,[15] recently acting as lieutenant. This shows our heavy loss since leaving winter quarters. We started out with four lieutenants; three of these have been killed and the [fourth] has not been seen or heard of for two months. At one time today there came a Yankee shell, which struck the middle horse of my limber right between its eyes, and bursting, took off the middle horse's head, cut off the hind legs of the saddle horse in front of him and the front legs of the horse just behind him, cut the pole of the limber in two pieces, passed through the limber box, which fortunately was nearly empty, and knocked Bill McDaniel[16] down, who was standing just behind the limber box. Bill was acting as Number 6. None of the drivers were hurt and Bill soon picked himself up, being more frightened than hurt. I don't see how Charley Taliaferro,[17] who was the driver of the horse that had its head carried away, could possibly have escaped, but he did most wonderfully. He was holding his horse close up near the bit, when the shell struck it, and, after the bursting of the shell, Charley was left unhurt, holding the reins and bit in his right hand, but covered from his face to his knees with the brains and blood of the horse. I could not help being amused at his appearance, yet it was an awful grue-some place to be amused. But Charles quietly went to the limber, gath-ered up a handful of cotton, dipped it into the sponge bucket and pro-ceeded to wipe his face and clothes off. Soldiers are never made cooler, or braver, than Charles Taliaferro. It is sad to think that such men are fall-ing around us every day. When will this cruel war be over? It happened on another part of the field today that at my gun, three men, one after the other, were shot down at my right hand: viz., Jim Pleasants, John

---

[14] Actually, Col. Thomas Hill Carter was chief of artillery for the larger part of the action that day. During the afternoon, however, he was wounded and turned over the bat-talion command to Colonel Nelson. Whenever Colonel Nelson acted as chief of artillery, Captain Kirkpatrick was usually placed in command of the battalion. (Wise, *Long Arm*, II, 887.)

[15] William E. Harris, of Hanover County.

[16] William L. McDaniel, of Lynchburg, Virginia.

[17] Charles Taliaferro, of Richmond, Virginia.

Graves and James Monroe.[18] Jim Pleasants lost his right foot, by a musket ball burying itself in his ankle; John Graves was knocked over, but the strap on his belt saved his life. Jim Monroe was wounded in the fleshy part of his right leg and will get well. These three men, with several others at our other guns, were wounded by Yankee shooters who had gotten up into trees and whom we could not bring our guns to bear on. I thought my time would certainly come next. A sharpshooter's ball went through my gaiter and scraped my ankle. Gen. Ramseur came up about this time, and I told him that if he kept us there much longer that every one of my men would be picked off by the Yankee sharpshooters. He then ordered me to retire to the hill just behind where we then were, and which we did very handsomely and without loss of men or horses.

*September 20.* We reached Strasburg, went into camp south of the town, and after feeding our horses and getting something to eat, we went back on picket duty on our infantry line of battle, which had been established about a mile south of the town of Strasburg. We put our guns in position and made some breastworks.[19]

*September 21. Wednesday.* Everything very quiet in our front. We are supported by Gen. Battle's Brigade.[20] Gen. Battle is one of the few brigadier generals who have escaped thus far. We started out of winter quarters with brigadier generals twelve in number and there are only two left, ten having been killed or wounded. Gen. Grant is reported to be in command of the Yankees in our front. I don't believe it. There is a Yankee officer who rides a white horse that has appeared frequently and conspicuously in our front. This officer is said to [be] Averell.[21] We went back to our camp to feed our horses and get some rations cooked.

*September 22. Thursday.* We went over to the front early this morning. The Yanks have been moving heavy columns of infantry to their right all day. We can see them plainly climbing up the side of North Mountain.[22] I suppose Gen. Early knows this and has troops there to

---

18 Of these, John B. Graves was from Hanover County.

19 Early established his forces on a line in front of Fisher's Hill, less than two miles south of Strasburg. Here he awaited the attack of the enemy, which did not come for two days. (*Early,* p. 429; *Official Records,* Vol. XLIII, pt. 1, p. 556.)

20 Brig. Gen. Cullen A. Battle, of Ramseur's Division.

21 Bvt. Maj. Gen. William W. Averell, commanding the Second Cavalry Division.

22 This was Little North Mountain, about three miles west of Fisher's Hill. It should not be confused with North Mountain, a few miles farther west. Sheridan had decided to turn the Confederate left as he had done at Winchester, and sent Brig. Gen. George Crook's command into the woods at the east side of Little North Mountain. No other account of Crook's movements being seen by Confederates could be found. When Crook attacked Early's weak left, where the undisciplined troops of Lunsford Lomax's command were dismounted and

meet them, and unless he has, we will have to get from this position, and very quickly too. At 4 P.M., or a little later, the Yanks, whom we had seen climbing up North Mountain all day, succeeded in turning our left flank and rolling up our line of battle; a very bad stampede of our left followed. When the fight began, our horses were a mile in the rear grazing. Mr. Gilmer, our chaplain, volunteered to go and bring up the horses, which he did very quickly and soon had them there. Gen. Battle's Brigade, which supported us, behaved splendidly and we succeeded in bringing off all our guns but one, which was lost by the limber's being turned over just as they were limbering up.[23] It was John Hill's gun. The horses at the wheel were both thrown down on their backs and it was impossible to get them up before the Yanks were on us. Our battalion lost two other guns, Braxton nine and King one.[24] This is very bad. John Hill lost his horse, blankets and all his clothes. All these traps were on his horse. His horse was tied some distance in the rear of his gun and when they started out John was cut off from his horse, and came near being captured. My messmate, Frank Kinckle, was shot about three inches above his right eye by a musket ball. His thick wool hat saved him. The wound was a slight one, but it bled very much. I got him in the ambulance and took his horse for myself. Maj. [Lt. Col.] Sandy Pendleton was killed this evening.[25] He is Maj. John Page's[26] nephew. He was a good and brave officer and a noble Christian gentleman. We continued our retreat up the Valley, until very late at night and encamped for the night right on the pike. It is said that the Old Stonewall Brigade was the author of this day's loss.[27] Alas! There

stationed as infantry, it was a complete surprise. Crook quickly rolled up the Confederate left, and the Confederate army retreated up the Valley. (*Early*, p. 430; Freeman, *Lee's Lieutenants*, III, 584.)

[23] Battle's Brigade was entrenched on the left center of the Confederate line. (*Official Records Atlas, Plate* LXXXII.)

[24] Early reported twelve guns lost and Freeman (*Lee's Lieutenants*, III, 584) accepts this number. Sheridan stated that he had captured twenty guns. Reports are so incomplete it is impossible to determine the exact number of guns captured by the Federal army. (*Official Records*, Vol. XLIII, pt. 1, pp. 27, 556.)

[25] Lt. Col. Alexander S. Pendleton, son of Lee's chief of artillery Brig. Gen. William N. Pendleton. "Sandie" Pendleton was mortally wounded while attempting to rally the disorganized Confederate troops and died on the evening of September 23 behind Federal lines, at the home of Dr. Murphy in Woodstock. Pendleton had been an adjutant general on Jackson's staff, then served under Ewell and Early in the same capacity. (Susan Pendleton Lee, *Memoirs of William Nelson Pendleton, D.D.* . . . [Philadelphia, 1893], p. 366 *ff.*; Freeman, *Lee's Lieutenants*, III, 584.)

[26] Major John Page was chief quartermaster, Artillery Corps, on Brig. Gen. Pendleton's staff.

[27] The Stonewall Brigade cannot be blamed for the loss that day. It was on the Confederate right. The author of defeat at Fisher's Hill, if it can be simply stated, was Lomax's dismounted cavalry on the left.

is very little left of that once splendid body of men, and one has not the heart to blame this poor remnant for its bad conduct this afternoon. We had a violent thunderstorm during our fight this evening. Surely the future looks gloomy and hopeless for the South just at present. May God help us.

*September 23. Friday.* We continued our retreat to New Market, where we made a stand and threw up some breastworks.[28] We got another gun and succeeded in putting our company in good fighting trim and are ready to measure strength again with these vile Yanks. I don't see why they don't go home and leave us alone. That is all we ask. But here they are with a vile mercenary army, burning our towns, destroying our crops, desolating our country and killing our people. I wish all the Yanks and all the negroes were in Africa.

*September 24. Saturday.* We began to fall back today from Rude's Hill,[29] which is about two miles north of New Market at 10 A.M., right in face of the Yanks. The country here is open in all directions and one can see for several miles in all directions. We fell back by alternate brigades. It was a grand sight and I never expect to see its like again. First, starting from our line of battle at Rude's Hill, the brigades, which consisted of the odd numbers, as 1, 3, 5, 7, etc., fell back for about a mile and formed a new line of battle. In the meantime, the brigades composing the even numbers held the line at Rude's Hill, until the odd brigades had established their line a mile in the rear. The bugles then sounded, and the even brigades fell back for two miles, passing through the odd brigades and after going a mile in rear of the odds, formed a line of battle, and then the odds retreated for two miles, and passing through the even brigades formed a line about a mile in their rear. This movement was kept up until sunset; every movement was made very slowly and deliberately and with perfect order.[30] There was some shelling, but at no time during the day did the Yanks make any attack on our line. About sunset, our last formed line held its position until about 9 P.M., giving our wagon train a good start. We then retreated, taking the Port Republic Road four miles

[28] With the defeat at Fisher's Hill, Early began a retreat up the Valley towards Port Republic to await reinforcements. On the afternoon of the twenty-third, General Lee had ordered Kershaw's Division with a battalion of artillery to the support of Early. (*Official Records*, Vol. XLIII, pt. 2, p. 878.)

[29] Rude's Hill is the proper spelling. HRB consistently misspelled it Rudd's Hill. It is located on the Valley Pike between Mt. Jackson and New Market.

[30] Of the withdrawal, General Early wrote, "The conduct of my troops was most admirable, and they preserved perfect order and their line intact, notwithstanding their diminished numbers, and the fact that the enemy was pursuing in full force. . . ." (*Early*, p. 432.)

south of New Market and marching towards Port Republic. Capt. Massie of our battalion was mortally wounded about sunset today by a fragment of a shell, and died at a farmhouse about 10 P.M. Another brave, noble and good man sacrificed on the altar of his country. This war is so very bloody, desperate and cruel now that our line of march is marked by the graves of the fallen.

*September 25. Sunday.* We continued our retreat to beyond Port Republic and encamped at the foot of the Blue Ridge Mountains right in the western entrance of Brown's Gap.

*September 26. Monday.* We remained in camp here until one o'clock in the day, when my gun went down on the Port Republic Road with Gen. Gordon's Division to look after some Yankee cavalry, which appeared in our front. There was some little skirmishing, but things soon got quiet and we went back to our camp in the gap of the mountain.[31]

*September 27. Tuesday.* We went round on our left this morning with Gordon's Division on a flank movement to drive off the Yankee cavalry.[32] We succeeded in driving them out of their camp and capturing a lot of nice beef, which I thought was the best I had ever eaten. We encamped for the night, on the west side of the [South] river very near Weyer's Cave;[33] but had no lights to visit the cave. Capt. Kirkpatrick and some four or five of our boys, having got hold of one little tallow candle, went a short distance into the cave, but the old guide refused to go very far. Yesterday, they say, our cavalry came near bagging a big lot of Yankee officers while they were in the cave.[34] We had a good supper tonight.

*September 28. Wednesday.* We marched from Port Republic to Waynesboro on the Central Railroad, driving some Yankees out of Waynesboro.[35] We went into camp about two miles south of that town. It was about at night when we got into camp.

[31] The enemy force engaged here was Bvt. Brig. Gen. Thomas C. Devin's Second Brigade, First Cavalry Division, commanded by Bvt. Maj. Gen. Wesley Merritt. (*Official Records,* Vol. XLIII, pt. 1, pp. 442, 477.)

[32] The force engaged here was again from Major General Merritt's First Cavalry Division. (*Ibid.,* p. 442.) This was one of the many maneuvers to prevent the enemy from strengthening their position before Brown's Gap. The enemy fell back to Cross Keys. Following this movement Gordon's Division and his artillery moved to Weyer's Cave to support the engagement mentioned in the entry for the following day.

[33] Weyer's Cave is located on the west bank of South River, less than three miles south of Port Republic. (*Official Records Atlas,* Plate LXXXV.)

[34] There was skirmishes near Weyer's Cave on the twenty-sixth, but there is no record of the cavalry's having threatened the enemy to the point of capturing any of their men in the cave. The cave is now known as Grand Caverns.

[35] Brig. Gen. James H. Wilson's Third Cavalry Division had been ordered to Waynesboro to destroy the railroad bridges there. This was the force driven out of that area by Early's

HENRY ROBINSON BERKELEY IN LATER YEARS

CONFEDERATE OFFICERS BARRACKS, FORT DELAWARE
Colored pencil sketch by Henry Robinson Berkeley

*September 29. Thursday.* We remained in camp all day at Waynesboro. Tom Henderson and I went out, and after walking some four or five miles south of our camp an old farmer gave us a nice supper, which we enjoyed very much. On our way back to camp, another old farmer's wife gave me a big piece of nice homemade soap. This was no poor gift to a soldier. One does not think it, but soap is a very important part of a soldier's rations.

*September 30. Friday.* We remained in camp all day at Waynesboro. Wrote to Nannie and Mollie.

army. Wilson states he was driven out of Waynesboro on the twenty-ninth but the evidence points to the twenty-eighth as the proper date. (*Official Records,* Vol. XLIII, pt. 1, pp. 519, 1029.)

# CHAPTER XII

# GENERAL EARLY NEEDED EVERY MAN

## Cedar Creek, 1864

*October 1, 1864. Friday.* We marched today from Waynesboro to Mount Sydnor [Sidney] on the Valley Pike through a very heavy and cold rain.[1] I never suffered more from cold in my life. We encamped west of the pike about a mile from Mt. Sydnor [Sidney] in an old farmer's new ground, just about an hour before sunset. It stopped raining soon after we got into camp. We soon had a nice bright fire burning, and after drying off a little we succeeded in getting up a right good supper. We, having dried ourselves and blankets as best we could, turned in about 10 P.M. and got a fairly good night's rest. I received a letter from Anna R. Berkeley giving me some of the details of her brother, Nelson Berkeley's death.[2] He was killed in [Lt. Gen. P. G. T.] Beauregard's battle with old Ben [Maj. Gen. Benjamin F.] Butler, near Bermuda Hundred. A brave and good soldier gone; but only one among the thousands who have fallen and are still falling around us every day. I must answer her letter and try to

---

[1] Mt. Sidney is located about halfway between Staunton and Harrisonburg. With the arrival of Maj. Gen. Joseph B. Kershaw's Division and Col. William E. Cutshaw's Artillery Battalion, on September 26, Early, finding that Sheridan was retiring to Harrisonburg, was ready to move on the offensive again. Also, he had the prospect of being further reinforced by Brig. Gen. Thomas L. Rosser's Cavalry Brigade, which reached him on October 5. (*Lieutenant General Jubal Anderson Early, C.S.A. Autobiographical Sketch and Narrative of the War Between the States. With Notes by R. H. Early* [Philadelphia and London, 1912], p. 435; *The War of the Rebellion: A Compilation of the Official Records of the Union and Confederate Armies* [Washington, D. C., 1880-1901], Series 1, Volume XXIII, part 1, pp. 556 *ff.*, and pt. 2, pp. 880-81. All citations will be from Series I unless otherwise stated.)

[2] A Nelson Berkley [*sic*] is listed as having received in a skirmish in May, 1864, a wound from which he died. (Confederate War Service Records, IV, 55, Virginia State Library.) The Berkeley noted was in Capt. John R. Bagby's King and Queen County Company, 34th Regiment, Wise's Brigade, which was under Beauregard in May, 1864. This Nelson Berkeley might be the one mentioned in Frances Berkeley Young, *The Berkeleys of Barn Elms* (New Haven, 1954), p. 112. No information could be found concerning Anna R. Berkeley.

give her and her family a word of comfort. Alas! A hopeless effort I fear it will be.

*October 2. Sunday.* We remained quietly in camp all day.

*October 3.* We remained in camp and washed our clothes.

*October 4 and 5.* We remained in camp. All quiet.

*October 6.* We marched down to Harrisonburg and encamped for the night on the west of the Valley Pike. John Hill went to Staunton this morning.[3]

*October 7. Friday.* We marched to New Market and into camp near that town on the Luray Pike.

*October 8. Saturday.* We remained in camp. Very cold and windy. A little snow.

*October 9. Sunday.* It is still very cold and windy. Bob Winston and I went to church in town at night. Church crowded with soldiers.

*October 10. Monday.* On guard over our horses while they were out grazing. At church in town that night.

*October 11. Tuesday.* I received a letter from Sister Bettie. Washed my clothes and went to church at night.

*October 12. Wednesday.* We marched from New Market to Woodstock and encamped for the night south of the town.[4]

*October 13. Thursday.* We marched to Strasburg. There was some fighting north of that town, but our battalion was left south of the town and went into camp on the east side of the Valley Pike. It was very cold and clear.

*October 14. Friday.* We remained quietly in our camp near Strasburg, south of the town, while the Yankee army was some two miles north, encamped along Cedar Creek, until the morning of October 19.

*October 19.* This morning about daybreak our army surprised the whole Yankee camp in our front.[5] Our men went through camp after

[3] Finding that the enemy had left Harrisonburg and retired farther down the Valley, Early prepared his army for a move forward which began the next day. (*Early*, p. 436.)

[4] Having heard that a portion of Sheridan's army was to be moved to Grant's Richmond-Petersburg front, Early set out towards the enemy and on the thirteenth found the Federals in strong numbers on the north bank of Cedar Creek. The fighting mentioned as taking place on the thirteenth was a result of Early's reconnaissance. Two brigades of the First Infantry Division, commanded by Col. Thomas M. Harris, opposed the Confederates in this engagement, and retreated in disorder. (*Official Records*, Vol. XLIII, pt. 1, pp. 371-72; *Early*, p. 437.)

[5] The Battle of Cedar Creek. Upon the recommendation of Maj. Gen. John B. Gordon and Maj. Jedediah Hotchkiss, Early planned a surprise attack on the enemy encampments north of Cedar Creek. By shortly after 9:00 A.M., the Confederate army had routed Sheridan's Eleventh Corps and captured about thirteen hundred prisoners and eighteen guns. The Sixth Corps had also been dislodged and the three Federal corps retired north of Middletown. Had the attack continued, the Federal army would probably have been destroyed; at least it would

camp, sweeping everything before them, capturing and killing a great many Yanks, often finding the men asleep in their tents or just in the act of getting their breakfast. We captured horses tied to their picket ropes and some three or four batteries in park. We drove them in great confusion for two miles beyond Middletown and had we not been stopped by our generals I believe we could easily have driven them into Harpers Ferry. Unfortunately, however, after we had driven them to this point, we were halted, just as Col. Tom Carter, our chief of artillery,[6] had gotten 45 pieces of artillery ready to open on the Yankee Sixth Corps, which had come up to the help of their routed friends. I don't believe there is one particle of doubt that had we been permitted to open on those Yanks with our forty-five cannon, but that we would certainly have put them beyond the Potomac River. It was only about 9 A.M. when they stopped us. We had captured twenty-two guns, two thousand prisoners and a great many wagons, mules and horses, and were picking up many prisoners. We remained quietly in line of battle about a mile north of Middleburg [Middletown], until about 3 P.M. when the Yanks, having received large re-enforcements attacked us on our extreme left flank, and here again the Old Stonewall Brigade proved false to us. For before the fight hardly began, it gave way without making the least effort and very soon our entire left wing was in a grand stampede, being frightfully panic-stricken, without the least reason for it, and, resisting every effort to rally them, fled from the field. The artillery acted splendidly and we easily kept back

have been pushed far down the Valley. But for reasons which have never been satisfactorily explained, Early decided not to continue the attack. Although Early placed the blame upon straggling, plundering, and poor discipline after an easy victory, he must have known it was his error that turned certain victory into defeat and humiliation. By not pressing the attack he allowed the enemy to regroup and gave General Sheridan, who had been away from the front, time to return and resume command of his army. At 4:30 P.M., the Federals began a turning movement in Early's left, and before long the Confederates were retreating in utmost disorder. The morning of October 20 found them defeated at New Market rather than victorious in Winchester. This was the real end of Early's Valley Campaign. (Douglas Southall Freeman, *Lee's Lieutenants: A Study in Command* [New York, 1942-44], III, 596-612; *Early*, pp. 437-52; *Official Records*, XLIII, pt. 1, pp. 52-54, 561-64.) The artillery played an important role in the day's successes and prevented the retreat from being more disastrous than it was. Ably commanded, the artillery gave ground grudgingly during the withdrawal of the artillery. Early stated in his report: "The Artillery throughout . . . behaved nobly, both officers and men. . . . I attribute this good conduct on their part to the vast superiority of the officers. Col. Carter and all his battalion commanders richly deserve promotion. They not only fought their guns gallantly and efficiently, but they made the most strenuous efforts to rally the infantry." (*Official Records*, Vol. XLIII, pt. 1, p. 563; Jennings C. Wise, *The Long Arm of Lee or The History of the Artillery of Northern Virginia* [Lynchburg, 1915], II, 890-92.)

6 Col. Thomas Hill Carter, who had been wounded at Winchester and replaced as acting chief of artillery by Lt. Col. William Nelson, returned to his command on September 25. (Wise, *Long Arm*, II, 889.)

the Yanks until dark, but after we crossed Cedar Creek, some Yankee cavalry broke into our artillery and wagon train and captured many of our guns and wagons. We, however, brought out our two thousand prisoners and much of the plunder taken early in the morning. We also lost many ambulances, but very few men. We had the pleasure of balling the Yanks this evening with their own guns and ammunition and brought two or three of their guns. Our whole army retreated in much confusion up the Valley. At one time, Yanks and Confeds were very much mixed up just south of Strasburg, and I made several narrow escapes from being captured. I, however, succeeded in getting out of the pike to its west side. Bernard Graves[7] and I happened to fall in with each other in the dark and kept together during the entire night. We came on up the Valley Pike, to its left coming up towards Mount Jackson, and made our way in the darkness through the fields; but this being very rough walking, we determined to try the pike. But being uncertain whether the Yankees or our men held the pike, we approached it very cautiously. We found a solid mass of men, moving perfectly quietly up the pike. Not a word was uttered for five minutes, and to save my life, I did [not] know whether they were Yankees or our men. At last, someone called out, "Whose division is this?" The answer came quickly and clearly, "Gordon's." We knew at once that we were all right and we soon joined this moving column and came on up towards New Market. Tom Henderson[8] and John McDaniel tonight, while walking up the pike, were overtaken by two cavalry men, whom Tom and John took to be our men, but very soon discovered them to be Yanks. Our boys, not being armed, jumped over a stone fence in order to escape. McDaniel was lucky and soon got away; but Tom Henderson, in jumping, landed in a lot of old tin roofing, which a farmer had taken from the roof of his house, and made a powerful noise, at which both of the Yankee horsemen riding up to the stone fence fired away at him with their pistols only about twenty feet off, while Tom was rolling about in the old tin roofing, he thinks for some five minutes, before he could get out. He finally succeeded in getting out of the old tin roofing and in escaping the balls and capture. He thinks these Yanks shot at him at least twenty times a piece and that an old tin roof never made as much noise in the world before, and that he owes his life to poor shooting. About

[7] Bernard B. Graves, a company member from near Beaver Dam, Hanover County.

[8] Thomas H. Henderson is listed on a company muster roll as having been enlisted by Captain Kirkpatrick in Culpeper on November 13, 1863. (War Department, Confederacy, No. 111, 88, Virginia State Library.)

day I crept into some bushes on the left of the pike and slept for about three hours. I then got up and came on up the Valley towards New Market. About three miles below New Market I met Sam Anderson, Jack Cooke and Charley Taylor[9] of the Hanover Cavalry. They said that if they were in my place that they would take a furlough and go home for a week or two. I told them that I did not think this was a time for men to be going home, that General Early needed every man which he could possibly get and many more than he had, and that if we did [not] stand to our guns, the Yanks might get to our homes before we did. I came on up to New Market, after talking with these Hanover boys for nearly an hour, and found about fifty of my company had gathered there with two guns and some twenty horses and [had] gone into camp about a mile west of town and that our whole army was rallying here in very good condition, much better than I had imagined it would.

*October 20.*  Our army continued to gather near New Market and our scouts report the Yankee army as having gone back to the neighborhood of Winchester. Both Early's and Sheridan's armies were badly used up on yesterday and now seem willing to play quits for a time.[10] Ah! This horrid war! When will it end? During October 21, 22, 23 and 24, we remained quietly in the same camp collecting men, guns, horses and ammunition, and trying to get ready for another struggle with the Yanks.

*October 25.*  We moved our camp across to the east side of the Shenandoah River in order to get better grazing for our horses. Phil Dandridge[11] joined our mess today. I consented to taking him, after being assured by our chaplain Mr. Gilmer, that he is a gentleman and a good fellow. My messmates at this time are J. H. Berkeley, P. Dandridge, Frank Kinckle, Dabney Williamson, Bob Winston and myself. The two last have recently returned to the company, having recovered from their wounds received on June 3rd in the terrible Cold Harbor fight. John Lewis Berkeley, who was wounded in the same battle, has not recovered sufficiently to return to his company. I am the only man in our mess who has never had to leave his post of duty. Frank Kinckle has only been absent

9 S. D. Anderson, John McP. Cooke, and C. A. Taylor of "Hanover Troop," Company G, 4th Virginia Cavalry Regiment. (Rosewell Page, *Hanover County: Its History and Legends* [Richmond, 1926], p. 82.)

10 After a hard-fought campaign, costly to both sides, both armies were ready to go into winter quarters. Sheridan felt that he had shattered resistance in the Valley and he was right. Early was to advance down the Valley once more, but it was a feeble effort followed by a quick withdrawal. (See November 10-12 of this diary.)

11 Probably the L. P. Dandridge listed on one of the company muster rolls in W.D.C., No. 111, 38, Virginia State Library.

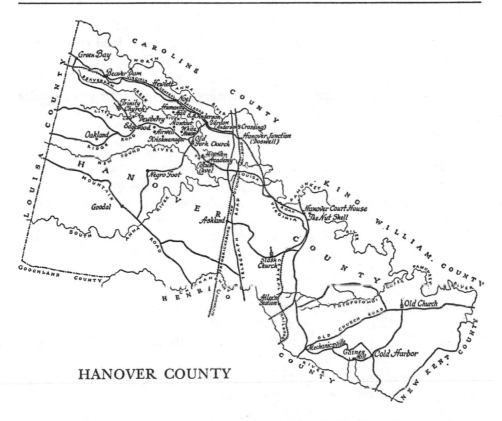

HANOVER COUNTY

two days and has been slightly wounded twice. J. H. Berkeley was absent
ten days while we were at Cold Harbor.

*October 26.* On guard. Washed my clothes. Bernard Graves, John
Graves and John McCary, who had been messing with us while our three
wounded messmates were absent, withdrew from our mess as two of our
wounded messmates had returned and our mess was getting rather too
large for convenience.

*October 27, 28 and 29.* We remained quietly in camp.

*October 30. Sunday.* Heard Mr. Gilmer. I was quite sick at night.

*October 31.* I am still quite sick. Heard Mr. Powers[12] preach in the
evening.

*November 1. Tuesday.* I am on guard today. I have about gotten
well.

12 Probably the Rev. W. C. Power, chaplain of the 14th North Carolina Regiment, which
was with Early at this time. (J. William Jones, *Christ in Camp or Religion in Lee's Army*
[Richmond, 1887], p. 514.)

*November 2.*  We remained in camp all day. Rained.

*November 3.  Thursday.*  It is still raining. I received two letters; one from Sister Bettie, and the other from Nannie [Berkeley].

*November 4.*  I answered Nannie's letter today.

*November 5.  Saturday.*  Our quartermaster issued us some apples today. Inspection by Col. Carter.

*November 6.  Sunday.*  On guard.

*November 7.*  All quiet.

*November 8.*  Got a letter from [Louisa] Carter [Berkeley].

*November 9.*  John Hill went up to Staunton. All quiet.

*November 10.  Thursday.*  We marched down below Edinburg and encamped near Woodstock for the night.[13]

*November 11.  Friday.*  We continued our march down below Middletown and came on the Yankees in line of battle, just this side of Newtown. We encamped on the right of the pike going down the Valley.

*November 12.  Saturday.*  We remained quiet all day. Just before sunset, we went to the front and placed our guns in position on our line of battle, sending our wagons back towards Strasburg. After dark our whole army came back and went into camp about two miles south of Strasburg for the night.

*November 13.*  We marched on up the Valley to Hawkinstown [and] encamped on west of the pike, for the night.

---

[13] Learning that Sheridan was preparing to send troops to Grant and that the Manassas Gap Railroad was being rebuilt, Early saw another opportunity to strike Sheridan. The Confederates arrived in front of Sheridan's army near Newtown and remained there until the night of November 12. The enemy was strongly entrenched and showed no disposition to come out of their fortifications, and since Early did not feel his force strong enough for an attack he retired on the night of the twelfth. There were several cavalry engagements during this movement. (*Early,* pp. 453-54.)

# CHAPTER XIII

# WHO WILL BE LEFT TO TELL THE TALE?

## *Winter Quarters, 1864-1865*

*November 14, 1864. Monday.* We came on up to New Market, and went into the meanest camp an officer could possibly pick out. It was very cold and windy and this camp was on the north side of a steep hill. The boys in the whole battalion seemed to think that it would be utterly impossible to choose a meaner camp in Rockingham County. They were abusing the officer who selected it pretty much all night, for it was so cold we could not keep warm and the hill so steep that we could [not] sleep in any comfort.

*November 15. Tuesday.* We moved our camp about four miles up the [North] River. Got a very good camp. We fixed up our tent quite comfortably and succeeded in getting a comfortable night's rest, a thing that we had not enjoyed for three or four nights.

*November 16. Wednesday.* A day of prayer and supplication. We had two prayer meetings and two sermons.

*November 17.* Cloudy. We remained encamped in this same place until the 29th of November, on which day we moved up to near Harrisonburg, encamping on the west of Valley Pike about a mile north of the town.

*November 30. Wednesday.* Nothing to eat this morning for either men or horses, our commissary wagons, which went out on a foraging expedition, not having gotten in last night. Beautiful weather. Commissary wagons came in late in the afternoon and men and horses got some rations.

*December 1.* We had beautiful weather until December 9, when it clouded up, turned very cold and began to snow very fast and hard about dark.

*December 10.*   It snowed hard all night, but stopped about sunrise and soon after cleared off, leaving quite a deep snow on the ground.

*December 11.*   We remained in camp. All quiet. Weather clear.

*December 12.*   Our poor horses have had nothing to eat for three days. All we could do for them was to turn them into a stalk field and to an old straw rack. The snow is still two or three inches deep. We received orders about dark to be ready to march by sunrise tomorrow morning. Quite cold.

*December 13. Tuesday.*   Very cold, and cloudy. Freezing all day. Pike icy and very slippery. We marched up to Mount Sidney and encamped on east of the pike for the night in a piece of oak woods where, very fortunately for us, there were several cords of nice seasoned oak wood. We scraped away the snow and soon had a big and hot fire blazing. The heat of the fire melting the snow, we soon had mud and water to deal with. The prospects for a comfortable night were gloomy. We, however, went into a stalk field near us, and each of our mess gathered an armful of corn stalks. These we put down on the wet ground. The stalks were then covered with some hay, which had been kept for a breakfast for our horses in the morning. On top [of] the hay we made our bed, putting our oilcloths on the outside as it looked very much like rain. Thank God I am not on guard tonight. We turned in about 9 P.M., first piling a big lot of wood on our fire.

*December 14.*   Last night, about midnight, it began to rain very hard and continued to rain for two hours. Very fortunately for us, the rain, which first fell, froze and formed on our oilcloths a thick coating of ice, which kept us perfectly warm and dry, not a single drop getting through to us, and we slept as warm and as comfortable as possible. A soldier, in freezing and cold weather, always sleeps with his head covered up. Had my parents known that their boys were sleeping outdoors with nothing but a blanket and an oilcloth to protect them, I doubt not that they would have been perfectly miserable, and yet we were perfectly comfortable. We were rousted out [of] our comfortable and warm bunk about [day] light. It was clearing off. The rain had put out our fire, but the cornstalks on which we had slept, being quite dry, with their help we soon had a good fire. After getting our scant breakfast, we pulled out and started for Fishersville, which is a small station on the Central Railroad about five miles east of Staunton. We went through Staunton about midday. We,

J. H. Berkeley and myself, stopped for two hours, [and] saw Uncle Carter Berkeley,[1] who got for us a very nice snack, which we enjoyed very much. We then went on to Fishersville and found our company encamped for the night about a mile northwest of the station.

*December 15. Thursday.* We slept very cold last night. We picked out a good winter camp in a big oak wood about a mile and a half northwest of the station on the farm of a Mrs. Bell.

*December 16.* We worked on our winter house all day. Very cold.

*December 17. Saturday.* Worked on our winter hut. Got things partly fixed up and slept rather more comfortably. Mr. Kinckle, Frank Kinckle's father, came to see us, bringing us some home grub and the boys a big and nice lot of tobacco.

*December 18. Sunday.* Mr. Kinckle gave us two sermons today, but I could not go to hear him as I was on guard. I got a letter from Sister Bettie, and also one from Nannie [Berkeley].

*December 19. Monday.* I wrote to Father and Nannie. We began to put up stables for our horses.

*December 20. Tuesday.* We finished our stables and got our horses in them.

*December 21. Wednesday.* We fixed our house up with some slabs, put up a door and made things much more comfortable.

*December 22. Thursday.* Very wet, snowy and disagreeable. We got a big lot of wood.

*December 23.* All quiet. Weather cold and disagreeable.

*December 24. Saturday.* We got letters today saying that Mr. Buck Winston was coming up to see us and to bring us some clothes and home grub. Bob Winston and I went to the station to meet his father, but he did not come.

*December 25. Sunday.* Christmas Day. The fourth Christmas since I have been in the army. Not so dry and hard a one as the last; but the future looks dark, gloomy, bloody and hopeless. I heard Mr. Gilmer, our chaplain, preach a very good sermon in the morning and [heard] a Methodist minister that night.

*December 26.* Mr. Buck Winston got to camp today. He brought us some clothes and a big lot of nice home grub and we are now living high. Had our Christmas things tonight for supper. Our army around

---

1 Probably the brother of HRB's father. He married his first cousin Ann Berkeley. (Frances Berkeley Young, *The Berkeleys of Barn Elms* [New Haven, 1954], pp. 111, 116.)

Petersburg is suffering terribly. I am very glad we are up here; but I expect the storm will strike us first in the spring.

*December 27. Tuesday.* Mr. Winston spent the day and night with us.

*December 28. Wednesday.* Mr. Winston went home.

*December 29. Thursday.* My furlough was made out today for ten days and sent to Gen. Early's headquarters for approval. Nearly the whole of Gen. Early's army has been sent to Petersburg. Only two regiments, the 62nd and the 63rd Virginia left here. We have also sent nearly all our guns to Lynchburg [leaving] only two guns to each company. Our battalion consists of three companies; viz.: Kirkpatrick's, Milledge's and Massie's. Since the death of Capt. Massie, Capt. [Charles G.] Snead has commanded Massie's old Company.[2]

*December 30. Friday.* I got a letter from Nannie. Heard Dr. Lacy[3] preach a splendid sermon.

*December 31. Friday.* Wrote to Carter. It snowed all last night and all day today until two o'clock in the afternoon. The snow quite deep.

*January 1, 1865. Sunday. New Year's Day.* The old year is gone with all its hopes, sorrows, losses, trials, dangers, sufferings, deaths, bloody battles and still more bloody heartaches and anxieties. Farewell, Old Year. Thou art gone, and with thee, many a noble and brave soldier. Who could count the vacant chairs in our southern homes, the bereaved and stricken fathers, mothers, sisters and wives? Alas, when will all this stop? The future looks gloomy, and almost hopeless. I wonder if I shall live to see 1866. I do not believe I shall. May God give me grace to do my whole duty to Him, my fellow man and to my country. I heard Dr. Lacy preach a most excellent sermon. Copeland Page took dinner with us. He is a first cousin of Frank Kinckle's and is on Col. Cutshaw's staff.

[2] Kershaw's Division had left Early's command for the Richmond front on November 15, and the divisions of Gordon and Pegram followed on December 9. Only Wharton's fragment of a division, a small battalion of artillery, and a cavalry force were left with Early. Lee hoped Early would make the impression that his force was larger than it was and thus keep Federal troops in the Valley and away from Richmond. (Douglas Southall Freeman, *Lee's Lieutenants: A Study in Command* [New York, 1942-44], III, 617; *Lieutenant General Jubal Anderson Early, C.S.A. Autobiographical Sketch and Narrative of the War Between the States. With Notes by R. H. Early* [Philadelphia and London, 1912], p. 459.)

[3] Beverley Tucker Lacy (1819-1900) was a native of Prince Edward County, Virginia. After graduating from Washington College, Virginia, and the Princeton Theological Seminary, he became a Presbyterian minister, being ordained by the Winchester Presbytery on May 16, 1847. At the outbreak of the war, he was the pastor of the Presbyterian Church in Frankfort, Kentucky. From 1863 to 1865, he was a chaplain for the Second Corps, Army of Northern Virginia. Immediately following the war, he served the Presbyterian churches in Wytheville, Virginia, and St. Louis, Missouri. He died in Georgetown, D. C. (E. C. Scott, *Ministerial Directory of the Presbyterian Church, U. S. 1861-1941* [Austin, Texas, 1942], p. 384.)

*January 2. Monday.* It is very cold and looks very much like we shall have snow.

*January 3. Tuesday.* Snowing fast. Got my furlough and fixed to go home on the early train tomorrow morning.

*January 4. Wednesday.* I came home. A very cold and disagreeable day. Reached home about 6 P.M. Had a hard and laborious walk from Noel's Station in a six-inch snow, which had a thick crust on it. I had to go down to Edmund Anderson's lower ford to get over the river. It took our train from 8 A.M. to 4 P.M. to run from Fishersville to Noel's. There were four Yankee prisoners on my train today to whom I gave nearly all my snack. I thought some day I might be in a like fix in a Yankee train. Such is the fate of war very often.

*January 5. Thursday.* I remained at home all day. Enjoyed the day very much, often thought that perhaps this might be my last visit home. War is a very uncertain trade; one never knows how it may end.

*January 6. Friday.* I spent the day at "Montout" with the family. Pleasant day. John Lewis [is] suffering very much with a boil under his armpit, caused by the use of his crutch.

*January 7. Saturday.* I spent the morning at home. Went over to [Rev.] Mr. [Horace] Stringfellow's after dinner. Quite a cool reception, I thought.

*January 8. Sunday.* I went up to Trinity Church with Papa and Eddie. Mr. Robert Nelson preached to eight persons. We dined at "Dewberry." Cousin Bettie Clarke[4] talked very much about white-livered men, cowards, etc. I wonder how she would face a Yankee battery and a Yankee brigade. I don't think our home people realize how near the end is on us, or what that end will most probably be. We got home about dark.

*January 9.* I dined at "Krishnanagar." Met with Miss Mattie Lockett, a young lady who teaches for Uncle Dick. Came home about dark.

*January 10.* It rained hard all last night and all day until just before sunset, when it cleared off. The girls, i.e. my sisters, gave me a supper, a very nice one, considering these hard war times. Nannie and Landon [Carter Berkeley, Jr.] came down to it in the horse cart with a mule.

*January 11.* Dined at "Montout" and spent the night there.

*January 12.* I spent the day at home. I saw John Lewis. He is looking thin and bad.

*January 13.* I remained at home.

[4] Elizabeth Cooke of "Dewberry," who married a Colin Clarke. (Interviews, Landon Carter Berkeley and Harrison C. Berkeley.)

*January 14. Saturday.* Cousin Nannie Wight and her husband came to our house this evening and will spend a day or two.

*January 15. Sunday.* Went to Fork Church today. John Hill, Lackey, and Bob Winston got home today on a horse-furlough, i.e. these men are furloughed on condition that they carry a horse home, feed it, and take good care of it, until they are ordered back in the spring. I think that their war life is over. They will hardly get back to their company. Lackey spent the night at the "White House" and then went on to his home in Lancaster County.

*January 16.* I went down with Carter to see Aunt Kate, who is now living at "Locust Level."

*January 17. Tuesday.* I went over with Carter to see Miss Kate Winston, came back to "Locust Level" to dinner and [went] up home that afternoon.

*January 18. Wednesday.* I remained at home all day, many sad and hopeless thoughts running through my active mind. Tomorrow I leave for the army under the darkest auspices I have ever done. I have but one wish, that is, that I may have courage, strength and grace, in this coming campaign, to do my whole duty to my God, my country and my fellow man. If I must fall, I want to fall at my post of duty. The future looks dark, bloody and hopeless; but our only hope is in God.

*January 19. Thursday.* I remained a day longer at home. Went up to "Montout" [to] tell them good-by.

*January 20. Friday.* Left home for my command at Fishersville on [the] Central Railroad. [The] train broke down in the Blue Ridge tunnel[5] and I did not reach camp until twelve o'clock at night. I only found Frank in camp. All the other boys except Phil Dandridge [have] gone home on horse-furlough. Dandridge is detailed on [a] foraging expedition out in south and west Augusta, looking for anything he can find to eat either for man, horse or mule.[6]

*January 21. Saturday.* It is raining, sleeting and snowing today. Camp exceedingly dull and gloomy.

*January 22. Sunday.* I went to church near Fishersville and heard a very good sermon.

*January 23. Monday.* A rainy day. Camp dull and gloomy.

[5] This tunnel goes through the Blue Ridge Mountains at Rockfish Gap, near Waynesboro.
[6] The drought during the summer caused a short corn crop, and Sheridan's forces had destroyed the crops during the Valley campaign. The food shortage, for both men and animals, was severe. (*Early*, p. 459.)

*January 24. Tuesday.* I went up to Staunton hoping to see Brother [Thomas Berkeley], but he was too sick for me to see him. Expected to come back on the freight train, but for some reason the freight went up to Millboro and had not gotten back at 4 P.M., so I had to walk back. I reached camp about 6 P.M.

*January 25. Wednesday.* Willie and Carrington Kinckle, younger brothers of Frank, who had spent some two weeks in camp with us and had brightened up our tent-life very much, went home.

*January 26. Thursday.* Very cold. Camp cold, dull and very gloomy.

*January 27. Friday.* Very cold. Freezing all day.

*January 28. Saturday.* Very cold and windy. Camp cold, dull and gloomy.

*January 29. Sunday.* Heard Mr. Robert Nelson preach in the morning and Mr. Gilmer at night. Mr. Nelson preached in the little Methodist Church near Fishersville and Mr. Gilmer in camp. A bright and pretty day; but quite cold. Men's spirits dull, gloomy and all are evidently hopeless, waiting for we know not what end.

*January 30. Monday.* I got a letter from Nannie. May God bless and keep her from the evils and dangers of our hopeless future. I wonder if I shall ever see her again in this world.

*January 31. Tuesday.* Heard Mr. Nelson preach. Received some letters from home.

*February 1.* A bright and beautiful day. Camp rather more cheerful.

*February 2.* Braxton's guns and horses were turned over to us, Cutshaw's to Massie and Milledge, and their battalions were ordered to Richmond.[7]

*February 3. Friday.* Frank went home. I am now doing the duty of a lieutenant, the orderly sergeant, a corporal, and a gunner. Things must be desperate when all these duties have to be performed by one man, and he only a private, but evidently this private is not in the rear ranks.

---

[7] Because of the poor condition of the animals, insufficient equipment, and too few soldiers, Early kept only a small force. Colonel Nelson's Battalion with six pieces of artillery remained. Guns from the other battalions were distributed to Nelson's batteries to insure his having good equipment, and the remainder were sent to the Richmond front along with the men from the battalions of Lt. Col. Carter M. Braxton and Lt. Col. Wilfred E. Cutshaw. (*Early,* p. 460; Jennings C. Wise, *The Long Arm of Lee or The History of the Artillery of the Army of Northern Virginia* [Lynchburg, Va., 1915], II, 920.)

*February 4. Saturday.* Camp quite cheerful. Weather bright and beautiful.

*February 5. Sunday.* Heard Mr. Gilmer, our chaplain, preach in the morning and a Methodist minister in the evening.

*February 6. Monday.* Got a detail from Capt. Armstrong, our quartermaster, to go to Anderson's Crossing, in Hanover County, to get his trunk for him, which he left some time ago at Buster Thompson's. Fixed to go home on this detail.

*February 7. Tuesday.* Came home. A very heavy snowstorm all day, turning to sleet and ice after midday. It took the train all day to come from Staunton to Noel's. Got home about dark.

*February 8. Wednesday.* Found Uncle Lewis Berkeley at home on furlough. I went to Mr. Thompson's this morning before breakfast to see about Captain Armstrong's trunk, and to get him to send it to Anderson's Friday morning, which he promised to do. Went over to Mr. Stringfellow's and "Montout" in the evening.

*February 9. Thursday.* I remained at home until after dinner and then went up to "Montout" to see them a little while and to bid them good-by. Came home about 9 A.M.

*February 10. Friday.* Came back to our camp at Fishersville, bringing Capt. Armstrong's trunk. Met with Bev Turner on cars, on his way to his home in Fauquier County. Bev told me he was going to be married. I don't [know] whether he was joking or in earnest. Also saw on the train Big Willson, one of my old schoolmates at the Hanover Academy. Both of these old schoolmates seem to think our cause is hopeless and the end must come soon. I parted with them at Gordonsville with sad, gloomy and hopeless thoughts of the future. I wonder if I shall ever see home and the loved ones there again?

*February 11. Saturday.* I remained very quietly in camp with Frank Kinckle and Phil Dandridge, the only ones of my mess now in camp.

*February 12. Sunday.* Frank Kinckle and I went to church at Tinkling Spring. Mr. Gilmer preached. This is a large brick church some three or four miles south of Fishersville and is surrounded by a large graveyard.

*February 13. Monday.* I remained quietly in camp and wrote a good many letters.

*February 14. Tuesday.* Frank went over today to some gentleman's house in Nelson County to a party. [He] is to come back tomorrow.

He went with some young ladies of this neighborhood, whose acquaintance he has made.

*February 15. Wednesday.* A snowy, wet and gloomy day. Read *The Golden Daggers,* a novel. Got a letter from Mollie.

*February 16. Thursday.* Frank got back from his Nelson trip. He reports a pleasant time, nice girls and plenty to eat.

*February 17. Friday.* It snowed fast all day. Camp cold and gloomy.

*February 18. Saturday.* It has turned very warm. Snow melting very fast. Boys are snowballing and enjoying it very much. It makes things a little more cheerful; but if this warm weather continues, the Yankees will soon be on us. We hear that the Yanks are collecting a very large cavalry force at Winchester and are expected to move up the Valley as soon as the weather permits. I don't see how it is possible for our little force to make any headway against them. We are only 1500; they are reported to be 15,000. They will run over us by sheer weight of numbers. Who will be left to tell the tale?

*February 19. Sunday.* A beautiful day. Heard Mr. Gilmer preach a good sermon from Romans, X, 10. "For with the heart man believeth unto righteousness; and with [the] mouth confession is made unto salvation."

*February 20. Monday.* I received five letters today and enjoyed them very much. Our letters are the one thing which we soldiers always enjoy very much.

*February 21. Tuesday.* We are still encamped near Fishersville on the Virginia Central Railroad. Everything is seemingly quiet, but rumors are daily heard of large cavalry forces of the Yanks gathering at Winchester, who will be on us as soon as the weather permits. I wrote to Carter today.

*February 22. Wednesday.* Our mess, now consisting of Frank Kinckle, Lem Dandridge and myself, cut and brought down to our tent on a hand sled a large pile of wood ready for our tent chimney. It took us five or six hours. This day three years ago I saw President Davis inaugurated. I don't think the future looks as promising as our President then painted it.

*February 23. Thursday.* We received two months' pay today. A wet and rainy day.

*February 24. Friday.* John Lewis Berkeley came up from home to go before a board of surgeons for a furlough. He is still suffering from his wound and not able to do field duty.

*February 25. Friday. [i.e., Saturday].*    I went up to Staunton and found Brother Tommy much better. Spent the day with him and Uncle Carter. I came back to camp about dark.

*February 26. Sunday.*    I went to Tinkling Spring Church today with Frank Kinckle. A bright, sunny day.

*February 27. Monday.*    Frank went down to Col. Bell's with Frank Bell to take supper and spend the evening and night, leaving me to do the duty of orderly sergeant.

# CHAPTER XIV

# CAPTURED

## Waynesboro to Prison, 1865

*February 28, 1865. Tuesday.* We heard that the Yankee cavalry were coming up the Valley with a very large force, said to be 15,000 strong. We are only about 1500. I don't see how it is possible for us to contend against such great odds. Ordered to be ready to move at a moment's notice.[1]

*March 1. Wednesday.* This evening we moved down to Waynesboro and encamped near town. A cold and disagreeable night. I feel very anxious about John Lewis [Berkeley]. I don't see how he can possibly keep up. The Yankees are in Staunton.

*March 2. Thursday.* I carried John Lewis down to Waynesboro this morning about day and put him on a train then waiting there, he with some three or four more being ordered to the hospital at Charlottesville. By this time, it was about sunrise, but the weather was cold and rainy. We took a position on a very high hill, north of Waynesboro, on the Port Republic Road. After remaining here until three in the evening in a cold and sleety rain and being nearly frozen, the Yankee cavalry, in a large and heavy body, forming almost a semicircle, appeared in front and on both flanks. After a short fight our little force being flanked and outnumbered by ten to one, gave way and attempted to get to the mountains.[2] We had

[1] Sheridan's cavalry moved out of Winchester on February 27, and began its march towards Early's camp near Waynesboro. The Federal forces included Maj. Gen. George A. Custer's Third Cavalry Division and Brig. Gen. Thomas C. Devins' First Cavalry Division. The force was under the immediate command of Bvt. Maj. Gen. Wesley Merritt, Sheridan's chief of cavalry. Merritt's orders were to destroy the Virginia Central Railroad tracks, capture Lynchburg, and then join Sherman in North Carolina or return to Winchester. (George E. Pond, *The Shenandoah Valley in 1864* [New York, 1883], p. 252, Vol. XI of *Campaigns of the Civil War.*)

[2] In this battle, the last one fought by General Early's army in the Valley, the Confederate

only one little narrow plank over the [Virginia Central] railroad bridge[3] by which we could retreat and it took so long to get over, that Custer's Yankee Brigade got ahead of us, and [did so] by a circular movement and by crossing a ford above the town. Wharton's two regiments behaved very badly and ran very disgracefully. Had they stood firm, we could have gotten back in the cover of the mountain and defended ourselves against Sheridan's whole 15,000. I was captured after I had gotten over the railroad bridge in a little piece of oak woods to the left of the railroad as you come east. Lem Dandridge made his escape. Frank Kinckle was taken before I was captured and sent back to the railroad. The Yanks treated us very well. When they overtook us, they simply told us to go to the rear. I never saw men in better humor than these Yankees were. They, however, could outswear any set of men I ever heard and were the most profane set I ever was so unfortunate as to be thrown with. When I got out on the railroad where Frank Kinckle was, he was very glad to see me. He first said: "Robin, I never was as glad to see a man before in all my life," and then after a little pause, he would clap me on the shoulder and say, "I swear to God, *I never was as glad* to see a man in all my life," and he told me this at least fifty times that day. There were thirty of my company captured with me, and some eight hundred prisoners from the infantry. I aimed and fired my gun five or six times that day. It looks now, as if they would be the last shots fired by the Confederate artillery in the Valley of Virginia. The Yanks took us back to Waynesboro and put us in a lot near

line was on the ridge just west of Waynesboro and ran across the Staunton Pike (Va. Rt. 250) from southwest to northwest. Brig. Gen. Gabriel C. Wharton's Division mustered little more than one thousand muskets, and with a small group of cavalry and Colonel Nelson's Battalion with six guns, Early's little army formed to fight the enemy, which consisted of Maj. Gen. Custer's Cavalry Division supplemented by a cavalry brigade from the Second Division. HRB's gun was located on the extreme Confederate right. (*Atlas to Accompany the Official Records of the Union and Confederate Armies* [Washington, D. C. 1891-95], Plate LXXI.) Although the Federals arrived before Waynesboro shortly after noon, only skirmishing and maneuvering took place until about 3:00 P.M. when the Union force suddenly flanked Early's left. The Confederate lines immediately broke and were routed in a short time. Practically all of Early's army was captured. Early and a handful of officers and men were the only ones who escaped. Col. William Nelson escaped, for not long afterward it is known that he was in Lynchburg. (*Lieutenant General Jubal Anderson Early, C.S.A. Autobiographical Sketch and Narrative of the War Between the States. With Notes by R. H. Early* [Philadelphia and London, 1912], pp. 462-64; *The War of the Rebellion: A Compilation of the Official Records of the Union and Confederate Armies* [Washington, D. C., 1880-1901], Series I, Volume XLVI, part 1, pp. 502, 505, 508, 516-17. All citations will be from Series I unless otherwise noted.) It is interesting to note that at least sixteen Union soldiers received the Congressional Medal of Honor for this affair. (*Ibid.*, p. 509.)

[3] The bridge spanned the South River, just east of Waynesboro. The boards had been placed there in case of a Confederate withdrawal. (*Official Records Atlas*, Plate LXXII; *Official Records*, Vol. XLVI, pt. 1, p. 516.)

town where we spent a very disagreeable night. It was cold, rainy and we had very little fire, while the trampling of such a large body of men on such a small area soon made the mud very deep, so that it was impossible for us to make a bed, except in mud, some three or four inches deep. We had a plenty to eat, but nothing left for tomorrow.

*March 3.* We remained at Waynesboro until three o'clock in the afternoon, all the Yankee cavalry marching past us. It was a grand sight, and for ten hours without the least interruption did this mighty stream of cavalry pour by us on its way of devastation, death and destruction. The end of this war is in the near future. Our Yankee guards are kind and considerate. A Presbyterian preacher and a lady from Waynesboro came, by permission, in among us prisoners, looking for the lady's brother. He was not, however, found. No doubt he had made his escape; for there was only one man killed yesterday on our side, and he was a Maj. Harman[4] from Staunton. I saw a very badly wounded Yank, whom, his companion said, had been hurt by a shell. It must have been my gun that hurt him as it was the only cannon fired. We gave this lady many letters for home people. I doubt very much whether the Yanks will let them be carried out and think they will all go in the fire. At 3 P.M. the Yanks started us back to Staunton under a Gen. Thomas[5] and a strong guard. We marched that night as far as Fishersville over the deepest and most awful muddy road I have ever seen. The mud was of the consistency of thick cream and was up to our knees and some places was even deeper. The 15,000 Yanks had worked it up into this pasty, cream-thick mud, which was just awful to wade through. We reached Fishersville about dark and encamped there for the night. Many of our men got away tonight, [the] Yankee guard being very careless and indifferent about it. I chopped off Frank Kinckle's overcoat on a stump with an ax; it had become draggled and very muddy.

*March 4. Saturday.* We reached Staunton about midday. The Yanks halted here for two hours and gave us time to get off the mud and to cook the little food which they had given us. They gave us a little coffee and some sugar. The coffee and sugar was given us because the wagon

4 General Early stated, "The only person killed on our side, as far as I have ever heard, was Colonel William H. Harman, who had formerly been in the army but then held a civil appointment; and he was shot in the streets of Waynesboro either after he had been made prisoner, as some said, or while he was attempting to make his escape, after everything was over." (*Early*, p. 464.)

5 HRB must be referring to Col. John L. Thompson, commanding the First New Hampshire Cavalry, who was charged with returning Confederate prisoners to Winchester. (For Thompson's report covering his march from Waynesboro to Winchester, see *Official Records*, Vol. XLVI, pt. 1, pp. 528-29.)

in which it was carried was stuck in the mud and its mules played out. They then destroyed the wagon. Gen. Thomas [Col. John L. Thompson], the Yankee general, sent the people of Staunton word that he had a thousand Confederate prisoners and had nothing for them to eat, and that the good people of Staunton would be permitted to give us food as we marched through Staunton and that we would come through about three o'clock this evening. We marched through Staunton at the appointed time. Both sides of the streets through which we marched were lined with citizens, old men, old ladies, boys, girls and little children with baskets, bags, boxes, etc., filled with provisions, which they handed to us as we passed with looks of the deepest sympathy and words of encouragement. One lady gave us a pillow case with about a peck of flour in it.[6] This flour was a God's gift to my crowd. We encamped tonight at New River Bridge. Our Yankee guards are still kind and considerate, taken as a whole. A few are sometimes cross and ugly. This is only human.

*March 5. Sunday.* We had a long and hard march today. Yanks gave us nothing to eat. They say all their commissary wagons have been lost and that they have nothing for themselves and horses. A large number of their horses are giving out. As soon as a horse gives out, the Yank shoots him and destroys his saddle and bridle. They seem determined not to leave anything behind them which can possibly do our war-afflicted people any good. We went north of Lacy Spring and encamped there for the night. The Yanks are evidently very much afraid of meeting with Mosby and McNeill.[7] Gen. Rosser is following us up from behind.[8]

*March 6. Monday.* We marched today to Rudd's [Rude's] Hill. Here the Yanks were stopped in their march by McNeill and his men, who had occupied the north bank of the river at Mount Jackson and were trying to prevent the Yanks from crossing, while Rosser was worrying

6 Colonel Thompson in his report gives a rather different picture of the reception of the prisoners by the people of Staunton. His account reads: "Major Schwartz was directed to inform the citizens of Staunton that a large number of prisoners would pass through town, and that they must supply them with food. On reaching Staunton I found a few females bringing out a poor pittance in small baskets. I refused to allow them to approach the prisoners, and told the citizens that they could have a half hour to provide food or I should take it from the insane asylum [Western State Hospital]. They brought none, and I took flour and bacon from the asylum. . . ." (*Official Records,* Vol. XLVI, pt. 1, p. 528.)

7 Col. John Singleton Mosby, of the famed "Mosby's Rangers," and Lt. Jesse C. McNeill, commanding another well-known company of partisan rangers, were active in the Valley and Northern Virginia harassing Federal forces.

8 Maj. Gen. Thomas L. Rosser with a small group of cavalry was following close behind the Federal prisoner-guard, hoping to find the opportunity of freeing the prisoners. (Pond, *Shenandoah Valley,* p. 253.)

them from behind. We remained here all night. At night Rosser and his few men charged the Yankee camp in an effort to release us, and got quite close up to us. The Yankee guards who were guarding us were doubled and we were told that the first man who put up his head would get a ball through it. No head was raised and after a short fight Rosser and his men were driven off and things remained quiet for the rest of the night. We got to this place about midday. At that time, I had a biscuit and an onion in my haversack. I ate the onion and thought I would keep the biscuit until morning, but I became so very hungry that I was compelled to eat the biscuit too. I did get a piece of bread in New Market. We have had nothing to eat since our capture, except what the people of the towns and villages have given us. I never knew what it was to be hungry before.

*March 7. Tuesday.* The Yanks drove McNeill and his men off early this morning. We then forded the river, which came up to our *armpits* and was very cold. I was afraid that some of us would get drowned, as I had seen several horses washed down; but we prisoners went in in a solid body and with our hands resting on the shoulders of both our right and left-hand man. We got over very well and I saw that we were stronger than the horses. A kind-hearted Yankee guard took Jake Steptoe up behind him on his horse to carry him over the river. The horse had too much, and the Yank, Jake and horse were washed down the river. I thought that both Jake and the Yank would be drowned, but after both had been badly ducked, they were rescued. The horse, relieved of his heavy load, soon recovered himself and came out. We all got soaking wet. It was quite cold and the ground was frozen right hard that morning, with a cold wind blowing from the northwest. In going through Mount Jackson, an old lady tossed two or three big loaves of bread out to us. George Bray caught one of them and gave me a big slice. I thought [it] the best thing I ever ate and went on the strength of that bread all that day. We continued our march on towards Winchester until midnight, only stopping after we had crossed Cedar Creek, which we had also to ford, but it only came up a little above our knees. Miss Mollie Haas of Woodstock, whom Frank Kinckle knew, and who had been very kind to Frank when he carried Lieut. Basye, Bolling Hewitt, and other wounded through Woodstock the summer before, gave Frank a snack, which did us a power of good. We had to sleep in our wet clothes soon after wading Cedar Creek and had no fire. No wood to make a fire. It was freezing weather. We piled up like hogs do in their beds when cold.

*March 8. Wednesday.* We got to Winchester about midday. We

were halted just south of town. Gen Hancock[9] and his wife in a carriage came out to meet us and many other Yankees came to look on. Here our Yankee cavalry guard was relieved and a Zouave infantry guard put in its place. We were then marched through Winchester and down to Stephenson's Depot, which we reached about four o'clock in the afternoon, passing on our way many large camps of Yankee infantry. When I got to this place, I was so tired and worn out that when we were ordered to stand up in line, so as to be counted for drawing rations, I was so tired that I could not stand up, having gotten so stiff in my limbs and knee joints that I could hardly move them. George Bray and Billy Breden lifted me up bodily and held me up in line. The Yanks gave us some rations of hardtack and mess pork. We had to eat the mess pork raw, having no way to cook it. Just after dark, we were placed on some box cars and carried down to Harpers Ferry, which place we reached about day. I got a right good night's rest on the train.

*March 9.* We were carried by rail to Baltimore and then carried to Fort McHenry, where we were put to sleep out of doors in mud a foot deep, in a cold, sleety rain. We got thoroughly wet and chilled, and when I woke up I felt so bad and feeble that I thought I would die before night. Two men were found dead under their blankets this morning. But fortunately for me, Maj. Halsey[10] came along with a bottle of whiskey and Frank Kinckle told him of my condition. The Major poured out a glass nearly full of whiskey and made me drink it very slowly. I never had anything to revive me more in my life. In an hour I felt like another man. Frank also managed to get me a cup of coffee. We had no fire and had gotten very wet and cold. I think the whiskey and the coffee saved my life on this occasion.

*March 10. Friday.* We remained all day at Fort McHenry. We were put in a big plank shed about midday. The mud in this shed was something like three or four inches deep. Fortunately, my crowd got by a pile of shingles, which was in one corner of this shed. We scraped away the mud as best we could with some of these shingles and made us a bed by putting others down and placing our oilcloths on the shingles and our

[9] Maj. Gen. Winfield Scott Hancock. This could not have been General Hancock, who was in Cumberland, Maryland, as late as 2 P.M. on the eighth, and did not arrive in Winchester until sometime on March ninth. The general referred to here could have been Bvt. Maj. Gen. W. H. Emory commanding the Nineteenth Corps and other forces at Winchester during Hancock's absence. (*Official Records*, Vol. XLVI, pt. 2, pp. 893-95.)

[10] Major Don P. Halsey of Lynchburg. He was on General Wharton's staff at the time of his capture at Waynesboro on March 2. For a biographical sketch, see *Southern Historical Society Papers*, XXXI (1903), 193 *ff*.

blankets on the oilcloths. In this way, [we] succeeded in getting a right good night's rest.

*March 11. Saturday.* A cold, bright day. We were put on two transports and carried by a tug to Fort Delaware, passing through the canal, which connects the upper Chesapeake Bay with the Delaware Bay. Fort Delaware is situated about the middle of the Delaware Bay on a small island out from Delaware City, where the canal comes out into the Delaware Bay. Our boat was very much crowded and we had little sleep or rest that night.

# CHAPTER XV

# SUCH AN AWFUL END

## Fort Delaware, 1865

*March 12, 1865. Sunday.* We reached Fort Delaware about sunrise, after spending a very rough and disagreeable night on the boat.[1] We were duly installed in the "bull pen," which is the name given by our men to what the Yanks call "barracks for enlisted prisoners of war." These barracks are simply plank houses, weatherboarded up and down and shingled. They are about twenty feet broad and five hundred feet long, and are intended to hold five hundred men each. They are called divisions. There are twenty of these divisions in the barracks, a large dining hall and a large kitchen, bakery and washing shed. The barracks are arranged with berths just like a steamboat, there being three stories of them one above the other. We were put in one of these divisions, which was divided into four companies of men, consisting of about a hundred men each. Frank Kinckle was made a sergeant of our company. His duties are to lead us into breakfast and dinner, to have barracks cleaned up every morning, the sick sent to the hospital, get our mail and to make a report every morning to Lieut. Ditz,[2] the officer in charge. This position gives Frank the right to choose his berth, or bunk we call it. He has chosen the upper one at the end of the division, which, being right in the middle [of] the roof, we can stand up and walk about on it. Our companions and bunkmates here are George Bray, Andrew Hardy, Billy Breden, Charles Taliaferro, Frank Kinckle and myself. We had hardly gotten in the bar-

[1]Fort Delaware is located on Pea Patch Island, which is in the midstream of the Delaware River near Delaware City. The fort there during the Civil War was built during the 1850's and is still standing, though it is not in use. See Isaac W. K. Handy, *United States Bonds; or Duress by Federal Authority; A Journal of Current Events During an Imprisonment of Fifteen Months, at Fort Delaware* (Baltimore, 1876), for an account of prison life at Fort Delaware.
   [2] Lt. Louis Ditz. See Appendix I, p. 148.

racks this morning when Ike [Sgt. Isaac W.] Rucker and some more of our company rushed out to greet us. These were the boys who had been captured at Gettysburg twenty months ago. These old prisoners are entirely ignorant of the state of things down in Dixie and it is hard for them to believe what we tell them. Ike Rucker took Frank and myself to "A Shebang" and gave us a cup of coffee and a ration each, which we enjoyed very much. "A Shebang" is a little prison restaurant, kept by a prisoner. Ike also gave us some hints on prison life, which he said would be useful to us, if we kept them in mind. We went into dinner about three o'clock, which consisted of three hardtack, a small piece of meat (about three bites) and a pint tin cup of bean soup. We only get two light meals a day.

*March 13. Monday.* Things here are not quite as bad as I expected to find them. They are, however, bad, hopeless and gloomy enough without any exaggeration. The men of our company who were captured at Gettysburg in July 1863, are never tired of asking questions about their homes and the state of things down South. I find men here who have been here three years and even longer.

*March 14. Tuesday.* Frank Kinckle quite sick. I wrote home to go by flag of truce. I doubt very much if the letter ever gets home. All the railroads, bridges and trains have been destroyed about Richmond. The end of the war is certainly very near us. And such an awful end it will be.

*March 15.* Frank Kinckle went out to the hospital. He is worse this morning. I feel very anxious about him.

*March 16. Thursday.* No news from Frank. Our Yankee guards are fairly kind; but I find some who are fiends incarnate. I shall try to get permission to go to [the] hospital tomorrow to see Frank Kinckle.

*March 17.* I could not get permission to go to the hospital. Frank is still there, but reported to be better this morning.

*March 18. Saturday.* Our division was cleaned out for inspection this morning. I was on the detail to do it.

*March 19. Sunday.* Capt. Ahl,[3] "the commandant of enlisted prisoners of war," came around inspecting our barracks. Our division did not pass inspection and they made us come out and clean it up a second time and we were not permitted to go back to our quarters until dark. I re-

[3] Capt. George W. Ahl. (*The War of the Rebellion: A Compilation of the Official Records of the Union and Confederate Armies* [Washington, D. C., 1880-1901], Ser. II, Vol., VII, p. 143. Captain Ahl was an assistant adjutant general and inspector. For references to Ahl, see McHenry Howard, *Recollections of a Maryland Confederate Soldier and Staff Officer Under Johnston, Jackson and Lee* [Baltimore, 1914], p. 309 ff., and Handy, *United States Bonds,* passim.)

ceived a note from Frank, who is still at the hospital. He reports himself much better, which I am very glad to hear.

*March 20. Monday.* I succeeded today in getting permission to visit the hospital to see Frank. I was to have gone out to see him at four o'clock in the afternoon; but Frank came back to us in the morning, looking quite pale and weak. He, however, says he feels much better.

*March 21.* I saw Mr. Thomas D. Anderson, a son of Dr. Tom Anderson of "Providence." It was at his father's that we were so often and so kindly entertained while at Pine Camp in 1862-63. He has been a prisoner here for more than a year. I also saw Gen. Page,[4] who recently commanded the defenses in Mobile Harbor. He and Lieut. Anderson are on a committee of Confederate officers to divide out some blankets and clothing among Southern prisoners of war at Fort Delaware. These blankets, shoes and clothing have been bought with the proceeds of a cargo of cotton, which the Yanks permitted the Confederate government to send to New York City and sell there for that purpose. Gen. Page gave me a new blanket. Our rations today were tolerable good.

*March 22. Wednesday.* I received two notes, one from Carter Berkeley of Staunton and the other from B. B. Turner of Fauquier County. I had parted with Bev Turner at Gordonsville on [the] tenth of February last. I am surprised to learn he is here. He must have been caught napping by the Yanks. Bev tells me, in his note, if I am much in need of clothes, shoes, etc., to apply to Mrs. S. Dickson[5] of Philadelphia for anything I may need. This good woman, it seems, is at the head of an organization to relieve Southern prisoners of war; but behind her is Mr. Henry Turner, Bev's uncle, and some other Southern sympathizers who furnish the money to carry on the good work. I am very much in need, but I hate to beg. I must think of this; it proves Bev's friendship and true regard for all his promises. Carter Berkeley sent me a dollar's worth of sutler's tickets, which means a great deal at Fort Delaware to an "Enlisted Prisoner of War from Dixie."

*March 23.* Prison very quiet. No news or rumors. The Philadelphia *Enquirer* is the only newspaper which the Yanks will allow to come in the "bull pen."

*March 24.* All quiet. No news.

---

[4] Brig. Gen. Richard L. Page. He surrendered Fort Morgan in Mobile Bay on August 23, 1864. (Robert C. Johnson and C. C. Buell, editors, *Battles and Leaders of the Civil War* [New York, 1887-88], IV, pp. 408-10.)

[5] See one of Mrs. Dickson's letters to HRB in Appendix II, p. 149.

*March 25. Saturday.* I got Billy Breden to wash my clothes while I went to bed. Later on in the afternoon, I took a bath myself and put on my clean clothes. The weather quite cool for the season.

*March 26. Sunday.* It is the third Sunday in Lent. I have kept Lent very strictly this spring, but it is due to "Uncle Sam" and his vile minions.

*March 27. Monday.* This is my birthday. A beautiful, bright and lovely day. But a day full of sad thoughts of the past, and sadder forebodings of the future. May my next birthday be as joyous and happy as this one is sad, gloomy and hopeless. God has been very gracious to me and I try not to repine. The end of this long and bloody war is certainly drawing to a close and that very rapidly. And what an awful close it is going to be. A great many of our people have seen it, since ill-fated Gettysburg; but they would not acknowledge it, even to themselves. Maybe I ought not to write it down even in this little diary.

*March 28.* Nothing new; all quiet. I spend my time reading, when I can get anything to read, and in watching the waves and the boats from my little bunk's window. From this little window one can see the Delaware Shore, Delaware City and up the Delaware Bay towards the mouth of the Delaware River as far as New Castle. The hospital dead-house, and a shed where the plain, pine coffins are made for our dead can also be seen. It is a gloomy and sad sight, those high piles of coffins, and they carry [away] from eight to a dozen of them every morning, filled with our poor dead boys, whose loved ones down in Dixie are anxiously watching for, and bury them on the New Jersey shore. It has passed into a hackneyed phrase among the prisoners, to say "That poor fellow will soon be in Jersey," when one sees a poor prisoner whose end is not far off.

*March 29. Wednesday.* I wrote to Bev Turner and sent the note via overhead route. By this route, the note is tied to a lump of coal and thrown over into the officers' barracks. The officers' barracks are situated parallel to our barracks, with only a narrow alley between them, and one can throw a lump of coal with a note tied to it across this alley into the officers' barracks and the officers can throw likewise back into our barracks. This is the usual way of communication between the officers and privates. A good many of the Yankee guard see these notes coming or going and generally take no notice of them. It is only when a mean Yankee sees them that he seizes and destroys them.

*March 30.* No news. All quiet. I wrote home by flag of truce.

*March 31. Friday.* A rainy and gloomy day.

*April 1. Saturday.* We received orders to have a roll call and daily inspection at one o'clock in the day.

*April 3.* We heard last night of the evacuation of Richmond by our forces.[6] There was great joy among our Yankee friends and guards. There are various rumors as to the state of things in and around Richmond. All our men are very low down; but I still hope and trust in God.

*April 4. Tuesday.* The Yanks fired a hundred guns in honor of the fall of Richmond. Some new prisoners arrived here today, who were captured near Petersburg, Virginia, on last Sunday, but cannot tell us much of the condition of things in Gen. Lee's army. We have been unable to get a paper from some cause. I suppose all Yankeedom is so joyous over the capture of Richmond [and] its burning that they have bought up all the papers and have left not even one copy for a poor Reb.

*April 5. Wednesday.* I received two letters today, one from Mr. Frank M. Page[7] who says that he will do all in his power to help me and that Dr. James M. Minor[8] would very soon send me assistance. The other letter [is] from Mrs. S. Dickson of Philadelphia, who very kindly offers to supply me with necessary clothing and anything else which I may need. This Mrs. Dickson is evidently acting as an agent of Mr. Henry Turner of Philadelphia, my friend B. B. Turner's uncle.

*April 6. Thursday.* I answered Mr. Page's and Mrs. Dickson's letters. A great many rumors of Lee's army being captured.

*April 7. Friday.* Our division was white-washed. A great many rumors about Gen. Lee's army and its hopeless situation. I know exactly how things are. It is impossible to be otherwise. That Grand Old Man and his noble army have simply worn out fighting numberless foreign hirelings. God help them. We are very near the end.

*April 8. Saturday.* I wrote and put in an application for clothing this morning. It is to be supplied by Mrs. Dickson of Philadelphia.

*April 9. Sunday.* A very cold and disagreeable day. Many rumors of Lee's surrender.[9] The very thought of such a thing is heart-sickening.

*April 10.* Yanks tell us Lee has certainly surrendered his whole army, at least what remained of it. There are some eight or ten thousand of his hire at Fort Delaware.

---

[6] General Lee's forces evacuated their Richmond-Petersburg lines on the night of April 2.

[7] Frank Mann Page, who was living in Brooklyn, New York, at the time. He was orginally from Hanover County, Virginia.

[8] Probably the James M. Minor referred to in John B. Minor, *The Minor Family of Virginia* (Lynchburg, Va., 1923), pp. 20, 47.

[9] Lee surrendered his army to Grant during the afternoon of April 9.

*April 11. Tuesday.* Surely the last twenty-four hours has been a day of the most intense mental anxiety I have ever experienced. Thousands of thoughts have passed through my mind as to what fate awaits my country, my family, my neighbors, my friends and myself. May God who has cared for, and protected them during the last four bloody years of war and destruction, continue his fatherly care and protection over them is my most earnest prayer. Lee has certainly surrendered. The Yanks are firing four hundred guns in honor of Lee's surrender. The firing of these guns makes my heart sink within me. To think that all the blood and treasure, which the South has so unsparingly poured on the altar of our country, should have been shed in vain. Oh! How many unhappy mothers are now mourning throughout the South for the useless slaughter of their sons.

*April 12. Wednesday.* Thousands of rumors are going the rounds in prison. No faith to put in any of them. I can only look to God in this hour of dark despair and utter hopelessness. Oh! May he help and comfort my poor people. A rumor tonight says Gen. Johnston has surrendered. I think this is very probable.

*April 13. Thursday.* There is no confirmation of Johnston's surrender. No papers came in the "bull pen" today. Prison life becomes more lonely every day. We have lost all hope.

*April 14. Friday.* Good Friday. It is a beautiful and lovely [day]. Would to God I were out of this vile Yankee prison. A great many of our men made application to take the oath of allegiance to the United States government, on condition of being permitted to go home. I received a letter from Carter Berkeley of Staunton containing a dollar and forty-five cents in sutler's tickets. May God bless him. He has been very kind to me ever since he learnt I was here. A dollar and forty-five cents is a royal gift to a Reb living on Yankee rations at Fort Delaware. No news today.

*April 15. Saturday.* Yesterday was Good Friday. Oh! What a different day I spent four years ago. We heard at twelve o'clock today that Old Abe Lincoln had been shot and killed last night in a theatre in Washington City by John Wilkes Booth, a play actor. Some of the prisoners think that his assassination will make the Yanks hard on us. I don't see why they should take revenge on us. We certainly could not possibly have had a hand in it. He ought to have been at church instead of at the theatre as it was Good Friday. Lieut. Ditz, the Yankee commandant of our barracks, came into our barracks beastly drunk about 5 P.M., having in his hand a club about five feet long; and wherever he saw a group of two or three prisoners talking together he would rush up to them with his club and strike right and left at them. Two or three of our men got severe blows, but most of them soon got out of his way. It is cold and rainy. The waves are quite high. The wind is blowing stiffly from the east. I have been watching the boats all the afternoon from our little window.

*April 16. Sunday.* Our division did not pass at inspection this morning. It had to be cleaned up the second time and we were kept out of it until roll call at one o'clock. It is a cool and windy Easter Sunday.

*April 17. Monday.* Very cool and bright. Heard Sgt. Wilson preach a good sermon. Sgt. Wilson is a Methodist minister who belongs to Morgan's Cavalry. He is a good man and a good preacher. He is, and he has been, doing a splendid work here for eighteen months or more. He is greatly beloved and highly esteemed here by all the Southern prisoners, and even these mean Yankee officials cannot help admiring his noble qualities, both of head and of heart.

*April 18. Tuesday.* Reports this morning say that Johnston has certainly surrendered and that Mobile has fallen and that Dick Taylor's forces have also surrendered, that Fitz Lee, Rosser and Mosby have all surrendered on the same conditions as Gen. Lee's army.[10]

*April 19.* A beautiful spring day. The Yanks have refused to let us have our money, our mails or anything else from the outside since Old Abe was murdered. Wonder how long they will keep this up. It is meanness in the extreme.

*April 20.* A rainy day. We have had no mail for a week, and no newspaper has been permitted to come inside of our barracks since Old Abe was murdered.

*April 21. Friday.* Rainy and gloomy in the extreme. Still no mail or newspapers permitted to come in our barracks.

*April 22. Saturday.* Bread for breakfast this morning; quite an improvement on hardtack. Sgt. Cox[11] notified Frank Kinckle that our mails would be hereafter given us regularly every day, as heretofore. Sgt. Cox, who is a right good and kind Yank, says it was a piece of old Stanton's

[10] Gen. Joseph E. Johnston surrendered his army to Gen. William T. Sherman on this date. Lt. Gen. Richard Taylor did not surrender his army until May 4. Maj. Gens. Fitzhugh Lee and Thomas Rosser and parts of their commands broke through the Federal lines at Appomattox after learning of Lee's surrender plans. Fitz Lee surrendered at Farmville, Virginia, on April 11, but Rosser was not captured until May 2 at Hanover Court House. Col. John S. Mosby disbanded his force on April 21 at Salem, Virginia, and surrendered himself at the end of June.

[11] Sgt. C. Cox, from Pennsylvania.

meanness that stopped our mails, boxes and papers. "Surely oppression maketh a brave man mad."

*April 23.* *Sunday.* Very cold, mail given.

*April 24.* *Monday.* I received a kind letter from Dr. James M. Minor[12] of Brooklyn, New York, containing ten dollars, which is a very acceptable present. No one who has not been in a Yankee war prison can possibly appreciate such a kindness. Dr. Minor is a brother of Cousin Lucius Minor of "Edgewood," Hanover County, Virginia. May God ever bless him and his, is my most earnest prayer.

*April 25.* *Tuesday.* A beautiful day—quite warm. Prison very tiresome. It gives one too much time to think.

*April 26.* *Wednesday.* Today I have had to decide for myself one of the most important questions of my life. God only knows what mental anxiety I have suffered. I have tried to act as I think for best interest of my country and my family. We surrendered to these people as prisoners of war, and now they wish and are trying to thrust their vile oath of allegiance down our throats on bayonets. It is a vile piece of tyranny of which they ought to be ashamed. Yet these people cannot take from us our liberty without destroying their own. They pretend to have made war on us to save the Union; but is a Union pinned together by bayonets worth saving? I think certainly not. We are very near hopeless, and it is not wise for the United States government to render us desperate. It can certainly afford to [be] liberal and magnanimous; but the question is, will it be liberal and magnanimous? I hope so, but very much doubt [it]. There are here some six thousand prisoners of "enlisted men of war," as the Yanks call us, and some fifteen hundred officers. Of these, nearly all have agreed to take the oath on condition of being permitted to go home. When first approached on this subject, they all refused with one or two exceptions.

*April 27.* *Thursday.* Quite warm, I received a note from Carter Berkeley advising me *not* to take the oath.

*April 28.* *Friday.* I received a kind letter from Miss Evie Vernon and answered it. She is a Maryland lady who taught school at Mr. Stringfellow's and to whom my sisters went to school. She used to be a frequent visitor at the "White House."

*April 29.* *Saturday.* The papers this morning confirmed the surrender of Johnston's army. Yanks have somewhat gotten over Old Abe's murder, and are not quite as mean about it. As if a lot of men, imprisoned on an island and surrounded by soldiers and warships, could by any possi-

---

[12] The letter referred to here is included in Appendix II, p. 149.

bility, have had anything to do with the murder of Old Abe in Washington City, one hundred miles away. It was meanness in the extreme, the way in which they treated us about it.

*April 30. Sunday.* All the prisoners were turned out of barracks at sunrise this morning to have the roll called on the taking of the oath. We got no breakfast, but they gave us double rations at dinner. Most of the men agreed to accept the oath on condition of being permitted to go home. It was just about this time that the Richmond *Whig* made its appearance at Fort Delaware. This paper gave long lists of the names of the most prominent men of Richmond and [the] South generally, who had taken the oath of allegiance to [the] United States government. After this our boys no longer hesitated to take the oath. We also learnt that it was necessary to take the oath before one could engage in any trade or business, and that if we did not take it here, we would have to take it when we reached our homes. *Vae victis.* We be men without any rights.

*May 1.* A cold and rainy day.

*May 2.* A beautiful and bright day. The pen very muddy from yesterday's rain. I wrote home to Sister Louisa. The Richmond post office has been opened and there are now regular mails between here and Richmond and the Richmond boys are getting and sending letters home. About one third of the whole city was burnt at its evacuation. I have written to Cousin Mary Herring.

*May 3. Wednesday.* No news. It is a bright and sunny day. The wheat fields on the Delaware shore look beautiful. Crowds of citizens from Philadelphia and other places come here now, and, walking around on the platforms, which are on the top of our barracks, look down on us as if we were wild animals. This practice does not improve our tempers and gives a rather poor opinion of the men and women who do it. The children are excusable perhaps, but their parents should know better with their boasted higher civilization. We prisoners look on it as an insult in our misery. I always go to my barracks when they appear. Some of the men come down among us looking for rings, toothpicks and other trinkets, which our men make in great numbers for sale.

*May 4. Thursday.* I received a letter today from Sister Bettie. This letter was mailed in Washington City by a Yankee officer who is on Gen. Gary's [John W. Geary?] staff. Gen. Gary's Division had marched back to Washington by my home and Gen. Gary and his staff had eaten their dinner under the large oak trees in the yard at home, and this officer had kindly offered to take this letter and mail it when he reached Washington, which he did.

*May 5. Friday.* I received a letter from Sister Carter, mailed in Richmond.

*May 6. Saturday.* A rainy day. I put in a second application for a permit for Mrs. S. Dickson to furnish me some necessary clothing.

*May 7. Sunday.* I received two letters; one from Miss Evie Vernon, the other from Mrs. S. Dickson. Miss Evie sent me five dollars. Mrs. Dickson sent me five and informed me that she had sent me by express a suit of clothes and a hat and a pair of shoes.

*May 8. Monday.* The express agent informed me that my package had reached here. I answered Miss Evie's and Mrs. Dickson's letters, thanking them as best I could for their great kindness.

*May 9. Tuesday.* A close, rainy day. All quiet and gloomy.

*May 10. Wednesday.* A bright and pleasant day. All quiet.

*May 11. Thursday.* A very rainy day. All quiet. Talks of release and home.

*May 12. Friday.* I received today a suit of plain, heavy gray clothing from Mrs. Dickson; also a hat, a pair of shoes and a prayerbook. All these articles are very acceptable for they are much needed. I can go home now in a decent way, thanks to Bev Turner and his relations.

*May 13. Saturday.* No news. All quiet. Talks of release.

*May 14. Sunday.* A beautiful day. A great many rumors as to our release.

*May 15.* A beautiful and bright day. All quiet. President Davis captured.

*May 16. Tuesday.* Frank Kinckle received a letter from home. Post office has been opened in Lynchburg, Virginia.

*May 17. Wednesday.* I received a letter from Sister Carter, dated April 29, 1865. All well at home.

*May 18.* Our division was whitewashed. All quiet. Even no rumors about our release.

*May 19. Friday.* A cloudy, cold and drizzly day.

*May 20. Saturday.* This day four years ago I left home for the army. It has been four years of blood, hardship, sickness and danger and its end finds me a prisoner of war at this horrid prison den, and my country desolated, pillaged, plundered and conquered by these vile Yankees. Yet I believe we Rebs are going to be proud of these four years of war. It was only "by overpowering numbers and resources," as Gen. Lee puts it in his good-by order to the Army of Northern Virginia. We put up a bully fight, if we did go under. And we have no excuses to make for our actions.

*May 21.  Sunday.*   I heard Mr. Wilson preach a fine sermon from Romans III, 18. "There is no fear of God before their eyes." He advises us to be strong and show ourselves as brave men, that we can gain nothing by any other course. This day four years ago, I [was] enlisted in the state service of Virginia at Richmond by John B. Baldwin.

*May 22.*   A cloudy day. All quiet. Everyone talking of our release and of going home. It must come very soon, we all think.

*May 23.  Tuesday.*   Frank Kinckle broke out with the mumps. A good many other cases of mumps.

*May 24.*   A beautiful day. Everyone talking about going home.

*May 25.  Thursday.*   I received today, by Gen. Page, a note from Wash Nelson[13] in which he tells me that he has received a letter from his sister and that all at my home are well. A good many cases of smallpox have broken out in last few days. Yanks are taking every precaution to prevent its spread and to stamp it out. The prisoners, however, fear the scurvy much more than they do the smallpox. The scurvy is mostly confined to the men who have been here for two years, or longer, and is caused by a long diet of hardtack and salt meat without any vegetables. Its effects are curious and often very fatal. When the scurvy first attacks a man, all his limbs become swollen as if the skin would burst. After this swelling has lasted for a month, or longer, it goes down and the body of the man becomes covered with round spots, from the size of a ten-cent piece to that of a half a dollar. These spots are of a dark blue color, and look as if they had been caused by being bruised with a hammer. After these spots appear the man's limbs and whole body wither away and dry up, while every joint in his body becomes so stiff that he cannot move it. This withering process often continues until it ends in death. Hundreds here have died of it. A few vegetables and fruits would save their lives, and yet they are dying in the sight of these things. It is nothing but cruelty and tyranny.

*May 26.*   A cloudy day. All quiet.

*May 27.*   A cold, rainy day. All quiet. Boys talking of release and home.

*May 28.  Sunday.* Frank Kinckle is twenty-one today. A poor place to celebrate one's birthday. Fifty-two galvanized Yanks were set free. These galvanized Yanks are men who were captured as Confederate soldiers and surrendered as such. They have, however, turned traitors and gone over

[13] George Washington Nelson, the second and last captain of the Hanover Artillery, was captured on October 26, 1863, at a friend's home. He was first imprisoned at Johnson's Island and was moved to Fort Delaware in June 1864. His account of his prison life is in *Southern Historical Society Papers*, I (April, 1876), pp. 243-56.

to the Yanks. I pity them, even under our present conditions. They are utterly scorned and despised by the other Confederate prisoners, and are held in the utmost contempt by all Yankees. They are, however, men of the very lowest standard and have little or no sense of honor, or of a good character.

*May 29.  Monday.*   Frank received a long letter from his father to day. The old gent has accepted the inevitable and taken the oath of allegiance to Uncle Sam and gone on with his regular work.

*May 30.  Tuesday.*   I wrote to Miss Evie Vernon. All quiet.

*May 31.  Wednesday.*   No news. Everyone talks of release and about going home.

*June 1.  Thursday.*   I received two very old letters today, one from Sister Bettie and the other from Nannie Carter Berkeley. These letters had started by flag of truce and been hung up somewhere when the end came.

*June 2.  Friday.*   Gen. [George] Doles of Georgia was killed one year ago near Cold Harbor right in our battery. No news. All quiet. Boys talking of going home.

*June 3.*   This day one year ago Edmund Anderson was killed, John Lewis Berkeley, Dabney Williamson, Robert B. Winston and W. Hoge wounded. George Latham received a letter today informing him that his release had been ordered from General Grant's headquarters and that it would reach Fort Delaware in a few days.

*June 4.*   Whitsunday. No news. All quiet. Everyone talking of release and home.

*June 5.  Monday.*   A very hot day. No news. Our nights are always cool and pleasant, there being always a pleasant breeze up the Delaware Bay at night.

*June 6.*   A report says that an order has been received here from Secretary Stanton for our release. It, however, lacks confirmation.

*June 7.  Wednesday.*   The sick at the [hospital] were given the oath and those who were well enough have been sent home.

*June 8.  Thursday.*   Frank Kinckle, much to his surprise, received a special release. I received a letter from Cousin Mary Herring, who gives me some news from home and who tells me Uncle Lewis Berkeley has gone to Mississippi.

*June 9.*   Frank Kinckle got off home today on a special release, obtained by some of his Lynchburg friends from Gen. Grant. He has just started, and thus it is that I and my friend and companion in hardships, sufferings and danger part, he for his home, I to remain here in this horrid

Yankee prison for a few more weeks of awful ennui. May God protect, defend and guard him and permit us to meet again under brighter and happier auspices. No truer, nobler or braver man has worn the Confederate uniform. He says he is going straight to see my parents and let them know how I am situated and that I will soon be at home, and he will be certain to do it if he has to walk from Richmond to Hanover. Carter Berkeley of Staunton and George A. Latham of our battery left for home today on special releases. We hear that Gen. Schoepf[14] has the order for the release of all the prisoners in the privates' barracks, and that no more special releases will be granted as it interferes with the general release.

*June 10. Saturday.* The general order for our release was made known to us today. It says that the prisoners from the more distant states must be released first. This of course puts us here until the very last, as there are more Virginians here than from any other state. The Arkansas, Louisiana, Kentucky, Tennessee and Texas boys left for their homes amid long and loud cheers, and hearty good-bys.

*June 11. Sunday.* Mississippi, Alabama, Florida and South Carolina soldiers left this morning. Happy boys!

*June 12.* Rest of the Mississippi boys left for their homes.

*June 13. Tuesday.* Our officers were given the oath today and allowed the liberty of the island. The island of Fort Delaware, they say, contains only twenty acres. I received two letters, one from Mr. Peterkin[15] of Richmond, and the other from Sister Carter. They are all well at home.

*June 14. Monday [i.e., Wednesday.]* Alabama boys called out, but did not get off.

*June 15.* Taliaferro and Mercer[16] left this morning for their homes, also all the Alabama boys. All the Virginians from the Valley were carried out, but had to be brought back as the boat was too much crowded for them to get on.

*June 16.* A very hot day. All the Georgia boys left for home. It is very lonesome and tiresome to me now, since Frank left. Yet there are some two or three thousand prisoners still here. My favorite amusement is watching for new faces. The boys promenade the prison streets late in

[14] Brig. Gen. Albin Schoepf, commanding officer of Fort Delaware. General Orders No. 109, dated June 6, provided for release of prisoners of war (enlisted men and officers not above the grade of captains) upon their taking the Oath of Allegiance. As many were to be released daily as could conveniently be placed on the rolls. Prisoners from points most remote from the prison and those longest in captivity were to be released first. Transportation was to be provided to the nearest accessible point to their homes. (*Official Records,* Ser. I, Vol. VIII, p. 641.)

[15] Probably the Rev. Joshua Peterkin.

[16] Corbin Mercer of Williamsburg and Charles Taliaferro of Richmond.

the evening and by twilight by hundreds, and I sit and watch them and it seems to me that I see new faces every evening, although I have been here in the pen with all these men for more than three months. This promenading is usually kept up until 10 or 11 P.M. Our Yankee guards have become very friendly and easy to get on with.

*June 17.* All quiet. No releases. Yanks tell us it is because there are no transports to take us away and that we will have to wait for the return of the boats, which carried the boys already released away, and that it will be several days before they can get back.

*June 18.* Some six hundred officers, who, up to this date, had declined to take the oath of allegiance, accepted it and were given the freedom of the island on their parole. Some of them visited our barracks. None of the officers have yet been released, except a few by Gen. Grant on special release; and these all belong to the Army of Northern Virginia.

# CHAPTER XVI

# MY WAR LIFE ENDS

## *Fort Delaware to "White House," 1865*

*June 19, 1865.* I signed the oath of allegiance today to the United States government. God grant I may be enabled to keep it, without any temptation to break it. All our people at home are taking this oath so I suppose it is the proper thing to do. I received a letter from home, mailed in Richmond and dated June 14th. Frank Kinckle was at home and they were all to dine at "Montout" with him the next day.

*June 20.* North Carolina boys went home this morning. About fifteen hundred of them. About dark I was called out with some thousand other prisoners and given my oath of allegiance, which I had signed, and transportation to Richmond, and put on board the Baltimore boat. We were very much crowded at first, but after a while I succeeded in getting a very good seat and had a very pleasant trip. We were not guarded after leaving Fort Delaware; but on the boat they would not allow us to go in the dining room or salon. Andrew Hardy bought six nice rolls from one of the servants on the boat. He gave me one, which I enjoyed very much. When we left Fort Delaware, the Yanks gave us three days' rations of hard-tack and mess pork. We came through the canal which connects Delaware and Chesapeake bays and reached Baltimore about 7 A.M.

*June 21.* On landing at Baltimore, we went to the quartermaster's office, as we had been directed, to get transportation to Richmond. He informed us that there was a large steamboat at a certain wharf, which would leave for Richmond in two hours and that all Confederate prisoners of war who wanted to go to Richmond must go and get on this boat at once. He sent a courier to show us the boat. This old boat was called "The Eagle." She was a buster, and although there were about one thousand of us, we were not in the least crowded. These prisoners were from all parts of the South and were men who had been released from various Yankee prisons. We left the wharf about 10 A.M. and, going a short distance out into the harbor, we anchored there and the captain went off in a small boat to the city. We remained here until 3 P.M. in a very hot sun. At three, the quartermaster visited us in a small boat. He got as mad as Old Nick on finding the captain absent, and sent off to the city for him and told the men he sent to bring him *at once,* if they had to bring him in chains. These fellows brought the Captain back very soon and the quartermaster gave him fits, because he had not started at 10 A.M. as he had been ordered to do. The quartermaster wound up by telling the captain if he was not off in ten minutes, he would put him in prison and in chains. The Captain took it all very meekly and started at once, which was nearly 5 P.M. We had [a] pleasant run down the Chesapeake Bay. The old boat did not make more [than] six or seven miles an hour.

*June 22.* At sunrise, we passed Point Lookout near the mouth of the Potomac River. After a very tedious trip we reached the wharf at Fortress Monroe about 4 P.M. We prisoners were not allowed to get off of our [boat] at Fortress Monroe and about dark we went up to Newport News. It was a bright moonlight night and the captain told some of the men that if they would help him coal his boat that he would go up to Richmond that night by moonlight; but after they had very quickly put the coal on board, the captain changed his mind and said that he was afraid of torpedoes and could [not] go until the next day.

*June 23.* We left Newport News about light and entered the James River just before sunrise and after a very slow trip we reached the wharf at Richmond about sunset. We passed a boat going down the river near Jamestown loaded with negro soldiers. These were the first and only negro soldiers I have ever seen. At least one half of the men on our boat got off at City Point and went by rail to Petersburg. They were North Carolinians. When we reached the wharf at Richmond we were met there by some Yankee cavalry, who started us up to the Chimborazo Hospital. I asked one of them where he was carrying and what he was going to do with us. He said they were going to give us something to eat and a place to sleep. I asked him to let me go, that I could take care of myself. His reply was, "Then you can go," and I immediately thanked him and left my fellow prisoners, bidding Billy Breden good-by, the last man in my company with whom I had acted, ate and slept. But no braver man, better friend or better No. 1 at a cannon ever handled a sponge-staff. Simple in his nature, but true and brave in heart and mind. May [God] be with him, even unto his life's end. I spent the night at the Powhatan House. Paid a dollar for a supper; but it was the first decent and regular supper I had sat down to since I left home the 10th of February last. I had eaten very little since I left Fort Delaware. I enjoyed my supper very much. I drank a glass of milk; it was the first milk I had seen or tasted since I left home in February.

*June 24.* I got up early this morning, hoping to be able to find Mr. Herring's, but after a hopeless effort, I gave up the search and went to the Custom House to see if I could get transportation home over the Central Railroad, which was then running trains to Staunton. The train left at 8 A.M. I found that the Custom House was crowded with men waiting for the quartermaster to get up and that there was no earthly chance for me to get home that day if I waited there for that Yankee quartermaster to get up; for there were at least three hundred men ahead of me and it was then seven o'clock. So I gave up and started for the Central Depot. As I had an hour, I thought I would walk a little way down Main Street and take a look at the burnt district. One could hardly tell where Main Street had been. It was one big pile of ruins from the Custom House to the wharf at Rocketts. At this point, the Yanks had collected all kinds of debris of war: cannon, muskets, bayonets, cartridge boxes, swords, broken gun-carriages, broken wagons, etc. I had never imagined that the Confederacy had one-half as many siege guns in and around Richmond. As I gazed sadly over all this war wreckage for a few moments, my thoughts were with our noble dead, "the unreturning brave." Is it better with them or with us? We hope, aye, we almost know it is well with them. But who knows what the future holds for us; only God. I turned away and with a sad and gloomy heart bent my steps towards the Depot. When I reached there the train was there ready. I went in one of the coaches and took my seat. Here I found some twenty other Southern prisoners on their way home. I asked one, who proved to be a man named Thompson and [who] was going to Verdon, if he had a ticket. He said no, that he had no ticket, transportation or money. He was just from Point Lookout and was trying to get home. I asked him if he expected to be put off the train. His reply was that he meant to do some hard begging before being put off. We started and I suppose that we were six miles from the city when the conductor, Capt. [Carter S.] Anderson, came in. I felt easy. I knew he had too kind a heart to put released Confederate soldiers off his train. He said we ought to have gotten transportation, but that he had positive orders from Col. Edmund Fontaine, the president of the road, to carry all Confederate soldiers home free. Everyone in the coach cried out, "Carry them home free, Carry them home *free*," and the coach was quite full, there being several Yankee officers and soldiers aboard. We reached Noel's about ten. Here I saw Mr. Edmund Anderson, Mr. James Fontaine, Sam Anderson and some others of our neighbors. After starting to walk home, I met Mr. John McLockton Anderson, with whom I had quite a talk. His brother Tom, whom I had met at Fort Delaware, had gotten home on a special release. I had to go down to Mr. Anderson's lower ford to get over the river. When I got over on the "White House" farm, I crossed some nice dewberries and stopped to eat some, for I had gotten very hungry, not having had any breakfast that morning. Everything was so quiet, still and peaceful. My thoughts were very busy, but very sad and almost hopeless. I looked around several times almost expecting to see a Yankee guard spring up out of the bushes. I reached home about eleven and half o'clock in the day. Frank, a negro man, was the first to see me. Then Papa, who was ploughing corn in front of the house, was the second and Carter the third. The whole family was soon crowding around me, giving me a most hearty and loving welcome. Old Francis, among the servants, was very hearty, and I believe, very sincere in his welcome. I found all well and hearty at home. The Yankee cavalry had been there in March and taken everything from them, which they could find. All the bacon, corn, flour, meal and nearly all the fowls had been taken and things looked gloomy for the future. It is today that my war life ends. It has been four years, one month and seven days since I joined the Hanover Artillery. Ah! What hardships, what sufferings, what trials, what deaths, what sorrows, what tears, what great losses both of men and of property have I seen and through which I have passed in these four bloody and awful years. Yet there is something within me which tells me plainly that it was not all passed through in vain. That there is, at the bottom of this fiery furnace of affliction, through which we Southern people have all gone, some pure gold left us. That this deep well of sorrow, suffering and affliction must contain some pure and clear waters of comfort, of resignation and of hope. With this belief I end here my little war diary. God grant that I may never see another war, with all its horrors, blood and desolation. And yet this war was not all blood, suffering, desolation and sorrow. Self was forgotten and the noblest impulses of the human heart were drawn forth by our common dangers and sufferings, while sublime examples of bravery and heroism were exhibited from the highest officer to the lowest private. Noble friendships were formed, which, I trust, time itself will never blot out, and that I may be permitted to enjoy the poet's beautiful thought, "That many friendships, in the days of Time (*War*) begun, are lasting and growing in Heaven."

# APPENDICES

## I.

*The following information concerning Berkeley's imprisonment is located at the end of the third volume of the manuscript diary.*

THE NAMES OF SOME OF MY FELLOW PRISONERS AT FORT DELAWARE, DELAWARE, AT THE CLOSE OF THE WAR IN SPRING OF 1865

U. S. MILITARY PRISON, 5TH DIVISION, FORT DELAWARE, APRIL 30, 1865.

C. K. Pendleton, Louisa County, Virginia
Corbin Mercer, Williamsburg, Virginia
W. S. Robertson, Richmond, Virginia
Sgt. Timberlake, Albemarle County, Virginia
Sgt. Taliaferro, Orange County, Virginia
Sgt. Cavialero, Mobile, Alabama
Pvt. Fletcher, Rockingham County, Virginia
Pvt. McNutley, Hampshire County, Virginia
A. S. Hardy, Middlesex County, Virginia
George S. Bray, Fredericksburg, Virginia
Frank A. Kinckle, Lynchburg, Virginia
George A. Latham, Alexandria, Virginia
William Breden, Henrico County, Virginia

Sgt. Kyrkendall, Romney, Virginia
Rev. Mr. Wilson, Montgomery, Alabama
W. A. Pence, Rockingham County, Virginia
W. Reed, Rockingham County, Virginia
Charles Taliaferro, Richmond, Virginia
Miller, Augusta County, Virginia
R. Wills, Shenandoah County, Virginia
B. B. Graves, Hanover County, Virginia
John B. Graves, Hanover County, Virginia
Langhorne, Portsmouth, Virginia
G. Berkeley Green, Mississippi
John S. Woodard, Middlesex County, Virginia

*N. B.* The above men were those with whom I was mostly thrown. Frank A. Kinckle, George A. Latham, A. S. Hardy, George S. Bray, [and] William Breden were my bunkmates and intimate friends. There are, at present, 5,935 privates and non-commissioned officers in the privates' barracks, about 1,500 in the officers' barracks and some three or four sick in the hospitals.

### YANKEE OFFICERS AT FORT DELAWARE

| | |
|---|---|
| Gen. A. Schoepf, Commandant of the Fort | Lieut. Wolf, in charge of officers' barracks |
| Capt. G. W. Ahl, A. A. General | Lieut. Louis Ditz, in charge of privates' barracks |

### YANKEE SERGEANTS AT FORT DELAWARE

These Yankee sergeants had charge of the divisions of our barracks. My division was the Fifth Division, in charge of C. Cox, a very good and kind man from Pennsylvania; D. Graham, a very good and kind man from New York; O'Neal, mean, brutal and tyrannical in the extreme; Leadbetter, a coarser devil than O'Neal.

Miller, paymaster, I saw very little of him; Randolph, Post Master; Adams, known as "Old hurry up," or as "Hyke-out," a good natured old man; Echolds, The dining room Sergeant, a big rascal; Williams, a bigger rascal than old Gen. Schoepf, which means much; G. Adams, Sutler to Officers and Prisoners of War, the biggest rogue that ever lived without any exception.

### GUARDS

In March by [the] 14th Maryland Regiment. In April by Brooklyn, New York Zouaves. In May and June by 202 Pennsylvania Regiment.

All of these Yankee soldiers, with some exceptions, were quite kind. The Marylanders were the worst and meanest; but were made up of foreigners and plug-uglies from Baltimore.

## II.

### LETTERS

A. *The originals of the following letters are pasted in Volume III of the manuscript of the diary.*

[Contemporary Scribe's Copy]

#### HEADQUARTERS VALLEY DISTRICT, OCTOBER 30, 1864

Colonel: I wish to express to the officers and men of the artillery my high appreciation of their good conduct and gallantry at Winchester, Fisher's Hill and on the 19th instant near Middletown. I had occasion to observe their conduct in person on all those occasions and I take pleasure in bearing this testimony to their gallantry and devotion to duty in all the actions fought at those places. The strictures contained in my address of the 22nd are not applicable to your command.

Respectfully,
J. A. Early

Philadelphia, April 4th, 1865
1127 Gerard Street

H. R. Berkeley Esq.

Dear Sir:

I have been informed through a friend that you were at Fort Delaware in need of assistance and without friends on this side of the lines. I write to say that if you will procure a permit for such articles as you require and enclose it to me, it will give me great pleasure to supply your wants. My impression is that Capt. Ahl will not refuse a permit to one in need of clothing and I trust you will be able to forward it to me without delay. Address as above,

Mrs. S. Dickson

100 Willow Street
Brooklyn
6th April, 1865

H. R. Berkeley
Co: A. Nelson's Artillery, 5th Division
Care of Capt. G. W. Ahl A. A. A. G.

Dear Sir:

It was with feelings of the greatest pain that I learned of your capture, through your letter to F. M. Page. I enclose *ten dollars,* Mr. P. not finding it convenient under the circumstances to do so. I do not know whether I have ever met you; if I ever have you must have been very young at the time; your name is one with which I am well acquainted from earliest life as well as connected through blood and marriage. God grant the time may soon come when I may once more see the good people of Hanover. "Coelum non animum mutant qui toons mare currunt" [*sic*].

Yours truly,
J. M. Minor, M.D.

I enclose to Capt. G. W. Ahl, A. A. A. G.

Fredericksburg, May 26th, 1868

I knew Mr. H. Robinson Berkeley during the war, being the Chaplain of the Battalion of which he was a member for two years, and a half, and I most cheerfully bear testimony to his courage and fidelity as a soldier, his modest, unassuming behavior as a gentleman, and his sincerity and consistency as a Christian. He was highly esteemed by all his comrades, and all his officers, and was always placed forward in times of exigency and danger. I have no doubt of his ability to discharge with the same faithfulness any trust committed to him and hope he may find friends wherever he goes.

Thomas W. Gilmer
Pastor, Presbyterian Church, Fredericksburg.

Hanover Academy,
May 27th, 1868

During the period that Mr. Berkeley was at Hanover Academy, I was an assistant teacher at that school, and taught several of his classes.

I fully concur in the testimonial given him by Col. Jones, and being a fellow countryman, can say that his character at school, was but the counterpart of that borne by him as a member of the community. Mr. Berkeley was, during the late war, a member of the Artillery company, in which I was a lieutenant. Consequently, I was enabled to observe his conduct under new, and trying circumstances. I always found him to be an earnest, patriotic, and faithful soldier, never falling short of his duty.

William M. Fontaine

Oakland, May 23d, 1868

Dear Robin:

I received your letter of the 14th instant a few days ago, and take pleasure in recommending you for any situation you may wish to get, as one every way worthy of the most important and responsible trust which may be committed to you. I do this from a thorough knowledge of your character, and that of your father and mother from your childhood up to the present time; and especially from my acquaintance with you during the four years of the late War, the whole of which period you were under my command, and it gives me pleasure to say, always faithful to duty, however disagreeable, difficult or dangerous.

I saw several members of your family last Sunday at Church, they were well.

With best wishes for your success in life,

I am very truly
your friend
W. Nelson

To H. R. Berkeley Esq.
Care of Mr. William Berkeley
Leesburg, Virginia

B. *The originals of the following letters are in the possession of Mr. Landon Robinson Berkeley of Yorktown, Virginia. Mr. Berkeley also has a few letters written to HRB by members of his family, but they are not published here.*

Lynchburg, June 5th, 1868

This is to certify that I am well acquainted with the bearer H. Robinson Berkeley of Hanover County, Va. and that it affords me great pleasure to bear my testimony to his high character for intelligence, strict integrity and fidelity to duty. I have never known a young man whose conduct was more uniformly honorable and upright and I can cordially commend him to the favor and confidence of any one who may secure his services.

Thos. J. Kirkpatrick.

Lewisburg. West Virginia
May 24th 1868

Mr. H. R. Berkeley was a student at the Hanover Academy while I taught there and by close application to his studies, strict conformity to all rules and a faithful discharge of all duties, gave earnest of future proficiency in his studies and I have no doubt but that he is fully competent to fill creditably any position that he may be willing to accept. It gives me pleasure to recommend him as a young man of good mind and irreproachable character.

Alexander F. Mathews, M. A. U. Va.

Line of Battle two miles west of
Cold Harbor. Wednesday evening
June 1, 1864 2 o'clock P.M.

Dear Sister,

I would have written to some one of you as soon as I reached this place, but I was so uncertain about the mails going up to Hanover that I thought it almost useless to write. But as Col. Nelson has just told me that he thought that the mails were going up to Taylorsville, I thought I would try a short one to let you know how I am. You ought to have written if you could send the letter; then I should have known if mine could have gone. I suppose the mails still go up to Negro Foot if they don't go to Verdon. All of us are tolerably well except Bob Winston who is a little unwell but is somewhat better this evening than he was this morning. My company is between Atlee's Station and Cold Harbor about two miles from the latter place from which our line of battle extends in the direction of Atlee's Station. Our present position is very disagreeable, the enemy's sharpshooters being very annoying. If you dare to put your head above the breastworks, two or three balls will come whizzing by your head. I am now sitting down in a ditch writing while they are flying over my head quite harmlessly. Two companies of my battalion were in a very hot fight day before yesterday, and lost one man killed (Lieut. Ancell) and three badly wounded. Lieut. Ancell was a fine officer and a good Christian man. He was killed instantly and died without saying one word, and as I helped to put him on a stretcher I could not help thinking that I too might soon be bourne breathless from some bloody field. Oh, God has been so good to me ever since I have been in this war that I am almost astonished at my own preservation, for it seems almost impossible to have passed through such dangers and not to be hurt. If you get this letter, please write at once and let me know if you get it. If the mail does not go to Verdon, let me know if it don't go up to Negro Foot. Bob Winston says please try and send his mother word [and] if you possibly can to write to him and let him know if he can get a letter to her. Write soon and let me know if the Yanks have been home and all about it. Good-by. God bless you.

"Robin"

Direct your letter to the Army as usual.

# INDEX

[Places and names only have been indexed. The introduction has been indexed only for more important information. The footnotes and Appendices are not indexed. Military units appear under their commanding officer.]